INDIANS OF THE NORTHWEST COAST

PHILIP DRUCKER is one of the leading anthropologists in this country and an authority on the aboriginal cultures of the American Northwest. He was born on January 13, 1911, in Chicago, Illinois, and was educated at the University of California where he received his doctorate in anthropology in 1936. From 1940 to 1955 he was a staff anthropologist with the Bureau of American Ethnology of the Smithsonian Institution.

Dr. Drucker has done field-work on the Northwest Coast since 1933, made an ethnographic study of the Nootka Indians in 1935 as a Social Science Research Council predoctoral fellow, and an ethnographic survey of the Northwest Coast for the University of California program in "Culture Element Distribution" in 1936. As National Research Council postdoctoral fellow in 1938, he made an archaeological survey of the Northwest Coast. He has also made archaeological investigations in southern Mexico. One of his more recent works is a study of the cultural adaptation and acculturation among Indians of the Northwest Coast.

Dr. Drucker is the author of many anthropological studies, among them *Rank, Wealth, and Kinship in Northwest Coast Society* (1939), *Archeological Survey of the Northern Northwest Coast* (1943), and *The Northern and Central Nootkan Tribes* (1951).

INDIANS OF THE NORTHWEST COAST

Philip Drucker

Originally published as an
Anthropological Handbook for
The American Museum of Natural History

AMERICAN MUSEUM SCIENCE BOOKS
Published for
The American Museum of Natural History

The Natural History Press
GARDEN CITY, NEW YORK

Indians of the Northwest Coast was originally published by the McGraw-Hill Book Company, Inc., in 1955. The American Museum Science Books edition is published by arrangement with The American Museum of Natural History.

American Museum Science Books edition: 1963

Unless otherwise acknowledged, all photographs for this book were provided by The American Museum of Natural History. All the line illustrations were prepared by the Graphic Arts Division of The American Museum of Natural History.

PREFACE

The American Museum of Natural History has exceptionally fine collections from the Northwest Coast of America, particularly from the Indian groups of the northern half of that region, that is, from the coasts of British Columbia and southeast Alaska. A good part of this material was collected in the closing decades of the nineteenth century when the Indians preserved ancient patterns and standards of values to a considerable extent, and there were still many expert practitioners of the rich and distinguished aboriginal art. Portions of these collections were made in connection with expeditions sponsored by the American Museum of Natural History for the purpose of studying the colorful, vigorous native civilization of the area. The purpose of the present work is not, however, to present a catalogue of the collections, nor is it to serve as a simple guide to them in the ordinary sense. Its aim is to sketch in the cultural background of the specimens by relating briefly not only how the various material objects were made and used, but recounting something of the general way of life of the makers and users. It therefore discusses at some length a variety of aspects of culture that cannot of themselves be displayed in a museum case: social customs, religious beliefs, and ceremonial patterns. The aim is to make the specimens on exhibition more meaningful by describing the way in which they formed a part of the lives of the aboriginal people of the Northwest Coast.

Only fragments are to be found today of the aboriginal civilizations described in these pages. Many of the Indians of the coast are nowadays commercial fishermen and loggers. Most of them are more at home with gasoline and Diesel engines than with the canoes of their forefathers. Membership in one or another Christian church is universal. The ancient art style has very nearly disappeared. Men no longer have time to carve and paint when they have to make a living in the competitive modern society. Here and there a few relics of ancient patterns have been preserved more or less deliberately. Some groups occasionally still give festivals and feasts in the ancient potlatch tradition; others retain certain of the ancient social forms, such as the clan organization. A few Chilkat Tlingit women weave the traditional type of robe. Among other groups the women still make basketry or cedarbark mats. But aside from these fragments and the people's pride in their identity as Indians, Northwest Coast culture must be regarded as having disappeared, engulfed by that of the modern United States and Canada.

PHILIP DRUCKER

CONTENTS

LIST OF ILLUSTRATIONS

Figures

Photographs

INDIANS OF THE NORTHWEST COAST

1 INTRODUCTION

The Land

Along the shores of northwestern North America
from Yakutat Bay in southeast Alaska to Trinidad
Bay on the coast of present northern California,
lived a number of Indian groups who participated
jointly in a unique and rich culture. It is an anthropological truism that development of complex, or
"high," culture among primitive peoples is linked
with, or, better, results from the notable increase
in economic productivity that accompanies the invention or acquisition of agricultural techniques,
and within limits, the domestication of animals.
This can be documented by archaeological evidence from various early centers of high civilization—the Middle East, the Indus Valley, Middle
America. The expansion of the economic base effected by agriculture raises the general standard of
living, permits increased settled populations, pro-
vides more leisure time to cultivate the arts, to
elaborate on religious, social, and political concepts,
and to perfect the material aspects of culture:
tools, dwellings, utensils, textiles, ornaments, and
the rest. The culture of the Northwest Coast, therefore, seems to be an anomaly, for it was a civilization of the so-called "hunting-and-gathering" type,
without agriculture (except for a few instances of
tobacco growing), and possessing no domesticated
animals other than the dog. In other words, the

Fig. 1. The map shows the Northwest Coast area in relation to the surrounding states and also locates the important cities, rivers, and bodies of water.

natives of the Northwest Coast, like the rude Paiute of Nevada, the Australian aborigines, and others of the simpler cultures the world over, were entirely and directly dependent on natural products for their livelihood. That they were able to attain their high level of civilization is due largely to the amazing wealth of the natural resources of their area. From the sea and rivers, fish—five species of Pacific salmon, halibut, cod, herring, smelt, and the famous olachen or "candlefish" (this last so rich in oil that a dried one with a wick threaded through it burns like a candle), and other species too numerous to mention—could be taken in abundance. Some of these fish appeared only seasonally, but were easy to preserve. The sea also provided a tremendous quantity of edible mollusks; "when the tide goes out the table is set," as the saying goes. More spectacular was the marine game: hair seal, sea lion, sea otter, porpoise, and even whale. On shore, land game too abounded. Vegetable foods were less plentiful, although many species of wild berries were abundant in their season. In other words, the bounty of nature provided that which in most other parts of the world man must supply for himself through agriculture and stock raising: a surplus of foodstuffs so great that even a dense population had an abundance of leisure to devote to the improvement and elaboration of its cultural heritage.

The Northwest Coast is a unit, not only in its aboriginal culture patterns, but geographically as well. The Japanese Current offshore moderates the climate so that extreme and prolonged cold does not occur even in the higher latitudes. The same ocean stream releases vast amounts of water vapor that is blown onshore by the prevailing winds, condenses on rising over the coastal mountains and hills, and produces the characteristic heavy rainfall of the area. Consequently, innumerable streams and small rivers with their sources in the Coast Range flow to the sea, as do the major drainage systems like the Columbia, the Fraser, and the Skeena, with sources east of the mountains. Likewise, the heavy precipitation produces a dense specialized vegetation, consisting mainly of thick stands of conifers—Douglas fir, various spruces, red cedar, yellow cedar, yew, and, at the southern tip of the area, coast redwood. Deciduous trees are smaller and more scattered, but include several hardwoods, such as maple and oak, and the soft but even-grained alder.

The terrain is of two major types, which grade into each other in the Gulf of Georgia–Puget Sound region. In the north, the Coast Range is composed of towering mountains of raw, naked rock. Deep cañons, gouged out by glacial flow and turbulent streams, cut into them. A general subsidence in ancient geological times has "drowned" many of these valleys and cañons, producing long narrow fiords flanked by sheer cliffs rising hundreds of feet. The scenery is spectacular; travel, except by water and over a few rare passes, is painful and slow. As one goes southward the terrain changes until, around upper Puget Sound and the Oregon and northwestern Californian coasts, one sees steep but rounded coast hills, not mountains; estuaries resulting from the building up of sand bars form at river mouths, indicating the gentler gradients of the lower portions of the stream beds.

The areal fauna, like everything else, is highly specialized. Varieties and abundance of marine forms have been mentioned. The principal large game animals were deer, elk, and, on the mainland from the Gulf of Georgia northward, mountain goats. Where long northern fiords cut entirely or partially through the Coast Range, hunters had access to subarctic faunal assemblages, including caribou and moose. Coastal carnivores included chiefly wolf, black and grizzly bear, and brown bear in the north, mountain lion, and a variety of small fur bearers: beaver, mink, marten, and land otter, among others. The problems related to the distribution of land species, especially in the island areas along the Inland Passage are intriguing, though they have little connection with areal culture patterns. For example, on the Queen Charlotte Islands there were black bear and a type of small caribou, but no grizzly bear or deer. (The modern deer population has descended from a few pairs imported by white settlers some forty or fifty years ago.) On Vancouver Island deer, elk, wolf, mountain lion, and black bear, among the larger forms, occurred, but neither mountain goat nor grizzly. A small "black bear" with an all-white coat, known as Kermode's bear, was found in the vicinity of Princess Royal Island, and apparently nowhere else. Up the coast, nearly every major island from Admiralty Island north seems to have its own distinctive subspecies of Alaskan brown bear. It is possible that the deer population of northwestern California tended to show much greater color variation than in other areas. To return from oddities of distributions to the general faunal picture, the Pacific flyway follows the coast for a great part of its length, and enormous flights of waterfowl of many species flew along it on their annual migrational round.

Few modern students of human society will subscribe to a theory of environmental determinism of culture. Yet, while the geographical background of aboriginal Northwest Coast civilization can by no means be said to have defined the culture patterns of the area, it can be shown to have had a certain influence, by permitting, and even inducing, development along some lines, and inhibiting that along others. Some of the environmentally affected cultural elaborations are included among the patterns that make the areal culture as a whole distinctive, as compared with other native civilizations of North America. It is true enough that in other equally important area-wide patterns no environmental factors can be detected, but those in which the physical setting played a part are worth discussing.

Marine resources may be considered first. We have seen that they were tremendously rich and, in addition, partly seasonal (that is, the "runs" of certain important species of fish, such as salmon, herring, smelt, and olachen, occur for a limited period each year). The abundance of these resources made a relatively dense population possible, once techniques had been devised to exploit them properly. Even more basically, it favored the orientation of the areal culture toward the water—the river and sea—with a consequent interest in development of water transport, that is, development of vessel construction and navigation. In fact, in the northern, more rugged half of the area it seems probable that a certain minimum proficiency in canoemanship must have been essential to the earliest human occupancy. It is difficult to see how people could have survived without it. At the same time, it is possible to interpret the richness of the fisheries resource as a limiting factor also: concentrated, as the "runs" of salmon and the other fish were, at the upper ends of bays and channels, or along the beaches, they may have restricted interest in water transport to the foreshore. It is certain that the Indians of the Northwest Coast were not deep-sea navigators in the same sense as the Vikings or the Polynesians. They sailed along the coast, from point to point, and hated to get out of sight of land.

Another feature of the natural environment that affected culture growth was the seasonal aspect of the principal "harvests" of fish. This made for periods of intense activity, put a premium on the development of techniques for the preservation of foodstuffs, and, once such techniques had been developed, permitted lengthy periods of leisure. In fact, once adequate preservation techniques had been developed, not only was there opportunity for leisure, but there was a certain force for seasonal immobility; even a large family group is unlikely to favor a nomadic way of life if they have half a ton of dried salmon to lug around with them. This leisure and temporary immobility was utilized by the Indians of our area for the development of art and ceremonialism. Here of course is where the strictly environmental interpretations of culture break down. The particular fields of interest that were seized on were determined by historical and social factors of human culture, and not by environment at all. All the environment did was to make possible the development of economic techniques that permitted considerable leisure. How that leisure was utilized was not defined by the natural setting—as far as environmental forces were concerned it might as well have been spent at studies of mathematics or crossword puzzles. The important thing is that the natural resources were such that they permitted the expansion of some luxury aspects of culture.

Another environmentally favored development was that of woodworking. As will be brought out, there were undoubtedly historical factors involved in the original interest in this activity, but the fact that the forests of the Northwest Coast were amply supplied with an abundance of readily worked woods made elaboration of this craft possible, and even might be said to have offered a certain inducement to such elaboration. Wood was beyond all question the most abundant type of material available. Moreover, other materials suitable for technological developments were scarce.

Some inhibiting factors of the environment may be pointed out. In the northern half of the area, unquestionably because of the roughness of the terrain, land hunting was a luxury activity, not a major field of economic endeavor. Another example: the mountainous northern coasts were formed of massive blocks of tough igneous rocks; work in stone was of minor importance throughout the area as a consequence, since stone that lent itself to working was relatively rare. There are exceptions. A very tractable form of slate occurs at a few localities in the Queen Charlotte Islands, but given the general absence of a stoneworking pattern, little or no use was made of it until historic times brought new cultural stimuli. Again, the northern half of the area has little land suitable for agriculture and even today agriculture is a very minor form of economy. Even if, in aboriginal times, contacts with agricultural areas had made possible the introduction of the art (as far as we know, there were no such direct contacts), it could never have had much effect on native culture, at least in the north. Even though there was a much-disputed plant—a tobacco or one resembling tobacco—supposed to have been cultivated in the Queen Charlotte Islands, and a true native tobacco was planted and harvested along the lower Klamath River in modern California, agriculture could never have reached a point where it would have modified the prevailing fishing and sea-hunting economy of the coast.

We may summarize our survey of the natural setting as follows: There were certain permissive factors in the environment that allowed cultural developments in certain aspects of native culture. Some of these—dependence on exploitation of marine resources, elaboration of canoe navigation, emphasis on woodworking—came to be distinctive of the areal culture. Some negative characteristics of the area, such as minor importance of land hunting, very rudimentary development of stoneworking, and the like, are due to inhibiting factors of the natural scene which did not provide adequate materials. However, many other features of coastal culture that served to mark it off as different from most other Indian civilizations of North America can be traced only to historical factors, or to the selection of certain solutions to problems posed by functional relationships of strictly cultural, not environmental, phenomena.

The People

Along this rugged but bountiful coast lived a number of Indian nations who differed among themselves somewhat in physical characteristics, differed considerably in language, but shared a

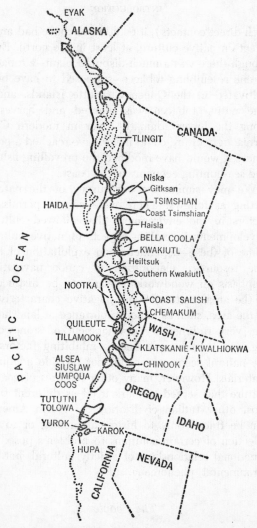

Fig. 2. This map indicates the linguistic groupings of the Northwest Coast Indians. The Niska, Gitksan, and Coast Tsimshian are considered sub-groups of the larger Tsimshian group; the Haisla, Southern Kwakiutl, and Heiltsuk sub-groups of the Kwakiutl. The other names (Bella Coola, Tlingit, Haida, and so forth) refer to similar language groups.

number of fundamental cultural patterns that, in combination, comprised Northwest Coast civilization. It must be noted that here, as elsewhere throughout this book, the term "nation" is used with certain reservations, for as will be explained below, there were no nations in the modern political sense. There *were* groups, however, who spoke the same language or dialect of that language, who resembled each other more closely in details of culture than they did their neighbors of alien speech, and who consisted of independent local groups, tribes, or even confederacies, but who were without any sort of over-all "national" political authority or even any sense of political unity.

Beginning our enumeration of Northwest Coast peoples in the north, the Tlingit, consisting of fourteen tribal divisions, occupied the coast from Yakutat Bay to Cape Fox. They spoke a language believed by most linguists to be related to the Athapascan stock of the interior. Shortly before the opening of the historic period they were pressing westward. Some of their divisions, probably the Yakutat, had driven the Chugachmiut Eskimo off Kayak Island, and the same or some related tribe established an outpost among the linguistically (distantly) related Eyak of the mouth of the Copper River. A small Tlingit-speaking group, the Tagish, on Tagish and Marsh lakes (inland from the Chilkat Tlingit), possessed a culture of completely interior, not coastal, pattern, and were apparently an Athapascan people who were in the process of becoming Tlingit-ized through aboriginal trade contacts. According to tradition, the ancestors of some of the Tlingit clans once lived to the south, around the mouth of the Skeena, and subsequently moved northward. Other ancestral divisions migrated from the interior, following the Stikine River to the sea. If the traditions are to be believed, they reached salt water only after a perilous journey under a glacier that bridged a section of the river.

The Haida, who also spoke a language believed to be related to Athapascan, although differing from Tlingit, inhabited the Queen Charlotte Islands, and the southern part of Prince of Wales Island in Alaska. It is said that the Alaskan Haida, known as the Kaigani, drove out some Southern Tlingit tribe or tribes a little more than two centuries ago. There are two principal dialectic divisions among the Haida. These are called "Masset" and "Skidegate" after two important centers where the speakers of each assembled during historic times, following the sharp decline of the population. Most if not all the Kaigani came from the northern or Masset-speaking villages. Haida traditions relate that some of their ancestors—those belonging to the Eagle phratry (of which more later)—came from the mainland, but claim that the other Haida, whom the newcomers found living on the islands, had been there since the creation of the world.

The Tsimshian nation lived on the mainland and the adjacent islands. Each of the three major subdivisions spoke a slightly divergent dialect, and differed somewhat culturally. The first were the Niska, or Nass River tribes. The second, the Coast Tsimshian, consisted of fourteen tribes who held salmon-fishing villages on the lower Skeena River, and olachen-fishing grounds on the lower Nass. Nine of these tribes had separate winter villages along Metlakatla Pass, just off the modern city of Prince Rupert, and three had winter villages, one off the mouth of the Skeena, the other two to the south. Two Coast Tsimshian tribes, the Kitselas and Kitsamxelam, wintered in their villages just below the cañon of the Skeena. The third major division, the Gitksan, inhabited eight villages above the cañon.

Some linguists classify the Tsimshian language with a proposed linguistic stock, as yet not certainly defined, for which they suggest the name "Penutian." The nearest fellow speakers of this stock were to be found far to the south, within the limits of modern Washington, Oregon, and California. According to Tsimshian tradition, most of their divisions came originally from a legendary place called Temlaxam ("Tum-la-ham"), "Prairie Town," located somewhere far up the Skeena. We are on surer ground when we consider more recent events: after the Hudson's Bay Company built Fort Simpson in 1834, the nine tribes who wintered on Metlakatla Pass shifted their winter quarters to Fort Simpson. In 1887 a large group, mainly from Fort Simpson, who were followers of the energetic missionary William Duncan, moved to a site on Annette Island, Alaska, where their descendants still live.

South of the Tsimshian were the Kwakiutl, with three major dialectic divisions: that spoken by the Haisla of Gardner and Douglas channels in the north, a second dialect called Heiltsuk, and Southern Kwakiutl. The Heiltsuk-speakers consisted of the Xaihais, the Bella Bella of Milbanke Sound, a historic confederation of several formerly independent tribes and local groups, and the Wikeno of Rivers Inlet. The traditional origin tales of all these people claim Rivers Inlet and lower Burke and

Dean channels as their original homeland. The Haisla, for example, maintain that their ancestors came overland from Rivers Inlet. After settling at the old site of Kitamat, they incorporated a wandering Tsimshian clan. It is interesting to note that the names of their principal villages, "Kitamat" and "Kitlope," are Tsimshian, not Heiltsuk words; a possible interpretation is that their ancestors infiltrated a Tsimshian area and engulfed the former occupants (contradicting the traditional claim that the Haisla were there first). The Xaihais consisted of a number of independent local groups who, as a result of their lack of political unity, were being ground to bits between the warlike Coast Tsimshian and their own equally warlike Bella Bella relatives. The Bella Bella tribes seem to have held their own against all comers. Their drastic historic decline in population was effected by disease, rather than enemy successes. The present Wikeno represent a historic amalgamation of the original Wikeno of the Inlet, with the remnants of two tribes: the Nohuntsitk and the Somehulitk, of the upper and lower ends of Wikeno Lake, respectively.

The Bella Coola villages were located in the upper reaches of Dean and Burke channels and the lower parts of the Bella Coola River valley. These people spoke a Salishan language, fairly closely allied to the speech of the Coast Salish to the south, from whom they were separated by a considerable distance. Bella Coola traditions assert that this nation was created at the beginning of the world in the same locality (which we have just defined) where Alexander Mackenzie found them in 1793. However, in view of their linguistic affiliations, it seems more probable that their ancestors split off from the main body of Salish and migrated to their northern location. Various aspects of Bella Coola culture suggest either that they have been exposed to Heiltsuk influences a relatively short time or, more likely, that they were remarkably conservative in certain culture traits. Their material culture, their ceremonials, and their mythology check almost point for point with those of their Heiltsuk neighbors. In the field of social organization, however, particularly with respect to rank and social status, they have apparently retained to a great extent the amorphous, loosely organized Salish patterns rather than the precisely and rigidly defined ones of their neighbors.

The Southern Kwakiutl consisted of a large number of independent local groups and tribes occupying the bays and inlets around Queen Charlotte Sound and the entire northern end of Vancouver Island, as far south as Cape Cook. Like the Bella Coola, they insist that their ancestors were created in the region they now occupy; the possibilities are that they have occupied it for a considerable length of time. There is little evidence of any major population shifts among them, other than the expansion of the southernmost tribe, the Lekwiltok, into the Cape Mudge area at the expense of the Salishan Comox, and the separation of the Matilpe from the Fort Rupert confederacy. The Lekwiltok deserve special mention as one of the most warlike groups of the entire coast. Their original territory dominated Yucluta Rapids and Seymour Narrows, passes between Vancouver Island and the mainland. They exacted tribute or attacked anyone who traveled these roads, whether the party was a peaceful one going on a trading expedition or to a potlatch, or whether it was a Haida war party bent on slave raiding in Puget Sound. They were, of course, frequently attacked in retaliation, but always gave a good account of themselves.

On the southwest coast of Vancouver Island, or as it is locally known, the "West Coast," and on Cape Flattery, the extreme tip of the present state of Washington, live the Nootka. The Nootka language is distantly related to Kwakiutl; in fact, linguists consider that the two represent a single stock termed the Wakashan. It has been suggested that this stock, together with Salish and some other languages of the interior, may ultimately be related to Algonkian, a relationship that has not yet been demonstrated. There were two, or possibly three, dialectic divisions of Nootka—Nootka proper, spoken by the people from Cape Cook down to Barkley Sound—and Nitinat-Makah. It has not been established as yet whether Nitinat and Makah were minor variants of a single dialect, or whether they warrant separation into two distinct dialects. The Nootka possessed a specialized form of Northwest Coast culture—one extremely well adapted to the region. Only they (aside from a few neighbors of the Makah who learned the art from that last-named division) hunted the largest game on the coast—whales. Their basic canoe pattern was widely copied, and Nootka-made canoes were bought with eagerness by most of their neighbors because of their excellent lines and seaworthiness. The only territorial changes known to us from historical records or traditions are internal ones in which one Nootka local group or tribe exterminated or dispossessed another in order to acquire the victims' territories.

The land of the Coast Salish, aside from that of the Bella Coola, included the circumference of the Gulf of Georgia, Puget Sound, a good portion of the Olympic Peninsula, and most of western Washington, down to Chinook territory at the mouth of the Columbia River. One Salishan group, the Tillamook, resided south of the Columbia on the Oregon coast. As the name indicates, these Salish-speaking people were part of a larger linguistic entity, the bulk of whom lived in the interior to the east of the Cascades. This coast versus inland division appears to have been correlated with a major dialectic break, as well as with a differentiation between cultures of coast and inland genre. Great diversities of minor dialectic variants are recognized among the Coast Salish—the inhabitants of almost every drainage system, or at most, two or three contiguous valleys, had their own subdialects. There was a certain amount of intercourse between these coast people and their interior relatives. It is generally assumed that the coast divisions were relatively late entrants into the area, pushing down the Fraser River and spilling over the Cascades into western Washington. Such scant archaeological evidence as is available corroborates this theory, although the length of time the Salish have lived along the coast is not yet known.

A number of small enclaves of linguistically diverse groups occupied western Washington. On either side of the Nootkan Makah on the tip of Cape Flattery lived small divisions—the Chemakum on the Straits, and the Quileute on the Pacific Coast. Both of these spoke closely related languages, or dialects of the same tongue, but one not closely related to any other native North American language, although some authorities suggest a distant affiliation to a proposed group that includes Salishan, Wakashan, and Algonkian. The Chemakum became extinct too early for us to salvage any significant amount of linguistic or cultural data. We know that the Quileute borrowed heavily on the cultural side from their Makah neighbors, so that in historic times they varied from the Makah only slightly. A now extinct group, the Klatskanie, is reported to have held a sizable tract of territory in the midst of the Salish Chehalis. We know virtually nothing of this group, except that they spoke an Athapascan tongue. Presumably, they were culturally fairly similar to their Salish and Chinook neighbors. They were reputed to have been very warlike. Some time during the early historic period, they are reported to have moved from their territory on the Chehalis River across the Columbia to take up residence on the Clatskanie River in present Oregon. Another small Athapascan-speaking enclave, the Kwalhio-kwa, about whom even less is known, held a tract along the Willapa River. One wonders if they may not have been a subdivision of the Klatskanie.

Along the lower Columbia, from The Dalles down to the sea, lived the various divisions of the Chinook. The exact relationship of their language to any other is unknown, although affiliation with the proposed widespread Penutian stock has been suggested. The great fame of the Chinook nation stems from the fact that they were middlemen in aboriginal trade north and south along the coast and between the coast and the interior. They traded slaves from the Californian hinterland up the coast for Nootka canoes and the prized dentalium shells, and exchanged many other products as well. It was through their hands that the strings of dentalia from the west coast of Vancouver Island eventually reached the Plains tribes east of the Rockies.

The central coast of Oregon, south of Tillamook territory, was occupied by several small groups now virtually extinct—the Alsea, the Siuslaw, the Coos, and the Umpqua. Very little information is available on these tiny divisions. Such as there is has been collected from informants who lived their lives in the cultural hodgepodge of Siletz and Grande Ronde reservations, on which all the Indians of western Oregon were assembled and thrown into intimate contact in the 1850s. Culturally these small tribes seem to have stood midway between the Salish-Chinook patterns and those of northwestern California; if anything, they inclined slightly more toward the former.

Another segment of the Athapascan linguistic family lived in southwestern Oregon. Villages of these people, who were sometimes referred to as the Tolowa-Tututni, after two of the better-known divisions, were situated along every stream course from the upper Umpqua to Smith River in northern California. These groups were culturally marginal to—that is to say, in many respects pallid imitations of—the civilization of the lower Klamath River. In this last-named region, representatives of three linguistic stocks—the Yurok of proven Algonkian affiliation, the Hupa of the Athapascan family, and the Karok of uncertain relationship—shared a set of cultural patterns modified from the basic motifs of the Northwest Coast and elaborated in a number of unique ways. Their civilization, simple and poor as it may seem in comparison with that of the northern tribes, was complex indeed as compared with that of their Oregon coastal neighbors and most of the native groups of California.

These, then, were the Indian nations participating in the unique patterns of the civilization of the Northwest Coast. Each group's manifestations of the fundamental motifs of areal culture differed a bit. All were not of the same intensity. Some groups were obviously borrowers, not elaborators, of ideas. Some may even have been "Johnny-come-latelies" to the coastal scene. Yet all shared and utilized a series of concepts that, like the weft strands in weaving, connect the various elements—in this context the local cultural variants—into a unit distinctive and unique among native American cultures.

Prehistory

The prehistory of the Northwest Coast, from which we may hope to learn the sources and development of the areal culture, has received relatively little attention up to this time. Excavations carried out around the turn of the century at sites along the lower Fraser River and on southeastern Vancouver Island indicated that there were at least two or three distinct cultural horizons there. The lower and older horizon was associated with skeletal remains of a longheaded population, quite different from the recent and historic Coast Salish. The latest level contained human remains of a broadheaded type, that resembled both the modern Coast Salish and the Interior Salish. This situation corroborates the assumption, based on linguistic and cultural grounds, that the Coast Salish were, relatively speaking, newcomers on the coast, having pushed their way out from the interior. These early researches did not succeed in defining any cultural differences associated with the population change. However, current studies in this region and in lower Puget Sound indicate that several marked cultural changes occurred and can be defined by use of precise modern archaeological techniques. Interestingly, the earliest horizon found appears to represent a culture oriented toward the sea and the utilization of marine resources, particularly the hunting of sea mammals. Considerable use was made of one-piece toggling harpoon heads of forms surprisingly like basic Eskimo patterns, used on bone foreshafts, and points and knives of ground slate. Heavy woodworking tools are absent on this early level, suggesting to one investigator that some sort of light composite water craft—possibly even skin-covered kayaklike vessels—may have been used. This early pattern was succeeded by others in which interior culture traits became more prominent, and the dominantly maritime aspect of the earliest culture was lost.

To the northward, only one extensive survey has been made. It produced no definitive results as to culture growth, but did demonstrate that archaeological sites are numerous, large, and deep, indicating a fairly lengthy occupation by people whose economy and material culture (particularly the canoe navigation complex) were oriented very much as were those of the Indians of early historic times. Since many of these sites can be identified by modern Indians and from early historical accounts as well, they offer an excellent opportunity to take advantage of the direct historical approach, working back from known identifiable cultures to the more ancient ones.

Somewhat more archaeological work has been done along the Columbia and the coast to the south. An investigation of the Dalles-Deschutes region indicates either that the Upper Chinook adopted patterns derived from the coast in relatively late times, or that they pushed upriver, driving out a group or groups whose culture was essentially of interior type.

At the extreme south of the area, on Trinidad Bay, a sequence of three horizons has been found so far: the uppermost, dating from historic times, is preceded by a late prehistoric period, and the latter by an early prehistoric stratum. At this writing full information is not available as to whether the two lower levels represent a developmental sequence or the replacement of one culture by a completely different one.

With the still scant amount of concrete evidence supplied by the archaeologist's shovel, trowel, and brush, it is useless to speculate at length on prehistoric sequences and developments. However, it may be pointed out that while it might have been theoretically possible for interior peoples gradually to have worked their way downstream to become the first human inhabitants of the northern California, Oregon, and Washington littorals, and of the Puget Sound–lower Fraser region, the first occupants of the rugged rockbound coasts to the north must, in all likelihood, have arrived with a sizable inventory of culture traits adapted to coast life. To survive they would have needed adequate canoe navigation, with all the appurtenances, knowledge, and skills for navigating those rough waters, tools and techniques for marine fishing and hunting and the like. In other words, the sea-hunting early culture recently identified in the lower Fraser region may have been the basic pattern for the entire coast. Later entrants might, and no doubt did, come from the interior, and were able to exploit the coastal resources by adopting the implements and techniques of the original population. It is to be hoped that eventually enough careful scientific work may be done throughout the area to clarify the problems of the origins and growth of its unique culture.

Physical Anthropology*

From the land of the Tlingit south to the Fraser River, or possibly to the Puget Sound–Olympic Peninsula region, the Indians shared, and still share, certain similarities of appearance. They tend to range from tall to medium stature, with group means from about 5 feet 8 inches, in the north, to 5 feet 3 inches (173 to 162 centimeters), and are rather "stocky" in body conformation, with broad muscular chests and shoulders. As a rule they have broad heads (that is, heads which are wide in relation to length) and broad faces. An especially noteworthy characteristic is lightness of skin color. Unexposed (that is, un-sunburned) areas of the body are scarcely distinguishable in shade from the skin of many brunet Europeans. This is definitely not a result of race mixture during historic times; many of the early European explorers, like Captain Cook and Captain Vancouver, were struck by this fact, and made particular note of it in their descriptions

* The data for this section were assembled from various published sources by Dr. Marshall T. Newman, Division of Physical Anthropology, U.S. National Museum.

of the people of the northern coasts. Hair tends to
be coarse in texture, varies from straight to slightly
wavy, and although popularly referred to as "black,"
is actually very dark brown. Men appear to have
more profuse facial hair (mustaches and beards)
than do other North American Indians. Well-de-
veloped "folds" at the inner sides of the upper eye-
lids are common.

Within this generalized physical type, there are
several variations, some of which tend to mark off
regional sub-types, and others that suggest results
of mixture of distinct Indian types. The picture is
complicated by the fact that the variant traits do
not all correlate regionally. Stature, for example,
shows an almost regular decrease from north to
south, between south Alaska and the Fraser Delta.
The Tlingit, when measured around the turn of the
century, were tall people—the tallest on the coast
—averaging 173 centimeters (5 feet 8 inches) in
height. The Haida and Coast Tsimshian were still
to be regarded as tall, averaging 169 centimeters;
the Niska were a trifle shorter: 167 centimeters. To
the southward, the series runs in the "medium"
range: Bella Coola, 166 centimeters; Southern Kwakiutl, 164; Coast Salish of the Fraser Delta, 162.
The Puget Sound Salish alter this trend by averaging 165 centimeters. Boas, who pioneered the investigation of the physical anthropology of the area
as well as those in linguistics and ethnography, interpreted this north-south stature trend as the result of gradual permeation of tall northern people,
possibly originally Athapascans of the interior,
southward along the coast, modifying an older
short-statured population.

In addition to the stature gradient, Boas distin-

1. Karok dipnetting salmon on the lower Klamath River. A. L. Kroeber photograph.

2. Haida hardwood clubs (about 15 inches high) used to kill hooked halibut and harpooned seal. The Tlingit, Tsimshian, and Northern Kwakiutl used similar implements; farther south, shaped but undecorated clubs were used.

3. *Various types of fishhooks. The two at the top are Haida "black cod" hooks, also used by neighboring groups for ground fishing. In the center are sharp-angled hooks from the Tlingit of the type commonly used for codfish and for salmon trolling. At the bottom, left and right, are Kwakiutl-Nootka type halibut hooks; the U-shaped shank is steamed and bent into shape. Bottom center is a Nootka hook used in offshore trolling for salmon. These hooks vary in size from about 2½ inches to 8 or 9 inches.*

4. *Spoons and ladles. The example at the top is Tsimshian and made entirely of mountain-goat horn; the others are Haida and are made of mountain-goat horn with mountain-sheep horn bowls. These spoons vary in height from about 6 inches to 10 inches. (See Figure 12.)*

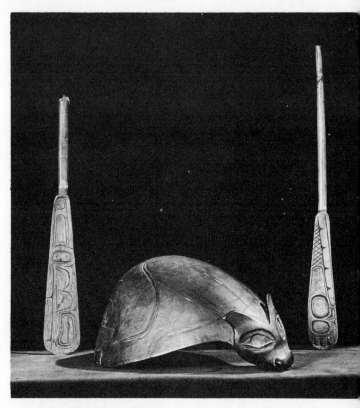

5. *The flat wooden spatula-like spoons were used to eat the popular sopalalli or "soapberry" mixture which consisted of berries whipped to a froth in a mixture of cold water and olachen grease. The carving on the mountain-sheep horn bowl, probably Tlingit, represents a Wolf, or Sea-wolf; the crosshatching on the right-hand spoon (16 inches high) suggests a reference to a Beaver.*

6. The old Haida village of Tanu, Queen Charlotte Islands, showing house frames and totem poles. C. F. Newcombe photograph, taken about 1900.

7. *A Southern Kwakiutl village of the 1880s. The vertical planking on the houses is one effect of the availability of iron nails. The boldly simplified carvings are typical of Kwakiutl art prior to the influence of northern "totem pole" art.*

8. *Yurok houses of redwood planks. Note the double slope of the roofs on the far side of both houses, which, with the slope nearest the camera, formed the typical "three-pitch" roof of the lower Klamath. A. L. Kroeber photograph.*

9. *A chief's house in a Bella Coola village (probably Kimsquit), near the turn of the twentieth century. The house combines alien influences: the framed doorway and windows are of European source; the false plates and nailed vertical planking are imitations of aboriginal custom. Note the difference in the rather ponderous carving of the crest-display pole as compared to the vigorous old-style Kwakiutl carving and as well to the more stylized carving of the north. The gill net drying on the racks in the left foreground is a type of European commercial fishing net. Courtesy of the Smithsonian Institution.*

10. A lower Klamath dugout canoe. Note the high steep ends, the identical bow and stern, and the rounded hull section that made this craft highly maneuverable in swift water, but cranky on the open sea. The chain painter is a modern addition. A. L. Kroeber photograph. (See Figure 14.)

11. The side of a carved Haida box, reported to have been used by a famous shaman for storing his professional kit. The carving on the box appears to represent a Beaver. The ends of the box were carved in the same manner. These boxes were made in many sizes.

12. An oil dish from the Haida (about 8 inches long), used to hold the grease they dipped their food in. This specimen represents a hair seal, the animal from which the grease came.

13. A Chilkat weaver putting the finishing touches on a robe. Note the "half loom" from which the blanket is suspended, the mountain-goat gut bags at the bottom to keep the ends of the fringe clean, and the pattern-board at the weaver's right.

guished three regional sub-types on the British Columbia coast. He described them as follows:

"Northern sub-type" [Haida, Tsimshian]: This sub-type is characterized by tall stature, with relatively long arms, short trunks and long legs. The head is both very large and relatively broad, and the face is correspondingly quite broad, and only moderately long. The nose tends to be low, concave in profile, with a low root and broad alae. The Tlingit probably fit in this sub-type, their principal deviation being that of their greater average stature.

"Kwakiutl sub-type" [Kwakiutl and Bella Coola]: Medium rather than tall stature marks this group off from the preceding. In addition, bodily proportions differ considerably, the trunk being much longer in relation to length of limbs. Chests and shoulders are commonly very broad. The dimensions of the head are about like those of the northern sub-type. Facial proportions differ sharply, however; faces are not only very broad, but they are also relatively and absolutely extremely long. Lower jaws are massive and wide. The nose form typical of this subdivision is very long, relatively narrow, and highly arched, with a convex profile rarely seen in the north.

There are virtually no data on Nootkan anthropometry, but casual observation suggests that they conform to this physical pattern, except that high convex noses, and low-bridged concave ones, seem to be about equally common among them.

"Thompson River sub-type" [Coast and Interior Salish]: Boas found no objective means of distinguishing between the physical type of the Salish of the coasts and that of their relatives of the interior.

In stature they are medium, ranging to the lower boundary of that category (165 to 162 centimeters). They also are broadheaded, but their heads are smaller in actual measurement, in both length and breadth, than those of their neighbors to the north. Their faces are broad, and proportionately and in actual measurement much shorter than those of the Kwakiutl. Noses are heavy, convex in profile, with a heavy long tip. The Salish also all tend to be slightly darker in skin color than the northerners.

One interesting feature of this survey is the thorough modification of the Bella Coola, who presumably once conformed to the physical sub-type of their Salish kinsmen. This fact suggests that not only were their closest contacts and intermarriages with the Kwakiutl, but that they may have maintained such contacts over a respectably long time period.

Such few archaeological data as are available indicate that the situation was not static. In the lower Fraser region, at least, there is definite evidence that an earlier population of different physical type, with relatively long narrow heads and narrow faces, and apparently of short stature, preceded people whose skeletal remains conform to the modern Salish ("Thompson River") sub-type. Occasional individuals of this ancient lower Fraser type appear as minor elements in historic Haida, Kwakiutl, and Coast Salish series. This probably means that this former population once occupied a considerable portion of the northern coasts.

An intriguing problem, which unfortunately probably cannot be resolved after more than a century and a half of racial mixture, relates to the occurrences of a few individuals with definitely brown (rather than the usual "very dark brown") hair color, and light-colored eyes. Alexander Mackenzie noted a number of such persons, with gray eyes, among the Bella Coola in 1793 (he was of course the first European known to have met this nation). We can only speculate as to whether these physical traits represent local mutations from the normal Northwest Coast genetic traditions, or whether some "Archaic White" strain, such as many human biologists believe occurs among the Ainu (the aborigines of Japan), might have been included in the racial heritage of the Northwest Coast Indians.

From western Washington south to northern California, there are few data on the Indian physical type or types. No studies were made in early days comparable to those by Boas in the north; since that time many small groups have dwindled to disappearance, and others have become so racially mixed that it would be impossible to define the aboriginal type. There are a few figures on stature, which show great irregularity, rather than a uniform trend as in the north. The Puget Sound Salish were in the medium category, with an average height of 165 centimeters—a little taller than their lower Fraser cousins. The Chinook on the Columbia were tall: 169 centimeters. The groups of the central Oregon coast seem to have been medium, around 165 centimeters; the northwest Californians varied from medium to tall. Some physical anthropologists have the impression that there was a strong strain of interior type, perhaps similar to Boas's "northern sub-type," in this region, which, in southwest Oregon and northwest California, was blended with a distinct longheaded California type.

History of European Contacts

Aside from the apocryphal voyages of Juan de Fuca and Admiral Fuente, the first Europeans to see the Northwest Coast were the Russian crew of one of the vessels of the Dane Vitus Bering, who made landfall in Tlingit territory in 1741. They sent a boat ashore which never returned. Presumably the boat crew was killed by the Tlingit, because a number of war canoes came out to threaten the ship itself, whereupon Bering sailed away. In 1774 a Spaniard, Juan Perez, hove to at a place he called San Lorenzo, which seems to have been Nootka Sound. Some natives came out in canoes and were given a couple of silver spoons. These ephemeral contacts had little effect on the natives, of course.

The first really important European contact occurred in 1778 on Captain James Cook's third voyage of exploration. He entered Nootka Sound where he spent some time before sailing on to southwest Alaska. While at Nootka Sound, some of Cook's party were given, and others traded for, sea-otter skins. When the expedition reached China, after Cook's tragic death in the Hawaiian Islands, they discovered that the lustrous brown pelts were highly prized by the Chinese, who were willing to pay—for that period—fabulous prices for them. When this news reached England, it was not long before a number of ships were fitting out for a voyage to the new land of treasure. Companies were formed in England for this new trade, and the East India Company assigned vessels to it. Hanna, Meares, Dixon, and Portlock were among the first ship captains to arrive on the coast. They explored hitherto unknown parts of it and then departed for China to dispose of their rich hauls of furs.

For the next few years, dozens of vessels visited the coast annually. They combed the bays and inlets in search of Indians who might have sea-otter pelts. English and American ships, the latter principally out of Boston, dominated the trade. Before long two other nations who had Pacific interests became alarmed at what they considered a threat to their colonial empires. The Russian-American Company had established its base on Kodiak Island in 1789. Up to that time, and for the next few years, the Russians confined their activities pretty much to the exploitation of the southwestern Alaskan fur trade; but the presence on the coast of so many vessels flying other flags eventually stimulated their expansion into Tlingit territory. Before this happened, however, in 1790, Spanish fear of the threat to her dominions created the so-called Nootka Controversy, which nearly brought England and Spain to war. These facts, of course, were of little immediate concern to the natives and are mentioned here only in passing. The effect of the fur trade on the native cultures is more important.

While Cook was in Nootka Sound, he noted that the Indians were quite familiar with iron, possessed a considerable number of tools and implements of this material, and—what proved of most importance to the later traders—were very anxious to acquire iron blades of any sort. For the next few years, the traders who succeeded Cook discovered that flat iron blades and chisels were the best possible trade goods. They filled their holds with pelts worth a king's ransom in China for a few barrels of adze blades, roughly made knives, and cheap glass beads given in exchange. However, they soon glutted the market, and in competing amongst themselves, taught the Indians to set higher and higher prices on their furs. Then there followed a period in which fads ruled the trade. A captain named Ingraham had his ship's armorer make some bracelets and neck rings of twisted wrought iron. These caught the native fancy and for a season or two following, the Indians spurned most other trade articles. The seafaring traders racked their brains to find things that might appeal to the Indians. Before long the Boston skippers came to dominate the trade. Their single great advantage was their ability to sell their cargoes directly in China. British traders could not take advantage of this because the East India Company held a monopoly on trade in Asiatic ports. The Yankee skippers developed an elaborate three-cornered operation. They sailed from Boston to the Northwest Coast, where they traded for furs which they sold in Canton and bought cargoes of tea, spices, and silk which they brought back to Boston. Eventually sandalwood from the Hawaiian Islands was included as a regular item for the Chinese trade.

The seagoing traders differed in one very important respect from traders ashore, who established posts which they planned to maintain for a number of years. The seafarers did not intend to return. The captain's share from a really successful voyage netted him enough to retire on, or at least enough to set him up in business ashore. Consequently, they had no interest in cultivating the good will of the natives. They did not hesitate to cheat or to rob them when they could obtain furs no other way. The warlike nature of the Northwest

Coast Indians was their only deterrent from out-right piracy. Even at that, there were innumerable affrays. Some traders fired at flotillas of canoes or villages on the beach at the slightest provocation; naturally, the Indians retaliated. If they could not revenge themselves on the attacking vessel, they were liable to assail the next ship that came along, for in their view all white men were of one tribe.

As time went on, faddism in trade goods de-creased and utilitarian articles were in greater de-mand, as well as a few luxury items that included exotic foods like molasses, rice, and, of course, rum —the traders' standby. Firearms came into great demand. Some traders discovered that certain na-tive products were reliable commodities, so they traded for tanned elkskins at the mouth of the Columbia and exchanged these for furs with the northern groups. Dentalia from Nootka territory, slaves from wherever they could be bought, and olachen oil from the Nass were all frequently car-ried aboard Boston vessels as trade goods.

Meanwhile, as the traders were stripping the coast of sea-otter furs, other events had taken place. Vancouver, in 1792 and 1793, had made his meticu-lous explorations and surveys and had discussed transfer of the Spanish establishment at Nootka to the British Crown with the Spanish commander Bodega y Quadra. The year 1793 marks the begin-ning of another era—that of the interest in the coastal trade that was ultimately demonstrated by land-based companies. The Northwest Company sent Alexander Mackenzie overland to search for a route of access to the coast. In 1799, the Russians es-tablished Fort Archangel near modern Sitka, which the Tlingit attacked and destroyed two years later.

In 1804 the Russians made another attempt and built a new fort near the same site, which they were able to hold.

The pattern for the expansion of land-based fur traders on the Northwest Coast came into existence in 1821 with the coalition of the Hudson's Bay and the Northwest companies. Sir George Simpson was designated governor of the "Northern Department," which included the Northwest Coast and the adjacent interior. The same year that the headquarters of the Company was moved across the Columbia to Fort Vancouver, at Simpson's orders a supply ship was sent to the Portland Canal, which had finally been established as the southern limit of Russian claims in Northwest America. In the course of the next few years, a chain of posts was built along the coast. Fort Langley, in the vicinity of modern Vancouver, British Columbia, was built in 1827; Fort Nass in 1831, abandoned and replaced by Fort Simpson in 1834, and Fort McLoughlin in 1834.

The purpose of the northern forts was to cut off the flow of furs to the American traders. By this time, the sea-otter population along the whole coast had been reduced to a small fraction of its original abundance. The traders were dealing mostly in land furs, beaver, land otter, and the like, that were obtained in the interior, traded to Indian middlemen on the coast, and by them to the white fur buyers. The fact that the Indians knew a good thing when they saw it was made abundantly clear to the representative of Hudson's Bay Company, Peter Skene Ogden, when he went to survey the possibilities of establishing a post on the Stikine River. Two Stikine Tlingit chiefs visited him and

told him, in what Ogden termed somewhat plain-
tively in his report "a tone I was not in the habit of
hearing," that they would not permit him to establish a post upriver where it would be in a position
to cut off their trade with the interior. A more em-
phatic demonstration of their belief in the importance of their monopolistic trade rights is reported
to have been made by the Chilkat Tlingit in 1852.
This group sent a war party nearly three hundred
miles inland on a mission, successfully carried out,
of capturing and destroying the Hudson's Bay Company's post of Fort Selkirk, at the junction of the
Lewes and Pelly rivers. The captured personnel of
the post were not massacred, but humanely released with the stern warning, however, that they
should stay out of Chilkat trading territory.

To return to the history of the coast, in 1839 the
Hudson's Bay Company leased the mainland coast
of southeast Alaska, from Mount Fairweather to the
Portland Canal, from the Russians for a period of
ten years. They established posts at the mouth of
the Stikine and the Taku rivers. For the next few
years, the policies of the Company, which involved
a minimum of direct interference with native cultures—other than supplying the people with trade
articles—prevailed for the length of the coast. The
Indians were enriched in worldly possessions and
free to make such use of them as they pleased.
More important still, the nations of southeast Alaska
and coastal British Columbia remained, and remain to this day, on their ancestral sites and have
never been subjected to the demoralizing effects of
segregated reservation life.

2 ECONOMY

Fishing was the basis of Northwest Coast economy. The rivers and the sea provided an abundance of foods. There are five species of Pacific salmon, some of which "run" annually in every river and stream along the coast. All of these could be taken in great quantity to be dried and stored for future use. Smelt, herring, and, in the north, the oil-rich olachen or "candlefish" also assembled in vast numbers during their spawning seasons, and were easily caught by the Indians. A variety of efficient devices was used by Indian fishermen. Traps, constructed like huge baskets, were set up in the rivers and sometimes at points along the coast where salmon congregate. Fencelike weirs of poles were constructed to turn the fish into these traps (Figs. 3, 4). For olachen, wherever they run, a special type of funnel-shaped net was used from the Kwakiutl area northward. The principal "runs" are in the Nass, the Kitamat, and the Bella Coola rivers, and the main rivers emptying into Rivers and Knights inlets. Ownership of olachen-fishing rights was highly prized, and people from far and near assembled at such places as the lower Nass River where Haida and Tlingit who had no fishing rights came to buy the oil.

All the coastal groups made dip nets, that is, bags of netting attached to a wooden frame on a handle, some like large editions of our fly fisherman's landing net, others on a V-shaped frame (Plate 1). These were used for salmon, and, in finer mesh and specialized forms, for smaller fish like herring and smelt. Long sections of netting suitable for seining or gill-netting (a special form in which the mesh allows the fish's head to enter, but catches under his gill covers when he tries to turn back), or that could be fashioned into huge bags for trawling from canoes, appear to have been ancient devices among the Coast Salish and all the groups to the south-

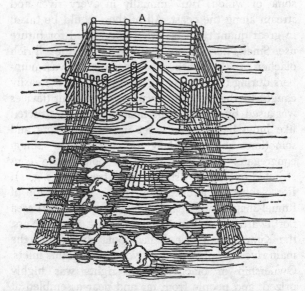

Fig. 3. The plan of a Kwakiutl salmon trap. (A) is a fence which generally extends some distance beyond the low-water banks of the river. Attached to this fence is a box-like structure (B) built of frames tied to stakes and located in the middle of the river. On each side of the box are two short frames with openings that lead into long, narrow fish baskets (C).

ward, but not along the northern coasts, with the
possible exception of the Tsimshian Niska. The
Coast Tsimshian and the Haida claim to have
learned the use of the Niska gill nets—in fact, obtained the finished nets—from the people of the
Nass in late prehistoric or early historic times.

The harpoon, a sort of spear with detachable
head connected to the shaft by a short line, was one
of the principal salmon-fishing devices. The northernmost groups used harpoons with a single, one-

Fig. 4. Kwakiutl salmon trap used in narrow streams.

piece barbed bone or horn point; from Kwakiutl
territory to northwestern California two-pronged
harpoons, armed with compound barbed heads,
were used (Fig. 5). There were many variations on
this two-pronged harpoon pattern, especially among
the Kwakiutl-speaking groups and the Nootka.
Lightweight short harpoons were made for throw-

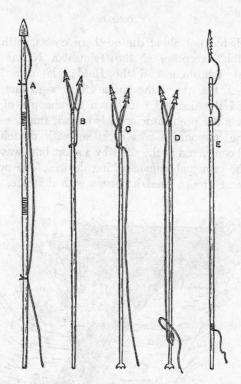

Fig. 5. Types of harpoons. In (A), a Nootkan whaling harpoon, the lanyard from the compound head was attached to the shaft at two points with light string, so that the weight of the lanyard and long line to which it was attached would not pull the head from the shaft before it was thrust into the whale. (B) is a common type of salmon harpoon, used everywhere except among the northern groups, who used a single tipped implement. The lanyards are joined and tied to the lower end of the shaft. (C) and (D) are examples of sealing harpoons used by the Kwakiutl and Nootka. The spurlike catches on the shafts held the heads in place during the harpoon's flight through the air. (E) is a Northern-type sealing harpoon with detachable foreshaft. Sometimes the line from the foreshaft was lengthened and attached to a float, rather than to the shaft. The whaling harpoons (A) were from 14 to 18 feet long, the sealing harpoons (D) from 6 to 7 feet long.

ing at salmon that swam with their dorsal fins out
of the water in the bays near river mouths. Shafts
that projected beyond the diverging foreshafts were
used for thrusting downward in deep pools; the
projecting main shaft served as a buffer, to protect
the points from breaking on rocks in the river bottom. Leisters—poles with two springy arms fitted
with sharp points projecting inward and backward
—were common from the Gulf of Georgia northward. Nowadays detachable gaffs, made of a heavy-
gauge steel hook attached to the shaft by a short
lanyard, harpoon-fashion, are popular salmon-fishing implements.

Angling was another method of fishing. Salmon
will strike a baited hook while still in salt water, before the spawning season; cod and halibut will take
bait at any time. The most nearly universally used
hook was the simplest form, with a straight or
slightly curved wooden shank to which a barbless
bone or horn point was lashed at an acute angle
(Plate 3). The groups living on the Olympic Peninsula above the Gulf of Georgia—the Nootka and
Southern Kwakiutl—used such hooks, baited with
fresh herring, in trolling for king salmon. Though a
hand-line technique was used, it took no small
measure of skill to boat a mature "king" (or "spring"
or "Chinook" in colloquial terminology) on one of
these barbless hooks. Cod were taken by bottom-
fishing with the same type of hooks.

Halibut were taken by bottom-fishing, also, from
the Olympic Peninsula north, but special hooks were
used. The Tlingit, Haida, Tsimshian, and the Northern Kwakiutl groups, Haisla, and Xaihais, made
halibut hooks of hardwood, shaped like a V with
one short arm, with a bone barb fastened into the

short side. The shanks of these hooks were often
elaborately carved with crests or figures intended
to have magical potency (Fig. 6). Two of these
hooks were attached by short leaders to the ends
of a cross-pole, to the middle of which a stone sinker
was attached. The cross-pole held the buoyant
wooden hooks clear of the line so as not to foul it.
Large hooks of similar form, but undecorated, were

*Fig. 6.   Tlingit and Haida V-shaped halibut hooks. The
Coast Tsimshian and Northern Kwakiutl used the same type
of hook.*

used by the Chinook for the huge Columbia River
sturgeon. The other Kwakiutl-speaking tribes, the
Nootka, the Coast Salish of the Gulf of Georgia and
Puget Sound, and the groups of northwestern
Washington, made halibut hooks of spruce withes,
steamed into U shape, and fitted with a sharp bone
barb (Plate 3). The springy arms of the hook
spread to permit the halibut to insert his snout to
take the bait, then helped set the barb. These hooks

ECONOMY 41

were attached to one end of a short rod, the other
end of which was made fast to the line, and also
supported a stone weight just heavy enough to hold
the rod horizontally, and keep the hook clear of the
line. Lines were commonly made of the long thin
stems of giant kelp.

A number of other minor fishing devices were
also in use along the coast. The "herring rake," for
example, was a long flat board with sharp bone
points set in one edge. While a companion in the
stern paddled, the fisherman used the rake with a
paddling motion, holding it edgewise, points to the
rear. As the canoe glided over the surfacing shoals
of herring, the fisherman followed through on each
stroke so as to bring the rake over the gunwale behind him, shaking the fish impaled on the points into
the canoe. According to local traditions, this device
was used for olachen fishing by the Niska before
they learned to make and use the special funnel-
shaped nets from the Haida.

In the Puget Sound area and along the Washington coast one's feet and a sharp stick were all
one needed to catch flounders. Parties of men and
youths waded about on the mud flats. When the
fisherman stepped on a flatfish resting on the bottom, he tried to hold the fish until he could spear it
with the stick. This sort of fishing was considered
something of a lark.

The northwestern Californians made a simple
gaff by lashing a sharp splinter of bone to a long
pole, and with this tool hooked out the lamprey
eels that run at certain seasons in the rivers.

In addition to the many varieties of fish, the sea
also provided numerous edible shellfish: clams of
many kinds, mussels, small abalones, and, in some

localities, oysters, and a great host of small gastropods such as limpets and periwinkles. Crabs, sea urchins, and the like were also abundant. That the Indians did not disdain these delicacies is proved by the fact that old village sites from Yakutat to Trinidad Bay are marked by great mounds consisting mostly of the shells discarded after meals made of the shellfish. Some shells also provided useful materials for tools or utensils. Large mussel shells were ground sharp to form the areally universal woman's knife. Deep clamshells made convenient spoons for sipping broth. Gathering shellfish was generally regarded as a woman's task, although men occasionally aided their wives. Specially made sticks of hardwood were used to dig up the mollusks or pry them loose.

While the hunting of sea mammals had a definite economic value, it yielded even greater returns in prestige to its participants. Among many of the tribes it approached a professional status; specific types of sea hunting were specialties of high-ranking chiefs. Chiefs of Northern Nootkan and most Kwakiutl tribes had special hereditary rights to the fat and flesh of hair seal taken in their waters, indicating the great importance they attached to sealing.

Hair seal, sea lion, and porpoise were hunted with the same type of equipment by most of the tribes. Special canoes, slim-waisted, with racy lines, were usually built for sea hunting. The hulls were scorched to remove splinters and sanded down to a glassy smoothness with sharkskin to permit them to slip through the water swiftly and noiselessly. Among the three northernmost groups, the harpoon had a single foreshaft with a long multiple-barbed bone point. Some were made with a detachable foreshaft: the point was connected to the foreshaft by a short lanyard, the foreshaft to the shaft by another, and the shaft carried a long line which the harpooner held or made fast to a canoe thwart (Figs. 5C, 7D). These several joints produced a sort of shock-absorber effect when the struck quarry lunged, minimizing the strain on each individual part. The northwestern Californians used a similar harpoon point, set in a socket in a very heavy shaft, to kill sea lions. The line was wrapped about the shaft for its full length and made fast to it so the shaft acted as a drogue, tiring the animal while the hunters followed.

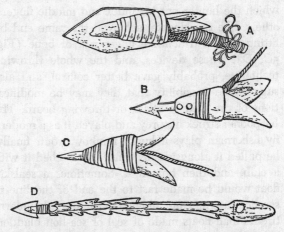

Fig. 7. Harpoon heads. (A) Nootkan whaling harpoon head; (B) Kwakiutl-Nootka sealing harpoon with iron cutting blade; (C) typical three-piece salmon harpoon head; (D) sealing harpoon head used in the north. Most Tlingit, Haida, and Tsimshian salmon harpoons were of the same general type as (D) but much less ornate.

The groups living between the two extremes of the area used harpoons with two diverging fore-shafts, on each of which was mounted a three-piece head with a sharp blade bound between two horn barbs. The line was held in place by a catch on the shaft, and extended from there to a coil that the harpooner paid out as he threw, just as a cowhand pays out a lasso in roping. Kwakiutl and Nootka sea hunters, and some neighboring Salish who had learned from them, did not throw these harpoons javelin-fashion, but steadied the shaft with the left hand (which also held the coil of line), and applied the propulsive thrust to the end of the shaft. Some Kwakiutl hunters fitted a butt-piece on to their harpoon shafts, with two perforations through which the hunter put his index and middle fingers; others, like the Nootka, achieved the same end by fitting a little tridentlike finger rest of bone (Fig. 5C, D). These devices, and the whole throwing technique, probably gave better control, and also suggest the possibility that they may be modifications of the Eskimo atlatl, or throwing board. The harpooner struck his prey and played it as a modern fly fisherman plays a husky rainbow trout; finally, he pulled it alongside his canoe, dispatched it with a club, and then boated it. Sometimes a sealskin float would be made fast to the end of the line in sea-lion hunting, and allowed to run until the quarry tired. Small floats made of seal or sea-lion bladders were fastened to the line by Southern Kwakiutl for all sea hunting, while some Heiltsuk used sealskin floats similar to those of the Nootka. In hunting porpoise, floats were always used by these groups, for the skin of the animal was so thin that too heavy a strain would probably cause the harpoon head to draw. Their neighbors did not use these buoys.

Sea otter, whose dense, lustrous pelts were so avidly sought after by European traders, were formerly hunted like hair seal. With the intensification of the trade, and the dwindling of the sea otter, mass hunts came into vogue, in which twenty or thirty or more canoes made sweeps along the coast, forming up in a circle around any sea otter sighted. Each time the animal surfaced volleys of arrows were loosed at it until it was killed. The efficiency of this broad coverage-and-surround technique is attested by the fact that the sea otter almost became extinct by the end of the last century.

Fur seal were probably unknown to most Northwest Coast Indians in aboriginal times, for the migration route of the herds is farther offshore than the natives ventured. The Haida and Coast Tsimshian were the main exceptions: they pursued the numerous stragglers from the main herd who came into Dixon Entrance to follow Hecate Strait between the Queen Charlotte Islands and the mainland. American and Canadian sealers began to recruit hunters, particularly among the Nootka and Kwakiutl, in the closing decades of the nineteenth century. From that time until the signing of the international conservation treaty regulating fur-seal hunting, shipping on sealing schooners came close to becoming a national industry for those two peoples.

The most spectacular sea hunting on the whole coast was the whaling of the Nootka and their neighbors of the Olympic Peninsula—Quileute, Quinault, Klallam, and perhaps the Chemakum, all of whom learned the art from the Nootkans. The whale harpooner was always a person of high rank, for the tricks of the trade—practical and magical—that contributed to the success of the hunt were cherished family secrets, handed down in noble lines only. Besides, only a chief possessed the necessary wealth to have a whaling canoe built, to outfit it, and the authority to assemble a crew. The whaling harpoon was a very specialized piece of equipment (Figs. 5A, 7A). The harpoon head was made of three pieces: a sharp mussel-shell cutting blade cemented with spruce gum between two heavy elk-horn barbs. A heavy lanyard of sinew twisted into rope connected the head of the 100-fathom-long line laid up of cedar withes. Four sealskin buoys were attached to the line at intervals. In historic times a huge reinforced cedarbark basket, in which the line was coiled, was made fast to the bitter end and served as a drogue, but this apparently was an improvisation modeled after the drogues of white seafarers.

The crew, with all the gear stowed according to a meticulous pattern so that the line and floats would run out without fouling, paddled out to sea. When they sighted a whale, they tried to approach silently from the rear so the animal would neither hear nor see them. They always came in on the whale's left side. The canoe had to lay close alongside, for the harpoon was much too heavy to be thrown, and had to be thrust home. The harpooner stood with his left foot on the bow thwart, his right forward on the gunwale, with the harpoon held crosswise in front of him at about shoulder height. He pivoted and struck, aiming just behind the cetacean's left flipper, then ducked down into the forward compartment to avoid being struck by the

floats or springy coil of line as they paid out and as
the whale rolled and thrashed about and the canoe
sheered off hard to port. This was the most dangerous moment. The whale might turn toward the canoe, smashing it to bits in one of his blind rushes;
a crewman might be badly injured by a blow from
a float or the rigid line, or even be caught in a bight
and dragged to his death. It was mainly for this moment that the whaler and his crew practiced long
drill sessions and carried out arduous rituals of ceremonial purification to forestall any mishaps. On the
beach, their families also observed certain rituals
for their good luck and welfare. Ritual behavior
before and during the hunt was considered essential
for all sea hunting, of course, but because of the
importance of whaling in native eyes its ceremonial
requirements were more elaborate and more rigid
than those for any other quest.

Usually a second whaling canoe, captained by a
kinsman of the chief whaler, accompanied the hunt
and often was conceded the privilege of planting
the second harpoon. A small, swift sealing canoe
might also be brought along, to take the first harpoon shaft back to the village as formal evidence
that a whale had been struck. The whaler and his
supporting canoe then followed the whale, running
in to drive home more harpoons with short lines and
floats, until the great creature was so weakened by
loss of blood, the drag of the floats, and its titanic
struggles that it lay quiet in the water as the hunter
came in for the kill. A lance with a very wide chisel-
like blade, much like a white whaler's "spade," was
used to sever the tendons controlling the flukes, so
that the cetacean lay hamstrung and helpless. Then
another lance with a long sharp bone point was

driven home behind the flipper to the heart. The cetacean rolled, spouted blood, and died. Holes were hacked through the upper lip and around the lower jaw to tie the mouth shut, so the carcass would not ship water and sink. Then all that remained was the wearisome chore of towing the quarry home. If luck was with the hunter, or, as the Indians interpreted it, if he and his crew had been punctilious in carrying out their rituals, the whale, when struck, would turn toward shore so it could be killed close to the beach. But frequently whales headed straight out to sea, so the crew had to pay for their ritual laxness by a day or more of steady paddling.

It is interesting to note that much of the impedimenta of the Nootka whale hunt, including the use of a special large canoe, harpoons with long lines and sealskin floats, the prestige associated with whaling, and many ritual elements to be described below, are very reminiscent of Eskimo whaling practices. Another kind of Nootkan whaler, or better, whale-ritualist, did not even approach the creatures at sea, but magically caused whales that had died from natural causes to drift ashore. Formerly Aleut whalers, in *bidarkas,* hurled lances with poisoned slate blades into whales, then went ashore to perform ceremonies to cause the carcasses to drift in. While the Aleut actually killed his whale and the Nootka whale-ritualist did not, the rites each performed in secret in some secluded spot were much alike. Both sets of ceremonies involved the use of human skeletons or corpses, who were supposed to call to the whale, or were propped up holding a line attached to an effigy of a whale. The basic idea was that through his rituals, songs, and prayers, each whale-ritualist induced the spirits of the dead to bring the whale ashore. The fact that the Nootka practiced both techniques of northern whaling (although such groups as the Tlingit, Haida, and Tsimshian knew nothing of them, even though they were geographically closer to Eskimo and Aleut) suggests some ancient connection between the Nootka and subarctic and arctic cultures.

Other Northwest Coast groups, although they did not use the same magical methods for causing whales that died from natural causes to drift ashore, enthusiastically utilized such bonanzas of oil-rich blubber and meat, "high" though the carcasses might be. Only the Tlingit turned up their noses, literally and figuratively, at dead whales washed up on their beaches.

Land hunting was practiced to a limited extent only, by most Northwest Coast tribes. It was of major importance to communities and small tribes living at some distance up the river valleys, away from salt water. The Chilkat Tlingit, for example, hunted a good deal and staged many caribou hunts on their trading trips into the interior. The Tsimshian division of the upper Nass River, who in former days are said to have come below the head of tidewater only rarely, are claimed to have been great hunters, as were the related Gitksan on the upper Skeena. Men of the upper Bella Coola villages, the Wikeno of Wikeno Lake above Rivers Inlet, and a few Nootka who lived on Gold River and about Sproat Lake were good woodsmen and hunters of land game. Up the Fraser and on the upper reaches of the rivers draining into Puget Sound lived Coast Salish whose way of life and economy was almost more like that of the Interior Salish than like those

of their congeners and blood kinsmen downriver
and along the coast. Lewis and Clark report that
the Upper Chinook hunted antelope on the plains
of eastern Oregon and Washington. The upriver
Yurok, the Karok, and Hupa as well, hunted extensively.

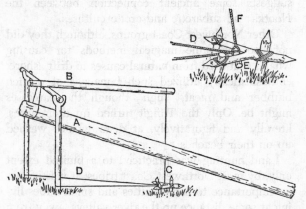

*Fig. 8. In this diagram of a type of deadfall trap used
by the Nootka for deer, (A) represents a heavy log which
drops on the quarry. The crossbar (B) supports one end of
the log and connects to the trigger (C) at the other end.
The kick lines (D) are attached to the supporting poles and
they trip the trigger and release the log. The smaller diagram
shows the detail of the trigger with (D) again representing
the trip lines that pull the small crosspiece (E) out through
the open arms of the forked branch, releasing the line (F)
and the crossbar (B) to which it is connected. After a drawing from the Smithsonian Institution.*

Naturally, hunting techniques and equipment
varied both according to the game sought and the
terrain. In the south, from the central Washington
coast down to northwest California, while snares
and deadfalls were known, pitfall traps were commonly set for elk, deer, and black bear. Farther

north, where the soils are shallow and rocky, pitfalls were rare, and snares and deadfalls (Fig. 8) were used almost exclusively. The bow and arrow was, of course, the standard land-hunting arm everywhere before the introduction of firearms, but pikes were also used on certain large game. Even the ordinary canoe paddle became a hunting weapon among the salt-water groups. If a canoeman encountered any land animal—deer, elk, bear, or the like—swimming across the channel, he overtook it, clubbed it with his paddle until he could hold its head under water with the same instrument to drown it, then rolled his quarry aboard, and continued on his way.

For waterfowl there were a variety of special devices: underwater traps with baited gorges for diving ducks, used by most Kwakiutl and Nootka divisions; small throwing nets mounted on pole frames that could be used from canoes on black stormy nights; spears tipped with many long diverging hardwood points that increased coverage like the spread of shot of a shotgun, favored by the Gulf of Georgia, Olympic Peninsula, and perhaps some Puget Sound groups. Many Coast Salish also made long nets (or perhaps used their long salmon seines and gill nets), stretching them across flyways between lakes and ponds where ducks were accustomed to come in low. The northwest Californian deerstalker used a device common to many of his non-coastal neighbors to the south and east—he wore a stuffed deer-head disguise on his head, so that, imitating the movements of a browsing deer, he could move in close enough for a perfect shot without alarming his victim.

Certain land animals, within the limits of their

range, were especially prized for their hides or other parts, and their successful hunting gave considerable prestige. Among the mainland groups, from the Chilkat south to the Gulf of Georgia, the mountain goat was highly esteemed for its "wool," for even though the Chilkat was the only group of late historic times to weave all-wool blankets, their neighbors all prized yellow-cedar robes with a few strands of woolen yarn run in. The jet-black horns were used to make spoons. The mountain goat is a wary animal, difficult even for the modern hunter with a high-powered rifle and telescopic sights. The Indian goat hunter, with his companions and their trained dogs, sought to climb above the animals and, without unnecessarily alarming them, gradually work them down from the cliffs into the rock slides, and if possible, into some cul-de-sac, or through some narrow sheer-walled pass in which snares could be set, or where companions could lie in wait. Such places were very valuable properties and were held by individual chiefs for their lineages. The usual weapon carried was a short hardwood pike, sometimes merely sharpened to a point, sometimes mounting a horn or bone blade. Apparently if a hunter ever maneuvered the goats to a place where he could get within bowshot, he could as easily close to spear-thrusting distance; besides, in inching along the goat trails on the cliffs and scrambling over rock slides, the more fragile bow and arrows were more liable to be damaged than the sturdy pike.

Skins of the whistling marmot were regarded as very valuable, particularly among Tlingit, Haida, Tsimshian, and the northern Kwakiutl divisions. It seems that anciently a robe made by sewing to-

gether many of the small soft-furred hides was
about equal in value to a sea-otter robe. Hunters
from the mainland groups climbed high above tim-
berline to set deadfall traps around the marmot
dens. Bone "triggers," carved with figures believed
to have magical power, were made especially for
these traps.

In northwestern California, the prize of prizes
was an albino deer. The hide of such an animal,
decorated with scarlet scalps of the pileated woodpecker and mounted so that it could be carried on
a pole in the wealth-display ceremonies, was a
treasure of tremendous worth. The lucky hunter
who brought down one of these deer thereby took
a major initial step on the road to greatness for himself and his family.

Over the larger part of the area, vegetable foods
were comparatively few and unimportant in the native diet. North of Puget Sound there are few plants
that produce and store large amounts of starch in
seeds or tubers. The rather spindly roots of a kind
of clover, and the tough fibrous ones of bracken
fern, were dug occasionally to lend some variety to
the diet. The "inner bark"—apparently the cambium
layer—of various trees was scraped and eaten by
most groups, from the Kwakiutl northward. All in
all, however, few sources of starchy foods were
available. It has even been suggested that the great
emphasis on oils and fats in the northern Northwest
Coast dietary may have developed to compensate
for the dearth of starches. Certainly these Indians had no innate dislike for starchy foods: they
promptly acquired a taste for white men's bread,
flour, and potatoes, and since early historic times
have planted potato patches on ancient middens

whose alkaline soil seems well adapted to this crop.

Berries of various kinds were fairly abundant, and they were utilized by all the tribes. The berries were eaten fresh, either plain or mixed with olachen or whale oil, or preserved. For storing, the berries were cooked to a pulpy mass, poured into rectangular wooden frames lined with skunk-cabbage leaves, and dried into cakes. Another storing technique was to stir them into a mixture of year-old olachen grease and cold water.

In the southern part of our area two plants that stored starchy materials in quantities were abundant enough to become staple foods. One of these was camas (*Camassia quamash*). On the upper reaches of rivers flowing into Puget Sound, and from western Washington down the Oregon coast, "camas prairies" occur, and the Indians dug quantities of the roots for food. Farther down the coast, in southwest Oregon and northwest California, native housewives collected acorns in the oak groves, soaked and hulled them, ground them to a meal in shallow stone mortars with basketry hoppers, leached the bitter tannins out of the meal, and cooked it into a nourishing, if rather tasteless, gruel.

In addition to being boiled in watertight boxes or baskets, food was steam-cooked in large shallow pits filled with hot stones by placing it on the stones and covering the whole affair with leaves and mats, then pouring water through to the stones. Fish and meat were also broiled over an open fire, or over a bed of coals. That the cooking techniques were few and simple does not mean that the native diet was monotonous. Around the turn of the century, a Kwakiutl housewife recorded some 150 different recipes for an anthropologist and there is no indi-

cation that her repertoire was exhausted. The long
feast mats were unrolled to serve as tablecloths.
From the Olympic Peninsula northward, dishes
were larger and more elaborately carved; sometimes four, six, or eight men would be seated at a
single dish. Ladles for serving food and oil were also
decorated with crests of the host's family, and
spoons of mountain-goat horn, carved and spread
open by steaming, were distributed among the
guests. The three northernmost tribes made huge
decorated ladles of mountain-sheep horn, traded
from the interior. For napkins, bundles of softly
shredded cedarbark were prepared and distributed.

3 MATERIAL CULTURE

Technology and Materials

From the northern to the southern extremes of the
area, the Indians utilized wood as a primary material for most of their manufactures. The products
of their carpentry were distinguished by neatness
of finish and, among the northern groups, by elaborate carved and painted decoration. This typical excellent workmanship was accomplished with
what would strike most of us as a rather limited
tool kit (Figs. 9, 10). Chisels of tough stone such as
nephrite, or of elkhorn, or of the dense shell of
deep-water clams, mounted in hardwood hafts,
were driven with unhafted pear-shaped stone mauls
for felling timbers. The three northern nations—the
Tlingit, Haida, and Tsimshian—sometimes used
heavy chopping adzes in their aboriginal logging.
Big logs were split, or sections were split from
standing trees, by driving up sets of wedges—usually of hardwood, such as yew, with grommets of
tough spruce root wrapped around the butt ends
to prevent splitting. The northwestern Californians
and their immediate neighbors made wedges of elk-
horn. The unhafted maul (Fig. 9) was usually
used for driving wedges, except in the north, where
heavy hafted stone mauls were used by the three
northernmost divisions, and by some of their Heiltsuk and Bella Coola neighbors. Besides the heavy
splitting adzes just mentioned, three types of small

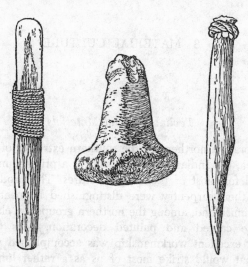

Fig. 9. Three examples of Kwakiutl woodworking tools. On the left is a chisel with a bone blade (about 7 inches long), center, a stone hand hammer (about 6 inches high), and right, a wedge made of yew wood (about 11 inches high).

adzes served for the fine work. Although their distributions overlapped slightly, the "elbow adze" in which the cutting blade was lashed to a T-shaped wooden handle was essentially northern, used by all the groups from Tlingit through the Southern Kwakiutl. The "D-adze" (Fig. 10A), in which the handle, of wood or whalebone, was shaped something like one of our handsaw handles, was common in the central region, used by the Southern Kwakiutl and the Nootka and their neighbors down the coast of Washington. South of the Columbia a "straight adze," which looked more like a chisel with a slightly curved handle, was in use. The Indians did a great part of their carving with these adzes, planing rough wood to smooth, flat, or curved surfaces, or to a decorated fluted finish. For the very finest carving short curved blades mounted in wooden handles, something like the Eskimo "crooked knife," were used.

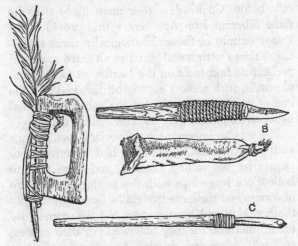

Fig. 10. Other Kwakiutl woodworking tools are (A) an adze with a bone blade (about 9 inches long over-all, (B) a metal-bladed knife (about 8 inches long) shown with its fawnskin sheath, and (C) a drill (about 12 inches long) with a bone point used for carving.

Anciently, the blades may have been of ground-down beaver incisors, but for many years, even before the coming of Europeans, iron was used. At Nootka Captain Cook noted that most of the knives and chisels were iron-tipped, and iron was eagerly sought after by the natives whom the early fur traders encountered from Tlingit territory to Trinidad Bay in California. Some ethnologists and historians have suggested that this pre-European iron may

have been found in the form of spikes, etc., from
the wreckage of ships washed up on the beaches
by the Japanese Current, and there is evidence that
such "drift iron" was used in early historic times.
However, few vessels in which iron spikes and bolts
were commonly used were sailing the western Pacific before Cook's day. It is more likely that the
same Siberian Iron Age center that provided the
Punuk culture of the archaeologically ancient Alaskan Eskimo with metal was the ultimate source of
prehistoric iron tools on the Northwest Coast. Simple drills, with a short cutting bit fastened into the
end of a wooden handle that the carpenter rotated
between his palms, were used for drilling holes.

Fire was an important woodworking tool, strange
as it may sound. The Indians had effective techniques for controlling burning, and were able to
hollow out large logs with fire in the manufacture
of canoes and the large troughlike feast dishes. Only
the Kwakiutl and Nootka claim to have scorned use
of this method, for they hollowed out their canoes,
etc., with adzes and chisels. The softening effect of
hot water on wood was well known; it was a common practice to widen the beam of a new canoe by
filling it with water, throwing in red-hot stones until
the water was almost boiling, then carefully driving
in thwartlike spreaders from gunwale to gunwale.
The Kwakiutl even had a device for softening small
pieces of wood to bend and shape them that came
close to the steam box of the modern boatwright.
They also made molds in which steam-softened
pieces of wood—for example, the shanks of the
curved halibut hooks—were forced and left to set
into the desired shape. To achieve the typical
smooth neat finish on wooden articles, fine sand-

stone, and then sharkskin, were used in lieu of sand-paper.

In a sense, the natural environment favored development of the woodworking craft, for the towering forests of the Northwest contained a number of useful and readily workable woods. The red cedar (*Thuja plicata*), which splits easily into wide straight planks, served a multitude of purposes (in northwest California the equally tractable coast redwood [*Sequoia sempervirens*] was used for the same purposes); yellow cedar (*Chamaecyparis nootkaensis*) and alder (*Alnus* sp.) were the sources of material when soft, easily carved wood without marked cleavage planes was needed, as in the manufacture of dishes and masks. Where tough, resilient wood was desired—for example, for bows, harpoon foreshafts, and the like—few better woods could be found than yew (*Taxus brevifolia*) or, in the southern part of the area, maple (*Acer* sp.) and oak (*Quercus* sp.). Only the more northerly Tlingit groups—those residing north of modern Wrangel on the mainland shore, and from Admiralty Island northward offshore, beyond the limits of distribution of red and yellow cedar—had to make shift with less easily split hemlock for planks, and tough but untractable spruce for canoe hulls, when they could not trade for good cedar from their southern kinsmen.

Another important material, particularly from the Columbia River northward, was the inner bark of the red cedar and, to a slightly lesser degree, that of yellow cedar. Even the northerly Tlingit, in whose territory neither red nor yellow cedar grew, found it necessary to import quantities of the bark, as well as of the lumber, of the two trees. One could very nearly describe the life of the individual Indian in terms of cedarbark: as an infant, he was swaddled in the bark, shredded and haggled to a cottony consistency; his pillow and head-presser were pads of the same material; woven robes and rain capes of shredded bark protected him from rain and cold throughout his life; checkerwork mats of red cedarbark were his principal household furnishings, serving as tablecloths at mealtimes, as upholstery for seats, and as mattresses for his bed. With the beginning of European contacts he learned to use sails on his canoe and, when he was unable to acquire imported canvas, he made sails of heavily woven bark mats; old worn-out mats served to protect his canoe from the checking effects of the sun on bright days. On ceremonial and festive occasions he wore turbans and arm and leg bands twisted and woven of shredded bark. He stowed his carpentering tools in a basket woven of the same bark. The Nootka whale hunter kept his precious harpoon heads in neatly made pouches of the same material. In historic times, our typical Northwest Coast native found shredded cedarbark to be an ideal gun wadding for the muzzle-loader he acquired from the white trader. And when he died, the chances were that unless he were a chief and entitled to special treatment, his body would be wrapped in a cedarbark mat for burial.

Most of this bark was stripped off standing trees. It is interesting to note that there was a conscious effort at conservation: only rarely was a tree stripped completely; instead, only part of the bark was removed, to permit the tree to recover and continue its growth. Long strips were pulled off, starting from a horizontal cut made near the base of the

tree. Then the outer bark was peeled off and the
inner bark rolled up into bales for carrying home.
When dried, the red cedarbark was split into strips
for mat and basket making, or shredded by feeding
it across the edge of an old paddle blade and hag-
gling it with a heavy blunt chopper of hardwood
or whalebone (Fig. 11). The bark of yellow cedar was treated by soaking it alternately in salt and
fresh water, drying it, then pounding it with a
whalebone or stone hammer until the fibers separated.

The Salish groups from the Gulf of Georgia southward, and their Chinook neighbors along the lower
Columbia, substituted sewn mats of tules, or reeds,
for the cedarbark mats of their northern neighbors.
They passed a strand of twine through a flat row
of reeds with a long wooden needle resembling an
oversize sack needle, then crimped the reeds down
with a special tool (Fig. 11) to prevent the stems
from cracking where the needle had split them.
The use of this technique spread during historic
times to adjacent Kwakiutl and Nootka who had
access to stands of reeds around lakes and muskeg
swamps; such mats are softer and more resilient
than those of cedarbark.

The regional flora provided a variety of materials
for basket weaving. The same red cedarbark used
for mats served for flexible but strong baskets,
woven with flat strips; for more rigid, tighter construction the same material was spun into stiff cord.
Spruce roots, from which long wiry segments could
be split, were widely used also. The bark of a "wild
cherry" (Prunus sp.), various tough grasses, and a
glossy black fern stem were frequently utilized for
decorative patterns.

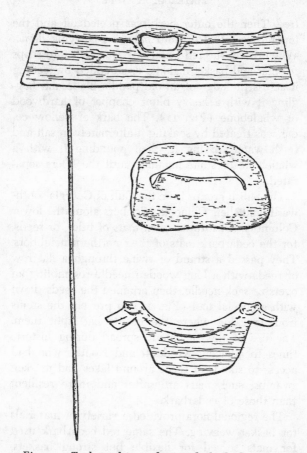

Fig. 11. Tools used in working with the bark of the red cedar. At the top, a hardwood shredder (about 24 inches long) used by the Kwakiutl. At the upper right is a whalebone shredder used by the Nootka (about 7 inches long) and below that a Coast Salish mat creaser. Also shown is a wooden needle, approximately 30 inches long, used by the Coast Salish in making mats.

14. An illustration of Tsimshian weaving in the Chilkat technique: at the top, the Killer-whale design on a goat-wool robe, and below, a geometric design used on a shirt.

15. The front (top) and reverse (bottom) of a robe collected about 1800 in Tsimshian or Northern Kwakiutl territory. This specimen is interesting for its geometric design and the variety of weaving techniques employed. Note that the left panel of the front is duplicated on the reverse side, whereas the color scheme of the right panel is reversed because of different weaves. The braided tassels on the front are also found in a few old Chilkat blankets. Courtesy of the Peabody Museum, Harvard University.

16. *A robe of duck down, collected from the Makah, who learned to make such textiles from their Salish neighbors. The warps, which run horizontally, were made of hanks of bark fiber into which quantities of down were caught. The down conceals the widely spaced cedarbark wefts. The predominant color is the rich brown of mallard down, with a few strips of white; the robe is remarkably light in weight, but soft and warm. Courtesy of the Smithsonian Institution.*

17. *A Coast Salish "nobility blanket," collected by Lieutenant Wilkes, U.S.N., on the lower Columbia River about 1841. The colors are chiefly native dyes: various tones of yellow and brown on a white ground, with a little black, blue, and red. The weave is plain twining; slanting design elements are formed by actually changing the direction of the weft elements from horizontal to the desired slope, and the undulating lines of the lower zone are formed by working the wefts in curves. The central panel, with the three broad stripes on the white ground, was apparently woven separately and sewed in along the sides, reminding one of the "panel weaving" of Chilkat blankets. Courtesy of the Smithsonian Institution.*

18. A Salish robe of dog and mountain-goat wool, collected in
the 1840s, which combines two very different weaves. The
central portion is woven in the twilled checker technique, and
could have been made on a two-bar loom. The sides are
closely woven in a plain twining, with wefts slanted to produce diagonal lines, as in the "nobility blankets." This specimen proves that the Salish utilized two distinct weaving
complexes; the side strips are not mends, but integral parts of
the original manufacture. Courtesy of the Smithsonian Institution.

19. An old Chilkat dancing skirt with a design area, woven of mountain-goat wool in the Chilkat blanket style, representing a Beaver. The design is mounted on a buckskin backing and the jinglers on the fringe are puffin beaks. Courtesy of the Smithsonian Institution.

20. An old Tsimshian dance legging which covered the leg from the shin to the ankle. Made of buckskin, the design is porcupine-quill embroidery and the jinglers are puffin beaks. Some leggings of this type were made with a design area woven of mountain-goat wool and mounted on buckskin.

21. *A chief's headdress, consisting of a mask of wood with abalone-shell inlays, and a trailer of cloth covered with ermine skins. The forehead masks in concept, though not in style, are reminiscent of some Western Eskimo ceremonial regalia. This example represents a Hawk and is from the Tsimshian. The mask rests on the forehead and the trailer extends midway down the back.*

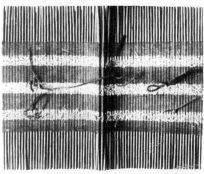

22. *Two kinds of Tlingit body armor: above, a painted moose hide with a design representing a Bear and, below, hardwood rods which were twined together with cord and wrapped around the wearer's midsection. Courtesy of the Smithsonian Institution.*

For textiles, in addition to the yellow cedarbark already noted, a few animal fibers were used. From Vancouver Island northward, mountain-goat wool was in great demand for weaving. The Salish groups of the Gulf of Georgia and on the shores of the Straits of Juan de Fuca had a special breed of little dogs whose wool-like hair they clipped to make into yarns for robes. However, the amounts of these animal fibers used were very small in comparison with those of vegetable origin.

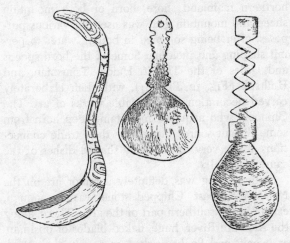

Fig. 12.   On the left, a Tlingit ladle of shaped and carved mountain-sheep horn (about 17 inches high). On the right, Yurok spoons of elk antler, showing typical lower Klamath decoration. (See Plate 4.)

Other materials were used for special purposes, of course. Cutting blades made of stone and shell have been mentioned. A tough, hard, bright-green nephrite found in southeast Alaska and along the Fraser River was extensively used for adze blades.

Horn and bone were ground down for many purposes. The use of the heavy shafts of elkhorn for wedges in northwest California has been noted. In the same region, neat little purses for shell money were carved of sections of elkhorn, as well as spoons for acorn mush, decorated with geometric designs (Fig. 12). Both horn and bone, particularly the compact hard material from the cannon bones of elk and deer, were used to make harpoon and arrow points, and perhaps in pre-iron times, served for the blades of adzes and other tools. Along the northern mainland shore, horn of both mountain sheep and mountain goat was used for various purposes, after being softened in boiling water to permit shaping and molding. Some of the horn spoons and ladles of the Tlingit, Haida, Tsimshian, and Heiltsuk (Fig. 12, Plate 4), with their elaborately carved decoration, are veritable works of art. The Chinook, who acquired mountain-sheep horn from some distant source tapped by their trade connections, made very distinctively shaped dishes of the same material.

Stoneworking was definitely a minor art on the Northwest Coast. Chipped stone was uncommon, except in the southern part of the area. There, along the Klamath River, huge, flaked blades of obsidian, as evenly and finely worked as any in the world, were made—not for utility but as valuables, comparable to crown jewels. Delicately flaked arrow points of chalcedony and agate, tiny and jewel-like in their perfection, were used by the Chinookan groups of the lower Columbia, but were trade articles made by the upriver interior tribes. Farther north, ground slate blades are found in archaeological sites, where, at the dawn of history, ground shell knives and harpoon blades were more common. In addition to the stone adze blades, mauls both hafted and unhafted, and the large, flat pile drivers with prepared grips used by the Kwakiutl and Bella Coola for driving stakes for fish weirs, a few stone vessels were made—paint-grinding mortars, "oil dishes," and in the extreme south, shallow mortars used with basket hoppers for grinding acorns. The lower Klamath River groups also made pipe bowls, set in tubular wooden stems, or, rarely, tubular stone pipes for smoking their tobacco.

Manufactures

Of the materials just discussed, wood served for houses, canoes, storage vessels, dishes, cooking utensils, cradles, and even—in the south—for pillows. The areally typical wooden houses fall into a series of regional subpatterns. In the north, the

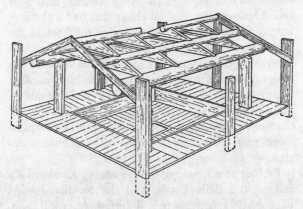

Fig. 13. A diagram of a Northern house type, showing joined construction, after a drawing from the University Museum, University of Pennsylvania.

Tlingit, Haida, Tsimshian, and the Northern Kwakiutl-speaking Haisla built large rectangular gabled-
roof houses, the elements of which were joined
together. Heavy horizontal members, or plates, ran
from corner post to corner post. These timbers had
deep channels or slots cut into them—the ground
plates along the upper side, and the roof plates on
their lower sides—into which the ends of the vertically placed wall planks of cedar fitted (Fig. 13,
Plate 6). Huge ridgepoles were supported by
heavy posts at front and back; these in turn supported the overlapping layers of roof planking. The
doorway, in the gable end facing the beach, was
often in the form of a round or oval hole cut through
the center post. Particularly among the Haida, an
elaborately carved exterior post that extended high
above the roof was set up in front of the house, and
the gaping mouth of some crest figure formed the
entrance. In many of these houses a deep pit was
dug some feet inside of the walls. In fact, traditions
tell of houses of renowned chiefs that had a series of
four or five benches or steps. Across the back of the
house, on the bench at ground level, if it had a deep
central pit, and sometimes along the sides were the
sleeping compartments of the important families
occupying it. These were small cubicles built of
planks—miniatures, even to their gabled roofs, of
the house. The front of the house-chief's compartment was sometimes painted with elaborate designs.

Farther south, among the remaining Kwakiutl divisions, the Bella Coola, and the Nootka, houses
were made according to a different structural plan.
Heavy posts supported ridgepole and side plates,
on which the roof planks were laid. So low was the

slope of the two sides of the roof that some early sources described the houses as flat-roofed. Sometimes a double ridgepole was used. The siding of the house was erected separately, only secondarily tied into the framework; that is to say, pairs of poles were set up just outside the corner posts and roof plate, and planks were placed horizontally, slung on withes tied between each pair of poles (Plate 7). These houses were particularly adapted to a custom of their owners, who commonly had house frames standing at various fishing stations, and would strip roof and siding off the house to take with them each time they moved. Elaborate crest designs were often painted on the house fronts. The Kwakiutl divisions, in recent times at least, copied the practice of the northern tribes in constructing plank-walled sleeping compartments inside the house.

Among some of the Bella Coola and Kwakiutl divisions, and the Coast Tsimshian and possibly among the ancient Tlingit, if descriptive ancestral house names may be taken as evidence, a specialized variant form of house was made by groups living on very narrow strips of beach in the steep-walled fiords. These were pile dwellings, built partly or entirely over the water. Alexander Mackenzie describes in some detail the Bella Coola houses of this type that he saw on his historic trip in 1793. A modification of the pile dwelling, known, on the basis of archaeological evidence, to have been used by some Tsimshian, and according to traditions by certain Kwakiutl, was the house raised above high-tide level on a cribwork foundation of logs and poles. In brief, regardless of which basic house type they used, these northern tribes had

sufficient mechanical ingenuity to adapt their dwellings to any peculiar local need.

The Salish groups living around the Gulf of Georgia and Puget Sound, and their neighbors in northwest and western Washington, built houses of the
same plan as the Kwakiutl, Bella Coola, and Nootka,
with horizontal siding structurally separate from the
house frame, but usually with shed, that is, one-
pitch, roofs rather than gabled ones. Wide raised
shelves that served as beds and for storage ran
along the walls. These houses were somewhat narrower than those of the gable-roof type, but some
were tremendously long—a whole village or tribelet
might occupy a single house of this kind. It must
be added that there was some overlapping of these
two related house types: some Southern Kwakiutl
and Southern Nootkans used the shed-roof type as
well as the gabled roof; a few of the Gulf of Georgia Salish built both gabled-roof houses and those
with roofs of a single slope.

At times, at camps and temporary stations, the
Salish groups also built mat lodges like those of their
interior cousins.

On the lower Columbia and along the Washington and Oregon coasts another house type prevailed. Although similar to those already described,
it was a variant of the areal pattern of rectangular
plank structure. A deep rectangular pit was dug
and lined with vertically set planks. Corner posts
and ridgepole posts supported long timbers on
which the roof planks were laid to form a steep-
sloping gabled roof, the eaves of which were just
above the ground. Raised plank shelves like those
in shed-roof houses were used as beds. The doorway
was at one of the gable ends; one entered and de-

scended a notched log ladder to the floor level. The Washington coast groups (except the Makah who built shed-roof houses), the Lower Chinook, and most Oregon coast groups had dwellings of this type. The Athapascan groups of southwest Oregon and the northwest corner of California built the same type of house, but with a pit only a foot or so deep, or without a pit, so that the house stood mostly above the ground.

The groups of the lower Klamath—Yurok, Karok, and Hupa—built still another kind of house. In some respects it was more like the structures of the extreme north of the area. The house had a deep central pit, but the walls stood back away from it, leaving a step or bench at ground level that served for storage space, as did a narrow anteroom between the double front walls. Poor men might build a house with a gabled roof, but a man of means and pride would have a three-pitch roof. A round doorway, just big enough to squeeze through, was cut through a big redwood plank on one side of the gable end (Plate 8).

There were few special structures in the area. The northwest Californians built large rectangular sweathouses that served as men's clubhouses. Certain features of these structures, as well as their use—the exit tunnel that also served as a flue for the fireplace, their use as a men's clubhouse, the direct fire-sweating rather than steam-sweating—strangely enough recall both the *kashim* or men's house of the western Eskimo and the *kiva* of the Pueblo tribes of the Southwest. The groups around Puget Sound and some of their Gulf of Georgia relatives made small domed mat-covered sweatlodges, in which they took steam baths by sprinkling water on hot stones in typical Plateau fashion. In this, as in so many other traits, they reflected their close ties with their Interior Salish kin. Along the mainland shores of the Gulf of Georgia from Point Grey to Bute Inlet, semisubterranean lodges of pure interior type were known and occasionally constructed. Traditions of both Bella Coola and Tsimshian refer to similar structures as having been used by their ancestors long ago.

It has been remarked previously that the Indians of our area preferred water travel to any other method of transport. While, unlike the Polynesians, they did not make long voyages over the open sea, many of the northern groups were sufficiently competent mariners to cruise coastwise on voyages of several hundred miles. Kwakiutl and Haida raided the villages around Puget Sound sailing down Queen Charlotte Sound and the Gulf of Georgia in their huge war canoes.

In the north, Tlingit, Haida, Tsimshian, all the Kwakiutl divisions, and the Bella Coola used a type of canoe with high projecting bow and stern, a sharp vertical cutwater or forefoot, and a rounded counter (Fig. 14A). The projecting elements, which served to repel wave crests that would otherwise swamp the craft, were separate pieces, scarfed and fitted to the hull, and sewed tight with withes threaded through drilled holes. Elaborate designs were painted on the bows and, anciently, carved figures representing family crests were sometimes mounted fore and aft on the bowsprit-like projecting pieces. Some of the large canoes—for example the Haida dugouts made of the tremendous clean-grained red cedar of the Queen Charlotte Islands —were more than fifty feet long, and seven to eight feet in beam, and could carry a considerable quantity of cargo or a large number of warriors. While all the northern tribes made both large and small canoes of this style, the Haida canoe makers were especially esteemed for their craftsmanship, and the mainland groups sought to buy the Haida-built craft when the tribes assembled at the olachen-fishing grounds on the Nass River every spring. Gulf of Georgia and Puget Sound Salish constructed what was essentially a small low-sided variant of this type (Fig. 14A) for cruising their more sheltered waters.

The Nootka were also renowned canoe makers. Craft built by their experts were traded far and wide among their Salish neighbors, and even to the Chinook of the lower Columbia and the tribes of the central Oregon coast. The Nootka canoe differed from the northern type in having a low vertical sternpost, and a graceful arc from the sharp-edged forefoot to the projecting prow piece (Fig. 14A). The bottom of the hull was flat and the sides were sheered, that is, flared outward to the gunwales, through a set of varying curves neatly calculated to ward off the seas instead of allowing them to come aboard. The graceful and practical lines of the Nootka canoe made it one of the finest seagoing vessels built by any primitive people. Some maritime historians believe that the flowing curve from forefoot to prow and the bold sheer of the bows of the Nootka craft inspired the New England designers of that queen of the seas, the American clipper ship, whose racy bow lines were nearly identical.

While dugout canoes were built on the lower Klamath, as in all the rest of the area, a special local pattern was evolved. These vessels were primarily river craft, round-bottomed, straight-sided, with high freeboard, and with blunt, upturned ends that made them exceptionally maneuverable even in swift currents (Plate 10). Nonfunctional yoke-like pieces attached to the blunt prow and stern suggest atavistic survivals of the separate prow and

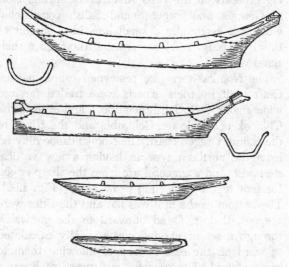

Fig. 14A. These are the principal types of canoes found on the Northwest Coast. All are shown with the bow to the right, the stern to the left. At the top is the "Northern" type and directly below, that of the Nootka. Beside each is a cross-section amidships, showing the important structural differences. Both these canoes were made in various sizes and proportions. For example, a seal-hunting canoe intended to carry two or three men swiftly and silently over the water would have the same general outline but be smaller and narrower than one intended to carry large quantities of freight or a war party. The third example is a Coast Salish version of the "Northern" type with low bow and stern, for travel on sheltered waters. The last is a small "shovelnose" canoe used by many groups for river travel.

stern pieces of the northern and Nootkan dugouts. Coast Yurok and their Athapascan-speaking neighbors immediately to the north put to sea in these craft, but for short trips only, for the canoes were better suited for river travel than for the deep sea.

The foregoing were the principal varieties of Northwest Coast canoes, but are far from completing the roster. A widely, if sporadically, distributed river canoe with round bottom, narrow, straight lines and bluntly pointed ends is usually called the "shovelnose" type (Fig. 14A). Most of the Coast Salish made and used these craft for river travel, even the groups living on the seacoast who had

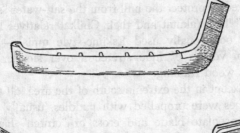

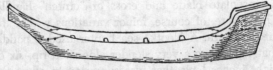

Fig. 14B. Two ancient types of canoes which have not been made for many years are (top) a war canoe made by the Southern Kwakiutl and perhaps by some neighboring Coast Salish and (bottom) a variant of the "Northern" type probably made by the Haida and traded to their neighbors. The high, wide bow piece on the top canoe served as a shield to the warriors and paddlers when landing on an enemy beach. The canoe on the bottom has, on the other hand, a deep boardlike bow which was usually elaborately painted. These craft may have been used principally for ceremonial occasions. (See Plate 10.)

Nootka- or northern-style canoes for use on salt water. In another part of the area, Lewis and Clark observed huge bluntly pointed dugouts, apparently oversized shovelnose models, with large carved figures mounted at bow and stern, among the Chinook of the Columbia. Farther north, the Southern Kwakiutl and a few Nootka and Gulf of Georgia Salish who traded with Kwakiutl had canoes with a wide, entirely vertical prow piece, and short vertical stern like that of the Nootka type (Fig. 14B). In the extreme north, the Yakutat Tlingit made a variant of the northern-style canoe with an underwater projection, something like the ram of an old-fashioned dreadnought. This feature may have served to protect the hull from the salt-water "scum ice." The Yakutat and their Chilkat relatives knew and occasionally used Eskimo-style umiaks—large open vessels of hide stretched over slender ribs and wood framing.

Except in the extreme south of the area, all these canoes were propelled with paddles, usually with a lanceolate blade and cross or "crutch" handle. There were, of course, minor variations within the areal pattern. A Nootka sea hunter used a paddle that tapered to a very slender elongated tip, six or eight inches long, that was supposed to allow the water to run off the paddle blade quickly and quietly instead of letting the drops spatter noisily with each stroke to frighten the seal or sea otter. In the north, especially among the Haida, paddle blades were often elaborately painted with family crests. Southward, many Coast Salish and Chinookan groups had special paddles for river travel with deeply notched instead of pointed tips. The purpose of the notch was to enable the canoeman to brace his paddle against snags, roots, and boulders. In northwestern California, a combination pole and paddle, that is, a pole with a slightly widened, flattish end, proved most practicable for river use.

After a few years of European contacts, the Indians began to step masts in their seagoing canoes, and rig sails of heavily woven cedarbark mats or of canvas. Before that time, however, they knew nothing of sailing. Even after they learned to use sails, they could only sail with the wind well astern, for otherwise the keelless canoes made too much leeway, and could not possibly beat into the wind.

Other canoe appurtenances include bailers, of a variety of local forms, and neatly made tackle boxes shaped to fit snugly in the narrowed spaces at bow and stern.

Household furnishings consisted chiefly of articles made of wood or woven of cedarbark. Wooden boxes that served a host of purposes were made from Tlingit country to the coast of Washington. The Indian carpenter selected a suitable thin plank of red cedar, cut it to a width corresponding to the height desired for the box, then, after carefully measuring with a set of measuring sticks, cut three channels as wide as they were deep across the board, a good three-fourths or even more of the way through. Then, using his steaming technique for softening wood, he bent the board into a right angle at each cut (Fig. 15). The two ends were scarfed and either pegged or sewed together with withes of spruce root. A rabbet was cut along one long edge of the board so that the bottom of the box could be fitted in snugly. Holes were drilled through

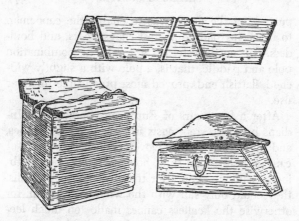

Fig. 15. *Kerfed (cut) and bent wooden boxes from the Kwakiutl. The "hunters' boxes" (lower right) tapered from top to bottom to permit stowage in the bow or stern of a canoe. As shown in the detail, the cuts in the wood were made on a slant. The boards for the box on the left (approximately 9 inches by 12 inches) were cut straight.*

sides and bottom, and dowel-like pegs were driven up hard to hold the bottom firmly in place. A box properly made in this fashion was absolutely watertight. It could be used as a cooking vessel by bringing water in it to a boil by dropping in a few red-hot stones, picked from the fire with wooden tongs. Fitted with lids, of the overlapping type in the north, or rabbeted among Southern Kwakiutl and Nootka, these boxes served for storage. In them were stowed all sorts of possessions: masks and ritual paraphernalia, valuables, furs and clothing, trade blankets in historic times, and even the prized oils rendered from candlefish and from whale blubber. In the north, the usual crest designs were painted on these boxes, and the Haida often carved these designs into the box fronts and sides (Plate

11). The northern storage boxes tended to be both squarer and squatter than those of Southern Kwakiutl and Nootka, who decorated their high narrow containers with tastefully spaced rows of fluting and inlays of sea-otter teeth and sea-snail opercula. There were many other uses for these boxes; they were made in different proportions according to their purpose. Very long narrow ones were slung from the rafters at ceremonials to serve as drums; small square boxes were made for water buckets. Quivers, babies' cradles, and trinket and tackle boxes were all made in the same technique (Fig. 16). The groups from the Chinook southward, who did not make these boxes with one-piece sides, made storage boxes by hollowing out big blocks of cedar or redwood and fitting snug lids to them.

Dishes were usually made in troughlike form, hollowed out of blocks of alder. The Kwakiutl and groups to the north of them often modified the

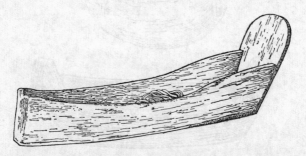

Fig. 16. *The sides of this Kwakiutl cradle were kerfed and bent like a wooden box. The cradle was padded with finely worked mats and shredded red cedarbark and the baby was lashed in securely so that he would not fall when the cradle was being carried or suspended from a rope and swung. Cradles of chiefs' children were often elaborately carved or painted.*

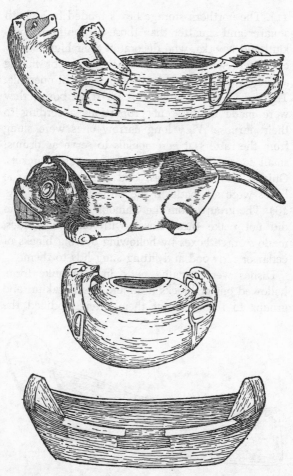

Fig. 17. Some examples of wooden feast dishes. The second from the top represents a Beaver and is probably of Tlingit origin. The remaining three are Kwakiutl, the top one about 27 inches long, the second from the bottom about 18 inches long.

basically simple dish shape into human or animal forms, especially in the case of the huge feast dishes (Fig. 17).

While elaborately carved and painted backrests were made in the north, only the people of the lower Klamath made seats—simple but neatly finished redwood stools. Elsewhere people sat on the ground, or on the ubiquitous checkerwork mats of red cedarbark. These mats should really be considered furniture too: as has been remarked, they were used to sit on, as mattresses, and as tablecloths. The Salish groups and their neighbors to the south used mats of tules for the same purposes.

The Northwest Coast dress styles were very distinctive. As in almost all other aspects of the culture of the area, even most of the minor regional variation that occurred was within the limits of the basic patterns. Fitted or tailored garments were not used, except by the northern Tlingit divisions. The Chilkat division and perhaps their kinsmen who trekked over the mountains into the frigid interior often wore one-piece trousers-and-moccasins of buckskin, and fringed buckskin shirts trimmed with porcupine-quill embroidery, typical garb of Athapascan neighbors. Elsewhere, when the weather permitted, men went about nude—except for the Tlingit, whose breechcloth was a type of garment almost surely borrowed from the interior. Women wore one- or two-piece skirts of buckskin among Tlingit and Tsimshian, of shredded cedarbark among their neighbors to the south, and of strands of shredded maple bark or buckskin in northwestern California. Tlingit women wore their skirts over a rather shapeless buckskin slip, at least on cold days. In northwest California, a close-fitting, neatly made twined

basketry cap was customarily worn by the women.
On Puget Sound and among the Upper Chinook,
women wore basketry caps of truncated conical
form, identical with those of the Nez Percé and
other Plateau groups. Throughout the area both
sexes usually went barefoot, although nearly all the
groups knew how to make rude moccasins for wear
on the rare occasions when they traveled back into
the mountains in winter. A number of early historic
sources comment on the way in which the Indians
walked about barefoot in the snow with no apparent discomfort. Whether this resistance to cold was
due to conditioning from childhood on, or to the
oil-rich diet, or to a combination of both, is unknown. For rainy weather the Indians from the
Columbia northward slipped on flaring conical
capes, woven of shredded cedarbark, that covered

*Fig. 18. Basketry hats are (top) a Kwakiutl-type with
painted design, (left) a Nootkan chief's hat with woven
design, and (right) a Haida example with painted design.*

them from neck to elbow but allowed considerable freedom of arm movement. Tsimshian and Tlingit relied principally on robes, and the Haida, Kwakiutl, and Nootka used rectangular rain capes of cedarbark matting. A tightly woven, wide-brimmed basketry rain hat (Fig. 18) completed the costume, although in cold weather a woven robe, twined-woven of shredded yellow cedarbark, might be worn under the rain cape. A robe of black bearskin, sea-otter pelts, marmot skins, or other warm fur was sometimes worn instead, especially by chiefs.

The woven robes of yellow cedarbark just mentioned were manufactured principally by the Nootkan and Kwakiutl groups, and perhaps by Coast Tsimshian, but were traded widely both to north and south. They were of a distinctive shape, being straight along the top and sides, with a curved lower edge that made the robe longer in the middle than on the sides. These garments were made of soft loosely twisted hanks of the inner bark of yellow cedar. To make a robe, the weaver hung the hanks of bark fiber, doubled over a cord suspended from a loom bar, and "twined" them together. In "twining," the wefts, or horizontal elements, were doubled, and each pair was crossed over about each suspended hank (or "warp" as the vertical elements in weaving are called) in turn, across the width of the blanket. The wefts were widely spaced, so that the surface texture was mainly that of the soft warps. In ordinary robes of this type the wefts were simply thin cords of tightly spun red cedarbark, but in better-quality products some wefts of mountain-goat wool were used. An added touch of luxury was given at times by sewing narrow strips of sea-otter fur along the borders of the robe.

A technically more elaborate robe, but one which in form, technique, and type of loom on which it was made was closely related to the cedarbark robe, was the so-called "Chilkat blanket" (Plate 14). This English designation was given the garment because for many generations—perhaps the major part of the historic period—these robes have been woven only by Chilkat women. There are indications that formerly some other Tlingit divisions may have made them, however, and that the technique may have been borrowed from the Tsimshian. According to one Chilkat tradition, the Tsimshian formerly made dancing aprons and half-leggings in the same technique. A Chilkat bride of a Tsimshian chief learned the art. At her death, a dance apron she had woven was sent to her home, where her relatives studied the weave, loosening and unraveling it bit by bit till they understood how it was done. They then began to make robes in the same fashion. This is of course not the only evidence of Tsimshian priority in the craft; some very old specimens, differing somewhat in style from recent Chilkat examples, have been observed among the heirlooms of Tsimshian chiefs. Also, as Lieutenant Emmons pointed out in his classic study of the craft, the Chilkat robes are decorated with the typically compact multi-element decorative patterns of the Tsimshian, whereas "dance shirts," a purely Chilkat development in the same technique, bear the more spacious and slightly more realistic Tlingit designs.

These robes, which are outstanding expressions of northern coast textile art, are woven by the women of yarn spun from mountain-goat wool (the warps are of goat wool with a core of yellow cedarbark twine; this latter material must of course be imported by the Chilkat). Men hunt the goats that provide the wool, make the "half-loom" on which the weaving is done (this is a loom with a single bar from which the warps are suspended with their lower ends free), make various measuring sticks and other devices, and paint the pattern boards from which the weaver copies her design. After months of spinning and dyeing her yarn, she is ready to set up her loom. First the warps are carefully measured and cut, so that their lower ends form the proper curve (in some specimens, the lower edge forms a shallow V rather than a true curve). Then she binds the warps together at the top with several rows of twined weaving, using a special variety of that technique. Her next step is carefully to measure the design panels of the pattern board, and to measure and count them off on the warps. Each lot of warps that will form a panel is tied into a bundle, and usually tucked into a container of dried mountain-goat or bear gut to keep it clean (Plate 13). One of the unique features of this weaving technique is that the robe is not woven as a single piece, but into separate panels which are joined together with sinew or wool-and-bark cord as the work progresses. These joints are concealed with a three-element false embroidery, which is also used to border each color area within the panel. Within the panel the weaving is done in a "twilled twining" technique; that is, the wefts seize two warps at a time, each row splitting the pairs of the previous one. The colors used are four: white, the natural color of the carefully washed wool; black, blue, and yellow. The three last-named were produced by soaking hemlock bark, copper, and lichen imported from the interior, respectively, in mordant solutions of urine, then dipping the yarns. The borders of the robe at sides and bottom are not woven, properly speaking, but are finished off in a sort of braiding technique. The long ends are left free to form a fringe, which is thickened by tying in additional strands.

The "dance shirt," a knee-length, unfitted tunic, usually sleeveless, has been mentioned as a peculiarly Tlingit garment. It may be a replica of an ancient type of moosehide armor. Authorities are not in agreement as to whether it is itself an ancient form, or one recently developed by the Chilkat. The methods of weaving used are identical with those used for the robe; it is simply woven on a higher and narrower loom. The dance aprons and leggings woven in the same technique are now quite rare. They have not been made for many years, perhaps since the Tsimshian abandoned the art.

It is interesting to note that the "Chilkat blanket" (and dancing shirt) is one of the very few ancient artistic products whose manufacture is still carried on. After a brief period of experimenting with cheap, imported colored yarns, the Chilkat weavers returned to their aboriginal materials and methods, which they use to this day. The chief innovation is that commercial dyes, particularly for blue, are often used. The robes and shirts are rarely sold to tourists, however, for they are extremely expensive. The purchasers are traditionalist Tlingit, who buy them to have at hand for sentimental reasons, to display at feasts, and to be buried in.

There are a few museum specimens collected in early historic times, either from the Tsimshian or perhaps slightly farther south, in which weaves used and type of design vary from that of the more recent Chilkat robes. The most well-known example, collected about 1800 somewhere along the coast, is distinctive because of its purely geometric patterns and the amazing variety of weaving techniques utilized (Plate 15). Probably in former times there were a number of local varieties of this same basic type of textile in the northern part of our area.

The Salish groups along the shores of the Gulf of Georgia and the Straits of Juan de Fuca possessed three distinct textile weaving complexes. This is one of the very few fields in which they could demonstrate technologic superiority over their northern neighbors. They also used a greater variety of materials in their robes. Not only did they spin yarn of mountain-goat wool, but they kept a special breed of small woolly dogs which they sheared at intervals, just like domestic sheep. The fine down of ducks and geese, and, as well, the "downy" pappus of cattail reeds or of "fireweed," was mixed into and caught up with the long hanks of vegetal fibers and wool to make yarn. Yellow cedarbark was used little if at all by these groups. Some or all of these materials were beaten together with a special clay that cleansed them, carded with the fingers, and spun into a thick yarn on a long hand-twirled spindle with a large decorated spindle whorl of hardwood or bone that served as a flywheel to maintain an even tension on the yarn as it was spun.

One of the Salish weaving complexes—that mechanically most elaborate—involved the use of a "full," or two-bar, loom, with the single continuous warp stretched over two horizontal bars set one above the other in a frame and looped over a string.

When the blanket was finished, the cross string was cut and withdrawn and the two ends of the robe came apart. The robes were woven in a twilled checker (over two, under one) technique, like the rabbitskin robes of many Plateau and Great Basin Indians of the interior, from which they differ only in use of the loom. Probably the basic method is a heritage of the Plateau–Great Basin cultural ancestry of the Coast Salish.

The other principal blanketmaking technique, which was used for two quite distinct products, utilized simple twined weaving similar to that of the Kwakiutl-Nootka yellow cedarbark robes. We have little or no information on manufacturing procedures except for what may be deduced from study of the finished specimens. Probably the work was done on the same type of "half-loom" or suspended warp loom as was used by Kwakiutl and Nootkan weavers, and the makers of the northern Chilkat robes. The Salish twined-woven robes are typically rectangular in form, lacking the curved or shallowly pointed lower edge of the yellow cedarbark robes and the Chilkat blankets. The two principal varieties of this Salish twined weaving were very different in appearance. One consisted of robes of wool and/or eiderdown warps with widely spaced cedarbark wefts (Plate 16). The major difference between these and the yellow cedarbark robes of Nootka and Kwakiutl neighbors was in the materials; a secondary difference was that the twining was usually done transverse to the long dimension of the robe, rather than parallel to it as by Wakashan weavers. The other variety of twined weaving, the so-called "nobility" or "organized" robes, was one in which wefts were closely spaced, so that they, rather than the warps, formed the surface of the finished robe. Some of these blankets in museum collections, acquired around the middle of the nineteenth century, include yarns of European make obtained from traders, and some strands of native materials colored with non-native dyes, but most of the materials and dyes seem to be of Indian origin (Plate 17). There are two characteristic features of the weaving that deserve mention: first, in a number of specimens a separately woven central design panel suggests relationship to the panel weaving typical of the Chilkat blanket; second, diagonal lines in design were produced by slanting the wefts (pulling the warps to one side or the other) rather than by stopping a series of rows of a color one space shorter or one space longer than the preceding, as is ordinarily done in textiles and basketry. This is a most unique method of achieving the desired slanting effect. One might appraise the two major kinds of weaving as products of two distinct cultures, were it not that in a few specimens both techniques, twilled checker and simple twining, were sometimes incorporated in one and the same object (Plate 18). Some belts and tumplines, collected from Coast Salish in the middle of the nineteenth century, were made with the same techniques as the "nobility blankets."

These Salish and Chilkat robes, and even the Kwakiutl-Nootka ones of yellow cedarbark that had a few strands of mountain-goat wool yarn woven in, were highly prized, and were traded widely along the coast, as far south as the Columbia River. Such luxury apparel was not worn daily, of course, but was reserved for festive occasions. Other articles of dress used by the three northernmost nations for special functions include dance aprons and knee-length leggings woven in the same technique as the Chilkat robes (Plate 19). Dance aprons of buckskin and half-leggings, painted and, at times, ornamented with a little porcupine-quill embroidery, were found among the same northern groups (Plate 20). They also used elaborate head-gear composed of a maskette mounted on a head-band, set with sea-lion whiskers, and with stream-ers of ermine skins down the back (Plate 21). Necklaces of various shells, especially the tusk-like dentalia regarded as highly valuable and dredged from a few offshore beds by the Nootka, were highly prized. In addition there were endless varie-ties of masks, carved helmets, and the turban-like rings of cedarbark that were the insignia of the dancing societies, in use among all the tribes from Tlingit territory to the Olympic Peninsula. (The Salish of the Gulf of Georgia had fewer masks and less in general of the elaborate festive equipment than their neighbors to the northwest and west; those of Puget Sound had few or none of such luxury items.)

In historic times the "button blanket" became a popular garment for formal wear. This was either a trade blanket or other piece of heavy cloth to which many large pearl-shell buttons were sewn, the usual design being the outline of a family crest. Occasionally appliqué designs in red flannel were also sewn on trade blankets.

The Oregon and Californian participants in the areal culture had different kinds of equipment for festivals, but, as in the north, much of their para-phernalia consisted of articles deemed to have an intrinsic value. Thus, the dentalia shells prized by the more northerly peoples, on the lower Klamath attained a status approximating that of money among ourselves. Many-stranded necklaces of these shells were worn in the Californian dances. Huge beautifully flaked blades of red or black obsidian, another form of wealth, were carried by certain performers. Headdresses were wide bands of deerskin attached to which was another form of currency, the scarlet-feathered scalps of the pileated woodpecker. In fact, it has been said that in the festivals of the lower Klamath the individual dancers were of slight consequence—they were little more than mannequins who modeled and displayed the wealth and treasures of men of importance who sat by as spectators.

Personal ornament was somewhat varied, although ear pendants and nose pins (passed through a hole made in the nasal septum) were widely used. Clusters of dentalia were favored for wear in the ears; in historic times squares cut from the iridescent shell of the abalone, brought from the central California coast by white traders, came to have great vogue. Tlingit, Haida, Tsimshian, Haisla, and Heiltsuk women wore labrets—elliptical plugs of wood or bone, grooved around the edge like a pulley wheel. These were inserted in perforations through their lower lips. Young Kwakiutl and Nootka women wore tight-fitting anklets, and sometimes bracelets of bands of sea-otter fur, to improve their appearance. Face painting for every day was usually for cosmetic purposes—an all-over type for protection against sun, wind, and cold. Elaborate and multicolored designs were usual only on festive occasions, although among nearly all the tribes gay young dandies adorned themselves with showy patterns for no reason but vanity. In the northern half of the area, ceremonial face-painting patterns usually referred to the family's heraldic crests. Apparently only the Tsimshian had mirrors other than a basket or box of water or a tranquil pool. They made keystone-shaped mirrors of ground slate, with constrictions at the middle. By pouring a film of water on the smooth surface, a vain Tsimshian could contemplate his or her reflection. On serious ritual occasions, Kwakiutl, Bella Coola, and Nootka washed their hair and bathed, using stale urine as a detergent. Haida and Tlingit followed the same practice at times. Combs—some of them very ornate —were made for hairdressing, but were not worn (Fig. 19).

Fig. 19. A wooden comb (about 6½ inches high) from the Tlingit. The carving shows a bear sitting on its haunches with a fish resting on its knees.

Some tattooing was practiced by most of the groups. The designs were often simple; the operation was casually performed. Crest designs, however, were tattooed on young persons of high rank in the north, particularly among the Haida, who used the most elaborate and extensive patterns and applied them on ceremonial occasions—that is, major potlatches. A high-ranking Haida man or woman was considered fully tattooed when the backs of the hands, both arms from wrist to shoulder, the chest, thighs, and lower legs, and upper surfaces of the feet bore crest designs. Sometimes the cheeks and back were also decorated. At the southern end of the area, girls' chins were tattooed with broad vertical lines; no representative designs were used.

Along the lower Columbia and northward, newly born infants' heads were flattened by binding a padded board at an angle against the forehead. This produced a wide, flat form of deformation, sometimes referred to as the "Chinook" type, but also found among the Coast Salish. The Nootka and Kwakiutl used head pressers that produced an elongated, tapering head form, sometimes called the "Koskimo" type, after the Kwakiutl tribe who carried this type of deformation to its most extreme form. A third variety, known as the "Cowichan type," was found among the Gulf of Georgia Salish, and was more or less intermediate between the other two forms. The northernmost tribes did not practice head deformation.

The arms used in the area before the introduction of European muskets and cutlasses were: bows and arrows; spears, or rather pikes, handled like fixed bayonets, not thrown; slings; and a variety of clubs and daggers for attack at close quarters. The same type of bow, in fact the same bows, were used interchangeably for war and hunting. The typical bow was made of a short, rather heavy stave of yew or other hardwood. It was worked down to a cylindrical grip at the middle, which gave into wide arms that varied from flattish to triangular cross-section, and was strung with a heavy cord of twisted sinew. In the extreme north, among the Tlingit, the upriver Tsimshian, and the Bella Coola, and in the south, among the Chinook and the Oregon coast and northwest Californian tribes, sinew-backed bows—that is, bows whose elasticity was increased by fastening a layer of dried sinew to the back or outer side—were used by some hunters and warriors. This trait clearly reflects influence from neighboring groups of the more arid interior. In the humid climate of the Northwest Coast, a sinew-backed bow, despite its lighter weight and greater potential driving power, was not a very practical weapon. It needed special care to prevent the dampness from making the sinew backing, which should give the bow its extra springiness, soggy and unelastic. A few Tlingit used long straight bows with wooden string guards, modeled after a common northern Athapascan form. The bow, whether "self" or backed, was characteristically held in a horizontal position that probably was better adapted to use from a slim-waisted, cranky, sea hunter's canoe than was a vertical grip.

The arrows used were commonly foreshafted, with ground bone or shell points. Chipped-flint projectile points were rare north of the Columbia, except for archaeological occurrences of relatively late prehistoric date around lower Puget Sound and the lower Fraser River, where interior influences extruded on the coast. The pikes used in warfare were usually short and heavy, tipped with bone or horn points or metal blades. In an emergency, of course, a man might defend himself with his fishing or his sealing harpoon, either of which would be a dangerous weapon in the hands of one accustomed to wielding it from boyhood.

Before firearms were acquired in quantity, slings are said to have been used in warfare from Vancouver Island northward. A flexible basketry pocket made of spruce root was fitted with long cords of some strong fiber, such as that spun from nettle bast, and was used to throw good-sized beach pebbles. In war legends it is claimed that an expert could crack the hull of an attacking war canoe with a sling-thrown cobble. Today, though the weapon has become a toy, lads develop sufficient accuracy to kill sitting birds and small animals with their slings.

The first European explorers to visit the northern tribes found double-bladed iron daggers, with one long and one short blade on either side of the central grip, in common use (Fig. 20). The fur traders had quantities of these daggers made by their ship's armorers for bartering purposes. Consequently, most of them now in museum collections are of late eighteenth- and early nineteenth-century workmanship. Many are of steel, but the basic de-

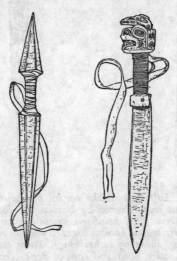

Fig. 20. Left, a double-pointed iron Tlingit fighting knife (approximately 24 inches long), and right, a single-pointed Tlingit fighting knife with an elaborately decorated haft (about 18 inches long).

sign has an Iron Age appearance that fits well with the hypothesis of an eastern Siberian Iron Age source for Northwest Coast pre-European metal. These great daggers, with the short blade above the handle for backhand passes, must have been very effective arms at close quarters.

From Vancouver Island south to northwestern California heavy clubs carved from whale ribs were in vogue, and were duplicated in iron by machete-like knives. Vicious-looking weapons, usually like short-handled picks in form and commonly referred to as "slave killers," were found along most of the coast (Fig. 21).

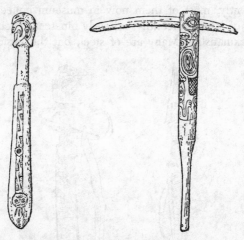

Fig. 21.   Left, a sword-like warclub of whalebone. Weapons like this were favored by Nootka and Kwakiutl warriors and were often heirlooms whose names and bloody histories were widely known. Right, a weapon of the "slave-killer" type (about 25 inches long). These implements of hardwood, antler, bone, and even of stone, some one-piece, some composite, were used by many Northwest Coast groups. Their name in English comes from the fact that they were often used to dispatch slaves on ceremonious occasions.

Various kinds of armor were also used. Wooden helmets, often elaborately carved, with separate visors, also of wood, and cuirasses of tough withes twined together or of short flat rods joined by sewing with sinew or tough rawhide, were used by Tlingit, Haida, and Tsimshian warriors (Fig. 22, Plate 22). Northwestern Californians also used

Fig. 22. Mode of wearing Tlingit armor and arms, from a catalogue of a collection of specimens made in 1867–1868. While the accuracy of old drawings is sometimes suspect, that of this one cannot be questioned. The specimens shown —wooden helmet and visor, cuirass of slats of wood twined together, and the weapons—are in the collections of the Peabody Museum, Harvard University, and are just as shown except that the designs carved on the helmet and visor are in conventional Tlingit style rather than in the sketchy manner of the drawing. The eye-holes can just be seen as shallow notches cut into the upper rim of the visor. The model was of the Chilkat division to judge by his fringed buckskin shirt and trousers with attached moccasins.

armor of the twined-rod type. Cuirasses of heavy hide, such as elkskin, caribou, or moosehide, traded from the interior, were used by the northernmost groups. Farther south, warriors wrapped themselves with wide strips of elkhide so that they were covered from armpits to hips.

In the field of textile arts, the various types of robes woven of cedarbark, mountain-goat wool, and dog "wool" have been described, and the many uses served by mats and baskets have been noted. A survey of the present type is not the place for a detailed technological account of basket and mat making, but a summary of outstanding traits is of interest.

The red cedarbark mats were woven principally in a simple checkerwork, that is to say, with the wefts, or crossing elements, being brought over the warps in an over-one-under-one sequence. Each weft, of course, reversed the sequence of the previous one, going *under* the warp that the previous weft had crossed *over*, etc. Decorative patterns were made, especially on borders, by "twilled" checkerwork, which is like the twilled twining of the Chilkat blanket, in that each weft goes over two warps and under the next one or two. In addition, patterns were made by dyeing strips of bark and working them in. A black color was usually produced by burying strips of bark in mud; red, by boiling the bark in water along with a quantity of alder bark.

A variation in mat-making technique consisted in weaving mats in a diagonal (simple) checkerwork. To do this, strips of cedarbark were folded over at the middle so that one half lay at right angles to the other end. Usually the folded strips were bound together by twining a light cord about them at the folds. The elements—in this case it is impossible to say which are warps and which are wefts—were interwoven in checker fashion, over one and under one. The point to making mats in this fashion was that new elements could be added in at the edges, where they would not create zones of weakness. While an expert could strip off very long pieces of bark from a tree, there is a limit to the length of a piece that a mat maker can handle conveniently. Therefore strips of bark were ordinarily cut to standard lengths. The length of the strips used as warps in an ordinary vertical-warp-horizontal-weft mat determined the length of the mat. Splicing in additional strips to lengthen the warps was unsatisfactory, for the strips would slip apart, unless they were knotted or twisted, which would create rough unsightly areas on the mat. By using the diagonal method, however, additional strips, caught in at the edge and doubled over to hold them in place, would not form a transverse zone of weakness at which the mat was likely to break in two. All the feast mats, some of them twenty, thirty, and more feet long, were woven in this way.

Strips of red cedarbark were woven together in the same simple checkerwork techniques to make baskets, also, from the Olympic Peninsula northward. Pieces of cedarbark were cut to a length that included the two sides and bottom of the basket to be woven. They were worked together in a simple checker weave at the midsections, forming a small mat with long loose ends at top and bottom and both sides. A light cord was ordinarily woven about the elements in a twining technique to hold them together, then they were all bent at right angles to the surface of the "mat," to form the "warps" of the sides of the baskets. Additional elements were then woven in, using the same checkerwork method, to form the sides.

Sometimes finely woven, flat wallet-like baskets were made of cedarbark in the diagonal checkerwork technique. The reason for making them this way was not to make them especially long, as in the case of the feast mats, but because the diagonal weave, like cloth cut on the bias, did not bulge and sag out of shape.

The best basketry on the coast was that made of thin segments of spruce root, or spruce root and cedarbark cordage woven in a twined technique. (This is the method in which the two parts of a doubled weft are crossed over each other each time they pass across a warp strand.) These baskets were so finely and closely woven that they held water. The elaborate ring hats of the Tlingit, Haida, and Tsimshian, and the Nootkan chiefs' hats decorated with whaling scenes, were all woven of these materials and in this way. The Northwest Coast, areally speaking, was the heartland of the development of twined weaving in North America. Technically, the groups at the extremes of the area—the Tlingit and Haida in the north, the Yurok and their close neighbors in the south—excelled in this craft, although the Nootkan women who wove the chiefs' hats, known from early historic times but not made for many a year, were not far behind in skill. (Only the Aleut, in all the continent, wove finer and tighter baskets, and Aleut culture, as will be shown, was related to that of the Northwest Coast.) However, most of the groups between the geographic extremes made twined basketry, except for the Coast Salish. These folk, in basketry as in so many other ways, continued an inland tradition. Their better baskets (some of them had learned to make twined baskets for special purposes) were made in the typical, and technically quite distinct, method of "coiling." Coiled basketry is, properly speaking, not a weaving technique at all, but consists in sewing together the rings of flat or ascending coils of rods or fibers. It is a method of making baskets which was especially characteristic of the Plateau, Great Basin, and Southwestern culture areas. In quite recent decades, some Nootkan groups who have had close contacts with Salish neighbors, through working alongside them in the Fraser River canneries and in the hop fields of the Puget Sound region, have learned to make this type of basketry, but they did not know the method in aboriginal times.

The well-made twined basketry was not left plain. Patterns were woven in, chiefly by a technique called "imbrication," which consists in laying flat strips of colored material over the weft elements to produce patterns. Angular, geometric designs were developed, for the most part, but a few of the better Tlingit and Haida basket makers were skillful enough to work in crest designs (Fig. 23).

Twining and coiling were both techniques that could be modified for special purposes. A competent weaver can not only make a basket that will be watertight, but, if the occasion demands, can also make an openwork one that will permit venti-

*Fig. 23. Tlingit twined-spruce-root baskets, noted for the
fineness of the weave. The decorative patterns are created
by what is called "false embroidery" done in bleached and
dyed grasses.*

lation—for example, for the storage of dried salmon
—in either technique. There were a number of
special openwork techniques in common use also,
along the coast, for making baskets for carrying
shellfish, smelt or olachen, and the like, where
drainage or aeration were desirable. Wrapped
twining, in which one pliable weft element was
given a round turn about not only each warp but
also around a rigid weft laid across the warps,
served to make quite sturdy yet open containers.
Ordinary twined weaving, in which thick weft elements, widely spaced, were used, of course provided a simple openwork technique. A three-
element checkerwork, in which the warps were
crossed at each passage of the weft, was, so far as
present information goes, peculiar to the Nootka,

Southern Kwakiutl, and the Aleut, in all western North America.

Musical instruments consisted principally of percussion instruments: drums and rattles (Plates 23–26). The tambourine drum, made by stretching a piece of rawhide over a narrow frame bent into circular form, was used only by Tlingit, Haida, and Tsimshian on the coast, though many groups of the interior, and Western Eskimo as well, used the instrument. The same three tribes of the northern coast, and all the groups to the south as far as, and including, those of Vancouver Island, made long narrow boxes of kerfed and bent cedar boards, which, slung from the roof and pounded with a sturdy fist wrapped in shredded cedarbark, boomed out the beat for dancers. Drumming with hardwood sticks on a long plank raised a few inches off the floor was another way of beating out time. The Chinook and southern Coast Salish reversed this: they used long poles, sometimes carved, and equipped with clusters of deer hoofs (so that they were also rattles), and thumped the ends against the roof boards overhead. Rattles were varied in form. Groups with considerable interior influence—Tlingit, Haida, Tsimshian, Coast Salish, Chinook, and northwest Californians—made considerable use of clusters of deer hoofs. The first three nations mentioned also used rings of withes from which puffin beaks, animal teeth and claws, and the like were suspended. Elaborately carved rattles of wood, the halves hollowed out and fitted together, were common from Cape Flattery northward. Rattles of mountain-sheep horn and of baleen, steamed and folded over and fastened to wooden handles,

were used by Kwakiutl and Nootka shamans
("medicinemen"). Gulf of Georgia Salish danced
to the accompaniment of rattles made of clusters
of large pecten shells on a cord.

Whistles of wood, some with and some without
reeds, were associated with the major ceremonials
of the Nootka and Kwakiutl, where they represented the voices of supernatural beings, as did the
bull-roarer, a flat stick whirled at the end of a string
to make a booming noise. The northwestern Californians were the only peoples of the coast to have
multi-toned instruments. They made simple little
flutes, on which a man could tootle a plaintive tune,
to amuse himself or to serenade a lady-love.

Gambling was a popular pastime among all the
coastal groups except the Wakashan-speakers, aboriginally, and these folk became enthusiastic dev-
otees of such games in late historic times. The
most popular game was one or another form of
"lahal," which consisted in guessing the relative
positions of a marked and an unmarked stick or
disk concealed in the hands of a member of the
opposite "team," who sang lustily to confuse the
guessers. Frequently two players on the same side
each held a pair of these objects. The opponents
had to guess the positions of all four pieces at once.
Dice, made of sets of four beaver incisors, were
tossed in a different type of game. Other contests,
sometimes bet on and sometimes not, included
wrestling, shooting arrows or throwing lances at
marks, foot and canoe races, tugs-of-war, and variants of shinny. Youngsters played most of these
games also, and like children the world over, many
games of make-believe that were patterned on the

activities of their parents. Myths were told both for education and entertainment. Of an evening, some old person would regale children and adults as well with the long, often humorous tales of the adventures and misadventures of such picaresque characters as Raven and Mink, or at times with the serious and important family traditions.

The cultivation of tobacco had a very peculiar distribution on the coast. The northwest Californians, probably most of the Oregon coast groups, and the Chinook sowed little plots of tobacco for smoking. Since the plant was widely used in aboriginal California, its occurrence along the lower Klamath is not surprising, although most California Indians did not cultivate it, but collected wild species. The reported use of a long-stemmed pipe with a stone bowl at right angles to the stem, among the Lower Chinook, hints most broadly at a trans-montane source for their tobacco and smoking habit, if they had not acquired the complex from the Californians before their ramified trade connections tapped sources so far east. However, the most mystifying and most isolated usage of tobacco was found among the Haida, where a plant, apparently a kind of tobacco, was sown and harvested and, mixed with lime, was chewed. Its cultivation was abandoned so early in historic times that we have only extremely meager information about it. Trade tobacco for smoking was obtained from white traders; its use became prevalent on the coast early in the fur-trade period.

The dog was the only animal domesticated on the coast. The dogs from which the Salish obtained their wool for weaving seem to have been a small, highly specialized breed; other dogs had no special attributes. Some hunters, particularly those who climbed the rugged mountains for mountain goat, trained their dogs to assist them in working the quarry within range.

4 SOCIETY

The Structure of Society

Superficially, the Northwest Coast presents a picture of considerable diversity in social organization. Some groups were divided into social units based on matrilineal descent; that is, membership in the social divisions, and also the inheritance of social position and of worldly goods, came to each individual from his mother and her side of the family. Other groups had no formalized unilateral divisions (social divisions based like the above on relationships through one side of the family only), but nonetheless stressed patrilineality (kinship through one's father) in group membership and inheritance. Still others followed a bilateral reckoning of descent, with, at most, a slight preference for transmission of position and rights in the male line. As regards the relationships of these varying social units to each other, among some Northwest Coast Indians the basic social units—a group of relatives, their spouses and children, aligned according to any one of the three methods defined above—were politically autonomous. Among others, several of these basic social entities were formally united into what may be designated a "tribe." In a few parts of our area, a number of such tribes might be confederated into larger groupings for social and political purposes. In the northern half of the area, roughly speaking, a system of hereditary rank and chieftainship prevailed; in the south, possession of riches nominally gave one social ascendancy.

However, when these apparently varied patterns are analyzed, it becomes clear that fundamentally all derive from a few basic concepts and societal forms common to all the peoples of the Northwest Coast. The two basic principles of areal society are, first, that the fundamental social unit (aside from the biologic family consisting of a man, his wife, and their children) was the autonomous local group consisting of a *lineage* (a formalized, named group of relatives who trace descent to a common ancestor exclusively through one line—in our area, through the maternal line), or an *extended family* (a social division less rigidly formalized and defined, in which descent may be reckoned through either line, or both). As will be shown, it made no difference whether formal alliances were made with similar social divisions, for while such units united at times for purposes of common defense or for ceremonial ends, they never surrendered certain highly important rights. Second, social status, involving the so-called system of rank, derived neither from heredity alone, nor from wealth, but from a combination of the two.

As an introduction to a group-by-group survey of socio-political organization, it must be re-emphasized that there were no true national entities among the Indians of the area. We have mentioned "the northern nations" and so on, but only after stating specifically that the term, in this usage, had no political significance, but referred only to linguistic units. That is to say, in these pages "the Tlingit nation" is a substitute for the clumsy phrase, "all the people of Tlingit speech." Terms like "Tlin-

git," "Nootka," "Yurok," and the rest are really linguistic designations, referring to all the independent political divisions whose members spoke those
languages. The Indians themselves recognized that
certain neighbors shared both the same language
and the same culture, but felt no unity or common
interest on that account.

The matrilineal type of organization just mentioned was found among the northernmost linguistic groups: Tlingit, Haida, Tsimshian, and Haisla.
Among the Tlingit and Haida there were two major
subdivisions to one of which every individual was
assigned at birth, on the basis of the affiliation of
his mother. Such twofold divisions of a national or
tribal group are called "moieties," that is, halves.
These divisions were "exogamic," to use a technical
term which means that it was compulsory that each
individual marry a person of the opposite division.
Since membership was matrilineal, or through the
mother, this meant that a man and his own children
were inevitably in the opposite moieties. The Haida,
for instance, were divided into two moieties, designated by the Indian terms for "Eagle" and "Raven."
A man who was a member of the Eagle moiety
had perforce to marry a woman of the Raven "side"
(as the Indians express the term in English). The
children of this couple automatically took membership, at birth, in the moiety of their mother; in other
words, they had to belong to the Raven division.
The same man's sisters' children, however, according to the same principle, of necessity belonged to
his side—they were Eagles, and were considered to
be, therefore, that much more closely related to
him.

The system is strictly comparable, though the

mode of reckoning is reversed, to our own inheritance of surnames. Among ourselves, when Mr. W. T. Door marries Miss Sally Doe, their offspring will all take the surname Door (patrilinear inheritance instead of the matrilinear system of the Haida and their neighbors), no matter whether the Does are more socially prominent or not. The fundamental difference between our system and that of the Haida is that among us all the population is not divided into the Doors and the Does, each group with formalized rights and duties. The Haida and Tlingit no more disregarded paternity than we disregard maternal rights and relationships despite our insistence on transmission of the paternal surname only. A Haida's or a Tlingit's paternal relatives had both rights and duties of great importance that affected him (or her) all life long.

Members of the Tlingit and Haida moieties shared, as well as the moiety designation, the right to use certain "crests"—representations of animals or supernatural beings that were reputed to have assisted the legendary ancestors of the social division, or, in some cases, were said to have been the original ancestors. These crests are sometimes called "totems." Actually, they were more like the heraldic devices of European nobility, used for display to show one's ancestry. We shall return to this subject of crests, for they were one of the most distinctive features of native culture in the northern part of our area.

The next smaller unilateral social division is the "clan." By definition, a "clan" is a formal, named, exogamic, unilateral societal unit, whose members trace their relationship from a legendary common ancestor. Clans may exist with moieties (as subdivisions of them) or without them. The Tlingit moieties, for example, were subdivided into clans. The Tsimshian, on the other hand, had no moieties, but had three, and in some places four, clans.

Despite all this variation, however, all these matrilineal societies were built up around "lineages," the basic units. A "lineage" is once more a unilateral group, consisting, among our matrilineal northern nations, of a nucleus of men related maternally. That is to say, the Tlingit, Haida, Tsimshian, and Haisla lineages were composed of, for example, a group of brothers and maternal cousins, their sisters' sons, and the sons of the sisters of the second generation. The sisters themselves also were members of the group, but since as a rule they lived apart from it, being married to men of other lineages (and other clans and/or moieties, according to the rule of exogamy), they participated in its functions only occasionally. The wives of lineage members, belonging as they did to other lineages, had only limited participation in lineage affairs. The men's own children, of course, belonged to the lineages of their mothers.

This social unit, among the northern nations, was ordinarily politically independent. Even where, as among the Tsimshian, it had entered into formal alliances with other lineages, it retained its important economic possessions—fishing stations, hunting areas, berrying grounds—had its own house or houses, its own chiefs, and operated socially—and, as a rule, ceremonially—as an independent unit. It had its own crests, in addition to those to which it was entitled through clan and/or moiety membership. Innumerable ceremonial prerogatives were also vested in the lineage.

Haida social structure shows this basic lineage pattern most clearly. As has been remarked above, there were two great moieties among the Haida, the "Ravens" and the "Eagles," each with its set of crests and origin traditions. (Curiously enough, the Raven itself was a crest of the Eagle moiety.) Each moiety consisted of a large number of named, localized segments, sometimes incorrectly referred to as clans. Each segment was a lineage, which held title to its lands of economic importance, occupied a separate village consisting of one or more houses, had its own chief and lesser chiefs. Each lineage waged war or made peace, staged ceremonials, and tended to its various affairs independently of any other.

Such a Haida lineage-village varied considerably in size. The shrinkage of population through the historic period, coupled with the tendency for survivors of decimated lineages to abandon their home villages and assemble at more populous centers, has obscured the picture somewhat, but early writers speak of villages of several hundred souls, as well as smaller ones consisting of one or two houses with forty or fifty inhabitants. It must be owned that these early figures are very rough estimates indeed, but we would probably not be far wrong if we used as an average thirty to forty persons per house. This would mean that there were anywhere from four to eight related adult males, about the same number of maternal nephews (sisters' sons), and a sprinkling of elderly widowed sisters or maternal aunts, in the average house. The other residents would be wives and children of the adult males of the lineage, plus a slave or two; these people of course were not lineage members. A large village, of eight, ten, or more houses, of course consisted of several sub-lineages, who still retained memory of their common relationship. The evidence indicates that in the course of time, if they prospered populationwise and economically, the sub-lineages tended to split off and become separate independent units, although retaining their feeling of relationship. For instance, the names of a number of traditionally related lineages on the Queen Charlotte Islands contain the term "Gitins." This word is meaningless in Haida, but it may contain the Tsimshian stem "Git-" or "Kit-," which means "people of." This linguistic hint is corroborated by the traditions of these lineages which agree that they are all descended from a single matrilineal family unit that came from the mainland later than the rest of the Haida, and may well have been of Tsimshian origin.

Each Haida village had a chief, who held that position by virtue of being the highest-ranking member of the lineage, and one or more house chiefs. The village chief (who was also the house chief of his own house) had a special title, the various versions of which translate either as "village master," "village owner," or "village mother." Each village was economically independent, owning its own village site, salmon streams, cod and halibut grounds, berrying and hunting tracts, and of course the camping sites that went with them.

The superficially similar structural pattern of Tlingit society differed slightly. There were two great moieties, named after the Raven and the Wolf. A slightly confusing feature was that, among the northern Tlingit, the Wolf division had many names and crests referring to the Eagle, and was commonly referred to as the Eagle moiety. In one of the southernmost groups, a small lineage called "Nexadi" ("Ne-hŭ-dee") also had many Eagle names and crests, and was regarded as a third division; that is to say, its members could marry into either Raven or Wolf groups. The origin of this little group is not known, but it is believed that it is probably of relatively recent alien source. Possibly an interior Athapascan or Niska lineage migrated to Tlingit territory and became Tlingit in language and culture. Many other Tlingit clans, according to their traditions, came originally from places outside Tlingit territory. However, these minor deviations in nomenclature and in accretion to the basic pattern cannot obscure the fact that the Tlingit had a true moiety system.

The first difference from the Haida pattern is to be found in the fact that the two moieties were divided into "clans." Some clans, like the Ganaxadi ("Ga-na-hŭ-dee"), the Kiksadi ("Kik-sŭ-dee"), and the Kagwantan, to mention a few of the larger ones, had a number of localized subdivisions, which were actually lineages exactly like those of the Haida. Although these local segments shared certain crests and traditions with the parent clan, they were politically and economically independent. There were also "clans," equated with the aforementioned units in the native mind, that consisted of a single local lineage group. Some of these were survivors of once larger units, whose other divisions had become extinct; others were clan subdivisions that, for one or another reason, had split off from the parent clan and, as it were, struck out on their own. In some cases traditions recall the original relationship; in others, that relationship has been suppressed or forgotten. These can be referred to as "clan-lineages."

Traditions of many of the clans indicate that their ancestors originally came from the south, near the mouth of the Skeena River, apparently prior to the arrival of the Coast Tsimshian, while others came from the interior, from what is now northern British Columbia. In connection with these traditions, it must be pointed out that while the Indians had no written records and had to rely on oral transmission of their clan and family histories, the traditions of all the groups from Vancouver Island northward are so specific and consistent—and, insofar as they can be checked, so correct—that there is little doubt that for the most part they are historically accurate, except for the occasional supernatural events that they recount, which we may regard as a sort of literary trimming.

The Tlingit were divided into fourteen named territorial divisions, or loosely confederated "tribes." Each tribe included one or more lineages (local segments of clans) of each of the two moieties. During the historic period, along with the decline of population, there has been a consistent trend toward consolidation of the "tribes" into unified villages. However, the evidence suggests that formerly each lineage had its own village, physically separate from those of the others of the tribe. Thus, one source reports that as late as 1880 there were eight villages of the Stikine tribe, five Kake villages, and so on. While the lineages of each tribe recognized certain mutual interests, there was no real unity. There was, for example, no tribal chief or over-all authority; each lineage had its own chief. Each lineage retained possession of its lands of economic importance, and exploited them individually. The lineages of a tribe might cooperate to make war, or for common defense, or they might not—they were under no compulsion to do so. The Indians insist, for example, that it was only certain of the Sitka lineages that attacked and razed the Russian fort in 1801, not the entire "tribe." Similarly, the lineage was the basic ceremonial unit. In other words, despite the nominal confederation of lineages in each region, Tlingit socio-political organization was quite like that of the Haida. The most important difference was that the Tlingit house-group, in cases where a lineage was of considerable size and had a number of houses each occupied by a sub-lineage, was somewhat more important than the comparable unit among the Haida. Traditions show that when a house-group prospered and grew, it tended to split off from the parent unit, move elsewhere, and become a new autonomous lineage.

The Coast Tsimshian and the Niska had a fourfold division, instead of the moiety or twofold division of Haida and Tlingit. Such divisions are sometimes referred to technically as "phratries," but we shall refer to them as "clans," since they were comparable to the major clans of Tlingit. These clans were named after the Eagle, the Raven, the Wolf, and the "Blackfish" (the killer whale and the black whale). The names of these divisions are interesting. Two of them, "Laxsgik" and "Laxgebu," mean "People (of the) Eagle" and "People (of the) Wolf," or "Eagle-people" and "Wolf-people," respectively. The names of the other two clans are meaningless in Tsimshian. The Raven clan is called "Qanada," a word probably derived from the name of the Tlingit clan "Ganaxadi" (and "Ganaxtedi"), which refers to a Tlingit place name and phrase, "People of (the village of) Ganax" ("Ganax" is also the name of a traditional Haida village site in the Queen Charlotte Islands). The designation of the "Blackfish" clan, "Gicpodwada" (gish-pod-wŭda), cannot yet be analyzed, except that the first syllable, "Gic-," is a variant of the previously mentioned Tsimshian "Git-," meaning "people" or "people of." The probable Tlingit (or Tlingit-Haida) origin of the name of the Tsimshian Raven clan points up the fact of the local shifts and migrations of population units back and forth across linguistic boundaries, especially frequent in the north. For example, one important Eagle clan among the Niska is known to have been of Tlingit origin; some ten or so generations back their ancestors, just before the epoch of European contacts, moved from Prince of Wales Island to the Nass, where they not only joined but adopted language and customs of the Niska. Several Tlingit clans can trace their genealogies to Queen Charlotte Islands Haida sources. Not only did some interior groups move out to the coast, but a few coast groups moved inland, up the Skeena, to join, and become Gitksan. The Tsimshian origin of one Haisla clan has been mentioned. Such population shifts of course must have been especially important in cultural transmission, and in leveling off the originally probably diverse culture patterns of the northern nations.

To come back to the Coast Tsimshian and their social structure, each of the four clans was represented by a local segment, or lineage, according to our terminology, in each of the fourteen Coast Tsimshian "tribes." Nine tribes had their individual summer and fall fishing villages on the lower Skeena, their separate winter village along Metlakatla Passage near the modern city of Prince Rupert, and olachen-fishing sites on the lower Nass. Two tribes stayed the whole year around on the Skeena, just below the cañon. The other three coast tribes lived south of the Skeena, each in a separate village. The difference between these tribes and the so-called tribes of the Tlingit is that the localized segments of the clans, that is, the lineages, were more firmly integrated. While each lineage had its own chief and owned certain properties, the lineages of each tribe were ranked relative to each other, and the chief of the highest-ranking lineage was the recognized chief of the tribe. It appears that the tribe as a whole held certain properties, including the winter village site. In recent times, at least, each tribe acting as a unit has built the house of its chief, and considers the structure tribal property. It is not certain that this was customary anciently, however. The tribe as a whole usually participated in both ceremonials and warfare in former days.

The nine tribes who wintered along Metlakatla Pass seem to have been approaching a still more complex type of political organization, which was hastened but not quite crystallized by the historic incident of the establishment of a Hudson's Bay post at Port Simpson. The tribes moved their winter villages there, and formed a loose sort of confederacy, although the individual tribes never quite gave up their old autonomy.

The organization of the upriver Tsimshian, the Gitksan, was essentially like that of their coast-dwelling relatives, except that they had but three large clans, whose names are translated as Frog-Raven (equated with the coastal Raven clan), Wolf, and Fireweed (equated with the Blackfish

division of the coast). A single localized clan, or
clan-lineage, at the village of Kitwanga, named
after the Eagle, had the right to use names and
crests referring to that bird. Tradition relates that
the ancestors of this group came originally from
the Nass River.

The Kwakiutl-speaking Haisla of Douglas and
Gardner canals were the southernmost people on
the coast to have a matrilineal type of social organization. There is no doubt but that these folk
acquired their social system from their Tsimshian
neighbors. In fact certain clans or clan-lineages are
traditionally reputed to have been of Tsimshian
origin, and many Haisla have Tsimshian blood
from recent intermarriages. There were two Haisla
tribes, with principal winter villages at Kitamat at
the head of Douglas Canal, and at Kitlope, up
Gardner Canal, respectively. (As has been noted,
both names are Tsimshian, not in the Haisla dialect
of Kwakiutl at all. "Kitamat," for instance, is said to
mean in Tsimshian, "People-of-the-snowy-place.")
There are said to have been a total of six clans
(including one clan-lineage), each with its own
crests and traditions: Eagle, Beaver, Raven, Crow
(extinct for some time), Blackfish, and Salmon (a
clan-lineage, found only at Kitamat). The lineages
of each of these units had their own chiefs, houses,
and fishing grounds.

The various possessions that have been mentioned as being vested in all the northern lineages:
crests, houses, and lands, were not the only forms
of lineage-held properties. Personal names, songs
and dances for ceremonial occasions, and ceremonies or specific parts of ceremonies were also so
regarded. It is true that where clans occurred, there

were certain crests and other prerogatives that were considered to be clan property. However, these things were handled in the same way that the lineage possessions were. The basic concept was that all the members of the unit shared in the joint right to these prerogatives, as they are often termed, but that the chief of the lineage was the custodian both of the intangible rights and of the lands and material possessions. The lineage chief was in this respect similar to the executor, in our own culture, of a large estate who manages its various enterprises for the heirs. It was the chief who decided when the group should move from the winter village to their fishing station and commence work on the weirs and traps. It was he who decided that a mask representing a certain hereditary crest should be worn by a dancer in a ceremonial, and that certain lineage-owned songs should be sung. The chief, once more, was the one who formally bestowed hereditary names referring to lineage crests on young members of the group. All these varieties of possessions, material and intangible alike, constituted the wealth of the social group. The better the use their chief made of these riches, the more was the well-being and prestige of the group enhanced.

South of the region in which matrilineal organizations prevailed, from the Heiltsuk to the Nootka and the Gulf of Georgia Salish, the formal social structure differed. There were no moieties, clans, or lineages. Descent was reckoned bilaterally, with only a slight preference for the male line. It is true that most Heiltsuk groups (both Xaihais and Bella Bella) had divisions named after the Eagle, Raven, Blackfish, and Wolf, which they themselves

equated with the Tsimshian clans. However, they
had neither a strict rule of descent determining affiliation in these groups, nor of exogamy, two concepts which are indispensable to true matrilinear
organization. A man and his wife might assign their
first child to the father's so-called "clan," the next
to the mother's, if she were of a different "clan,"
depending on the names and rights they wanted
each child to share—a procedure that would have
scandalized any right-thinking Tlingit, Haida, or
Tsimshian. Basically, these people, like their Southern Kwakiutl, Nootka, and Gulf of Georgia Salish
neighbors, were organized into extended families.
Each of these extended families had a series of land
holdings that included all-important economic resources—salmon- and herring-fishing grounds, hunting tracts, shellfish and berry tracts, etc.—and a host
of ritual and intangible possessions: the right to
use certain crests (not associated with clans), to
perform certain dances and ceremonies, to use certain masks, to bear certain names, and many more.
The chief of the extended family, like the chief of
the northern lineage, was the custodian of all these
rights. Membership in the extended family was inherited from one's parents. Although, when the parents stemmed from different local groups, a person
was considered more closely allied to his father's
side, he retained some claim to rights in the maternal line. On the marriage of his daughter, or the
daughter of any important member of the extended
family, it was not uncommon for a chief to bestow
certain of the family prerogatives on the groom,
thus in effect transmitting them to the bride's children when born.

The political units developed from this basic local

group-extended family pattern varied considerably. Some groups, like the Xaihais, a few of the Southern Kwakiutl, the Central and probably the Southern Nootka, and most of the Gulf of Georgia people, never developed more complex structures. On the other hand, just before or shortly after the dawn of the historic period, four Bella Bella groups, certain of which may have actually been tribes consisting of several local units, joined forces, establishing a common winter village at a place called Noluh. The Bella Coola likewise had several tribal winter villages at each of which a number of otherwise independent local groups assembled. Data on the Wikeno are fragmentary, but it seems likely that there was at least one tribal grouping on the Inlet, and two among the Wikeno Lake groups. Many Southern Kwakiutl divisions and Northern Nootkans also united into tribes, as did the Salish Homalco-Klahuse-Slaiamun divisions of the Gulf of Georgia. The hallmark of these tribal unions was the sharing of a winter village site, an established seriation or order of rank for the chiefs of the constituent local groups, and frequent, though not invariable, joint participation in ceremonials and in war.

A few groups went even further, creating confederacies. Some Northern Nootkan tribes, particularly those residing about a large inlet, assembled at a common summer village, established a fixed order of rank for all their chiefs, participated jointly in rituals (sometimes the highest-ranking of the chiefs represented the whole confederacy), and, on occasion at least, presented a solid front in war. Such a unit might have as many as thirty houses at their confederated summer site, and even well along in the historic period might include more than a thousand people. The four Southern Kwakiutl tribes holding the coast from Neweetee territory to the Nimkish River—the Walas Kwagiutl, the Kwexa, the Kwagiutl or Guetela, and the Qomkutis, and for a time the Matilpe—like the nine Coast Tsimshian tribes, formed a confederacy as the result of a historic stimulus: the establishment by the Hudson's Bay Company of a trading post, Fort Rupert, in 1849. Their difficulties in attempting to integrate their tribal system into a smooth-running confederacy will be described below.

The Puget Sound peoples and those of the lower Columbia were culturally disrupted so early by white settlement that much information on their social organization is irretrievably lost. However, it is fairly certain that the autonomous local group, consisting of an extended family, was the prevailing form. It is not clear whether they accented patrilineality in determining group membership and inheritance, or whether they permitted as much flexibility as did their bilaterally reckoning northern relatives and neighbors, although there are suggestions that they stressed kinship through the male line, as in western Washington.

In northwestern California the extended families were smaller. The tendency was for them to split up into small units of close kin. Several such groups, some vaguely related, others unrelated (or the fact of relationship forgotten), might share a village site. But each family group had its own lands, its own head man, and acted independently of the rest. Parts or all of a village might cooperate in ceremonies, particularly in the major festivals, but that was simply because no one family had either the personnel or resources to handle the performance unaided. Warfare likewise reduced itself to inter-family feuds; unrelated neighbors were careful to avoid involvement.

Northwest Coast society as a whole was distinctive in western North America because it graded individuals into a series of relatively higher or lower statuses. Examples of these ranked statuses were the chiefs, the nobles, the commoners, and the slaves. This phenomenon has been appraised superficially as indicative of the existence of a class or caste system which, to the Western mind, immediately suggests rigid sharply separated social strata within each society. Such an interpretation does not conform with the facts, except for the slaves, who formed, at least occasionally, a quite distinct societal unit. Actually, the members of each group occupied a series of social positions that were graded in minute steps from high to low. Within each graded series it is impossible to mark off a fixed point separating noble from commoner. Furthermore, despite the avowed rigidity of the system, it was possible for a person to modify his own status slightly, for better or for worse, and to improve or worsen that of his children (or that of his maternal nephews in the case of the northern matrilineal societies).

We may begin by examining the nature of the graded series of statuses just mentioned. It has already been pointed out that the basic social unit, the autonomous local group, invariably centered around a group of blood relatives, either a lineage or two or more sublineages, or an extended family. The chief or head of this unit was normally the oldest member of the group descended in the most direct line from the lineage ancestor or ancestress. It is true that among some groups, particularly the Coast Salish (Bella Coola conformed with the practices of their linguistic congeners in this respect, rather than with those of their Kwakiutl neighbors), there was some variation allowed, so that a more able junior relative might be awarded the chieftainship. Nonetheless, the native theory still held that the chief should stand in the relationship of the eldest to the other members of his group. The chief's younger brothers were his presumptive heirs and therefore next to him in rank. The formal rank of all the other members of the lineage or the related lineages was reckoned on the same basis— that of kinship to the direct chiefly line. The lowest-ranking individual, in other words the lowest commoner, was the most distant relative who was still counted as a kinsman by the members of the group.

As will be noted below, while social status was derived in this fashion from genealogical relationships, it was in a sense not automatically acquired at birth, but had to be formally assumed; that is to say, to take one's proper place in the group a person had to take or be given the proper name or title from the family stock of these honorifics. At a ceremonial occasion he had to present evidence of his right to use lineage or extended family crests and similar prerogatives on the same sort of formal occasions and so on. The names and titles that he might take, the crests he might display at once demonstrated the particular level of his rank in society and depended on the nearness of his blood kinship to the direct line of descent from the group ancestor or ancestress. Even the lowest-ranking commoner was entitled to certain categories of names that belonged to the group, and was entitled to participate in the all-important ceremonial affairs of the group. It is obvious, therefore, that within every social unit there was an unbroken, graded series of statuses from high to low. Informants have no hesitation in saying that "so-and-so was a noble," or that "so-and-so was a commoner"; but they find it difficult to define precise status for those who fit in between these two extremes.

Even among the groups on Vancouver Island and northward, among whom the system of graded ranking was most elaborated and theoretically most rigid, an individual could modify his social standing. A man of quite low rank who was a skillful canoe maker or mask carver or a bold warrior often became so valuable a member of the group and so esteemed by the chief that he might be given certain prerogatives beyond those to which he would have been entitled simply by reason of birth. Such privileges might include a higher-ranking name, a title of "war chief" if the man were a warrior, the right to use a special crest, or exclusive rights to some good fishing spot. At times, instead of giving these rewards to the individual himself, the chief might give them to him for his children or maternal heirs, as the case might be, or bestow them directly upon his heirs. Contrariwise, a man who fell into disfavor could expect only the barest minimum as his share of the honors and economic benefits of the group. The Coast Salish, including the isolated Bella Coola, permitted a great deal of such shifting up and down the social scale, according to an individual's outstanding qualities or lack of them.

The importance of properties in real and material

wealth and in intangibles, such as the right to use names and crests, has been mentioned several times. In the preceding paragraphs the significance of heredity, genealogically speaking, in fixing a man's social position has been stressed, but it is necessary to bring the intimate connection between heredity and wealth into proper perspective. In the final analysis, social status on the Northwest Coast did not depend entirely either on heredity or on wealth, but on the interrelationship between the two. The chief, by virtue of his noble birth, was the custodian of the lineage wealth and was entitled to use and manipulate these properties, particularly the ceremonial ones. Therefore in a sense he was the richest individual of the group. His noble juniors were also empowered to utilize certain of the group properties, but not those of the very highest rank or esteem. Low-ranking members were by birth entitled only to very minor rights from among the family properties.

Of course the manifestations of this concept—of rank as stemming from the interaction of heredity and wealth—were not identical throughout the entire area, although the basic forces were the same. The preceding discussion applies most specifically to the Indian communities from Yakutat Bay to Nootka territory. The Coast Salish, except for a few Gulf of Georgia groups strongly influenced by Kwakiutl neighbors, possessed far less wealth in the form of titles, ceremonial privileges, and crests to use—consequently they had fewer formal means of indicating each person's social position. There seems to have been less differentiation of status— less of a spread, as it were, between high and low. Nonetheless the chief's prestige, augmented or not

by personality factors, stemmed from his custodianship of group properties. Along the lower Columbia, early historical sources contain descriptions of
Chinookan chiefs of considerable power, and what
seems to have been a somewhat overdrawn picture
of variation of social rank. Certain chiefs were undoubtedly very powerful, but apparently their authority was basically the same as that of the Coast
Salish chiefs, exceptional powers deriving from two
factors: first, a strong personality on the part of the
chief himself, and second, a large and unusually
closely knit lineage standing solidly behind him.
In northwestern California, with the smaller social
nuclei, we get the impression of a greater accent
on individual ability. Yet in the final analysis, the
Yurok or Karok "rich man" or head of the little
family group attained his position because he had
inherited custodianship of the family's treasures of
white deerskins, great flint blades, and strings of
dentalia.

It would appear on the face of the information
available that the bases of the Northwest Coast system of rank statuses should have been fairly clear
to investigators. Nonetheless one finds many contradictory, ambiguous statements in the literature.
The principal reason for this seems to be that developments within the historical period superficially
modified the system. Two things happened during
the nineteenth century. One of these, which had
its beginning in the sea-otter fur trade, was that
varieties of material wealth became available from
a source external to the culture. Brass and iron
jewelry, abalone shells from California, blankets,
firearms and steel tools, all prized possessions, could
be obtained at the cost of little effort by anyone

who wanted to devote some time to hunting sea otter and, later, by trapping fur-bearing animals on land or signing on a fur-sealing schooner. Some groups—the Chilkat, the Stikine, the Coast Tsimshian and the Fort Rupert Kwakiutl, who were in a position to control trade with interior fur hunters or coast groups remote from the trading posts— netted tremendous profits by acting as middlemen in the fur trade. Hence great amounts of material wealth, such as was necessary for the prestige-giving ceremonials, was suddenly made available. More numerous and more spectacular ceremonials were, therefore, given in this period than ever before. The second factor was the sharp decline in native population brought about primarily by the introduction of European diseases, and secondarily by the increased efficiency of native warfare resulting from the introduction of firearms.

It eventually happened that among some dwindling groups there were more noble titles and crests available than there were people to bear them. Consequently, a man of low rank—one who was only remotely connected with the chiefly line of descent—might nevertheless find himself the heir presumptive to the chief's position or, as often was the case, one of two or three equally distantly related survivors. Were he an industrious fur hunter, he could assemble enough material riches to stage a great ritual at which he would announce his right to the high rank, titles, and crests—a situation that would have been completely impossible in the aboriginal era when the population was in a state of equilibrium. Quite as frequently, when there were several commoner survivors, they engaged in the bitterest sort of competition for the high statuses.

Therefore, during the past century there were innumerable prestige-claiming ceremonies, many more than would have been performed in prehistoric times, and a great many of them staged by people who anciently never could have performed them at all. The extent of the social gap between these *nouveau riche* claimants to high positions and unambitious commoners was falsely accentuated out of all proportion.

It has been remarked that slaves, as a group, came close to forming a distinct social stratum. Slaves on the Northwest Coast were primarily war captives, although in northwestern California a debtor could be reduced to slavery. A slave was a chattel in every sense, with no rights whatsoever. He was considered to be a valuable possession, not so much because his economic activities contributed to the riches of the group (although ordinarily he would be made to work and do menial chores), but because ownership of a slave indicated either success at war on the part of his owner or control of sufficient material wealth to purchase these unfortunates. In individual cases slaves might be treated well, but on their master's death they were likely to be killed. The sacrifice of a slave was interpreted to mean that the owner was so rich and powerful that he could unconcernedly destroy a valuable possession. Tlingit chiefs frequently crushed slaves to death under the enormous house posts set up at a ceremonial house-building. On the arrival of a visiting chief, Kwakiutl sometimes killed slaves on the beach in order to use the bodies "as rollers for the chief's canoe."

The enslavement of a relative was felt to be a disgrace to his entire lineage, so that his family made every effort to secure his freedom—usually by paying a ransom for him. Consequently, many war captives were sooner or later freed by their kinsmen; after a performance of ceremonials to cleanse them of the dishonor, they resumed their normal status in society. Ordinarily, therefore, it was only slaves who had been captured and carried a great distance from their homes—Puget Sound Indians enslaved by the Haida, or northern Californian natives captured and traded at The Dalles and down the Columbia to the coast—who had little chance of ultimate freedom. Slaves taken from nearby groups were usually either killed by the captors or ransomed by their kin. Hence, while slavery did involve a distinct separation from the rest of society, it was, in many cases at least, merely a temporary condition.

The Potlatch

The ceremonial at which the various prerogatives intimately associated with social status were assumed was called in Chinook jargon, which was the *lingua franca* of the Northwest Coast, the "potlatch." Each major cultural division, from the Tlingit to the Lower Chinook, had its own variations in procedure and detail of this performance, but the function was everywhere the same. The potlatch brought to expression basic principles involved in social status and also served as a major force for social integration. As has been stated, each individual in the social unit was born with an inherent right to use group properties of major or minor importance, but he could not exercise these rights— in other words, assume his proper status—until his title to them had been formally announced and validated. This formal announcement and public validation was accomplished during and by the potlatch. The heir presumptive to a chieftainship would be presented formally to a group of guests at such an affair. His relationship to the incumbent chief would be explained and he would be given a name or the right to use some crest specifically related to the position he would eventually occupy. Under some circumstances a man might, in the same manner, present himself as a presumptive heir. The guests who heard these claims announced, and recognized their validity, were regarded as witnesses to the proceedings. As such, they were rewarded and their subsequent good will was insured by giving them feasts and gifts. While at times the demonstration of privileges or the giving away of material goods might appear to overshadow the essential announcement and validation of rights and status, this last-named function was the essence and basic goal of the whole performance.

The contribution of the potlatch to group solidarity was achieved in various ways. The proper giver of the potlatch was, of course, the chief of the local group, although in some instances where progress had been made toward tribal solidarity, the ranking chief of the tribe might give the affair. The chief performed this function as custodian of the family's wealth in goods and intangibles. (When a tribal chief was the host, he used only his own lineage crests.) He was the principal host, but, in point of fact, all the members of the family assisted and joined him as hosts. The guests, who provided the necessary validation of the claims made, were nec-

essarily outsiders. They might be from another
group of the same tribe, or they might come from
an entirely separate and independent community.
Furthermore, since gifts and material goods—which
in historic times were synonymous with trade articles like blankets, guns, and other European imports, as well as cash—were essential, all the members of the host group contributed to make the
total quantity available for distribution to the
guests as large as possible. The host group also
cooperated with their chief in assembling foods for
the feasts, in providing dancers and singers for the
crest displays, and in innumerable other ways. In
fine, every member of the host group participated
actively and thus had many opportunities to demonstrate his membership in the group and to share
the prestige acquired from the ostentatious display.
Another contributing factor was the fact that not
only was the heir presumptive given titles and other
honors, but other members of the group had rights
to the public bestowal of whatever family rights
to which they might be entitled. Children of individuals of intermediate and low rank alike would
be given names from the family stock or have their
ears pierced at the potlatch, or in one way or another would be presented as members of the group.
Thus, in a variety of ways, the institution was a
group affair that affirmed or reaffirmed the group
affiliation of each of its members.

The basic pattern was embroidered on and elaborated in various ways by each of the northern divisions.

The Tlingit viewed the potlatch as a cycle of
rituals to mourn the death of a chief. It was not a
single performance, but one that might take several

years to carry to completion. It began with the reward to the group who had conducted the mortuary rites for the chief. These people always had to be of the opposite moiety from that of the deceased, that is, if the chief had been a Raven, a group from the Wolf side would take care of the body and bury it. In theory at least, this group should belong to the same lineage as the dead chief's father. In any case they were formally invited to a potlatch at which the new chief, the heir to the deceased, was presented. His rights to the position were explained and the origins of the various properties were recounted. For serving as witnesses, and for coming, as they said, "to console the (new) chief for his loss," they were given presents. At the same time, the chief who had been designated to take charge of the funerary proceedings was "paid." Subsequently, until the cycle was completed, the same people were summoned on various occasions: to rebuild the house of the new chief, and to raise a mortuary column in memory of his predecessor. Specifically, they were called upon to perform these tasks: to carve the mortuary column, to cut and carve the house posts, etc., so that some of the gifts were given to them in payment for their efforts, and some were given them simply as gifts.

The Tsimshian potlatch was essentially the same, although the overt expression of its purpose is sometimes stated as being that of inheritance—that is, the announcement of and validation of the position of the new chief—rather than to stress the mourning function as did the Tlingit. Actually the potlatches of both peoples were essentially the same, serving at the same time to honor and commemorate the departed chief and to establish his heir officially in his place. The Haida, as will be brought out, likewise staged such affairs.

The Haida, according to available published sources, seem to have given potlatches most frequently to establish the position of a younger person as the heir presumptive. That is to say, a potlatch might be given in a child's honor by his parents before he went to live with his maternal uncle, whose status and rights he would eventually inherit. Although the child's father appeared to function as a host, the actual hosts were the mother and her lineage, who provided the property—both the ritual prerogatives bestowed and displayed and the material goods distributed as gifts. The father's lineage were the guests. Eventually, on the death of the maternal uncle, the heir gave a potlatch in the house which he was entitled to inherit, using the prerogatives and wealth of his own lineage. These combination memorial–status-assuming affairs were probably the major ones given by the Haida, as they were amongst their Tlingit and Tsimshian neighbors.

Among the Kwakiutl, Bella Coola, and Nootka, potlatches were often given, like those of the Haida, to establish a child or youth as the heir presumptive. In addition, these three peoples very often combined the potlatch with performances by the dancing societies. The latter were elaborate dramas representing the abduction of certain individuals (with inherited rights to the performances) by supernatural beings who returned them, endowed with varied and often spectacular ceremonial prerogatives.

The Salish groups, who had fewer ceremonial

prerogatives to announce and validate, gave potlatches to confirm the status of their chiefs. To
demonstrate that he was worthy of the post, and
thereby validate his status, the headman of a Salish
lineage might stage such a performance years after
he had nominally attained his position as leader of
his extended family.

Too many years have passed since the last Chinook potlatch was given for us to have any detailed
information on such variations as may have been
made on the pattern along the lower Columbia. It
seems most plausible to assume, however, that there
was relatively little difference between their procedures and aims and those of their Salish neighbors.

The northernmost groups gave a minor variety
that has been called a "face-saving" potlatch. When
some misadventure befell a chief, or the heir to a
chieftaincy—for example, if he stumbled and fell
on some public occasion, or suffered any other
public indignity—the damage to his honor could
be repaired only by the formal distribution of gifts
and the reaffirmation of his honorable status. The
elaborateness of this performance depended to a
large extent on the nature of the accident. If it was
considered to have been a true accident and not
the result of malicious human intent to demean
him, a few small gifts sufficed to erase the damage
to his dignity. If, however, there was any reason
to believe that the affront had been deliberate,
either through physical or magical means, a large
and elaborate potlatch was called for. Among such
groups as the Nootka and many of the Kwakiutl,
where the function of the potlatch and its role in
social integration was overtly recognized, a high-
ranking guest at another chief's potlatch, when con-

SOCIETY 137

ducted to the wrong seat by the ushers, satisfied
his honor by giving a single blanket to one of the
hosts. In such a situation the host chief repaid this
gift later on in the proceedings.

Competitive potlatches have received considerable attention in ethnographic literature because of
their very spectacular nature. Two powerful rivals
might give away and destroy thousands of dollars'
worth of trade goods and money in the course of
the contest. The destruction of property, of course,
was to demonstrate that the chief was so powerful
and so rich that the blankets or money he threw on
the fire, or the "coppers" he broke, were of no moment at all to him. While such contests were held
occasionally among many of the northern groups,
they reached their highest development—or perhaps one should say their peak of bitterest rivalry
—in two places: Fort Rupert and Port Simpson. It
appears fairly clear that nearly identical factors led
to this development in the two localities. It will be
recalled that several neighboring Kwakiutl tribes
moved into Fort Rupert when the Hudson's Bay
Company post was established there, forming a
loose confederation. Each of these tribes consisted
of several local groups who, long ago, had formed
fairly stable political entities, even though the local
groups retained a certain independence of action
as well as their individual property rights. Once
the tribes occupied the common site, close to the
trading post, they were faced with a very acute
problem. It was inevitable that each tribe should
sooner or later invite the others to potlatches.

It is necessary to explain here that while the ranking of the individuals within each local group was
well known, and in each tribe the lineages, and

their respective chiefs, were graded in a well-established order of precedence from highest to lowest, there were no precise verbal designations for these sequences—that is to say, there were no native terms directly translatable as "first chief," "second chief," "third chief," etc. The crucial point, and the public recognition of a chief's claim to precedence, occurred at the time of the distribution of gifts to the guests. The highest-ranking chief was given the first gift—and ordinarily, to show respect for his rank, the largest single gift. The chief second in rank among the assembled guests was the recipient of the second gift, and so on in descending sequence. The chiefs of the newly organized Fort Rupert Confederacy had no precedents on which to base the relative rankings of the chiefs of the several tribes. This fact led them to initiate a series of potlatches in which certain of them asserted their claims to particular places—first, second, third, or fourth, and so on—in the consolidated precedence list. When two chiefs claimed the same place, the first one would give a potlatch, stating his claim; then the second would try to outdo him. Finally, one or the other gave away or destroyed more property than his opponent could possibly equal. The one who had been surpassed had no recourse. He could no longer contest his claim, for, in the native mind, it came to be regarded as ridiculous that an individual of few resources (and of course this involved not only the man, but his entire local group) should attempt to make a claim against someone who had demonstrated power and wealth.

The extremes to which these competitions were carried and the attitude that developed in Fort Rupert—that great expenditures were sufficient to validate any sort of a claim—are exemplified by the unique institution which those people created. This was the title of "Eagle." An Eagle was a person who had the special right to receive his gift before the highest-ranking chief was presented with his. At one time there were twelve Eagle titles at Fort Rupert. Investigation has revealed that most of these Eagles were not chiefs at all, but were men of intermediate or even common status who through industry and clever trading amassed great quantities of material wealth. Some of them, in addition, were backed by certain chiefs who recognized them as potential tools to assist in the downfall of some high-ranking rival. It is interesting to note that the Eagles made no pretenses at claiming tradition-hallowed names or crests, but assumed or tried to assume invented names that referred in some way to the privilege that they hoped to acquire—that of precedence in receiving gifts before the real nobles. There was even one individual who, in the early part of the last century, presumed to claim the right to receive his gift on the day *prior* to the pot-latch. The chiefs would not tolerate this effrontery; when he insisted on his claim, they had him killed. Others of this *nouveau riche* contingent, however, managed to keep in the good graces of the chiefs and maintained their anomalous positions for many years.

After the nine Tsimshian tribes assembled at Port Simpson, they were faced with almost the identical problem regarding potlatch protocol. The order of precedence of the clan chiefs within each tribe had been established for a long time and was not subject to question. The intertribal rankings were not definite. Competitive potlatches, very similar to and quite as bitterly contested as those of the Fort Rupert Kwakiutl, became common. It is entirely possible that such contests occurred occasionally among various groups in the remote past when certain local groups assembled at common winter villages in the process of tribal amalgamation. These prehistoric competitions never were so frequent or involved such quantities of valuables as at Fort Rupert and Port Simpson. An interesting sidelight on these specialized potlatches is afforded by the fact that among the Haida at Masset, fictitious competitions were staged solely to add a little spice to the occasion. The putative rivals agreed, in private, to expend identical amounts so that the affair would come out a draw. Some Southern Kwakiutl chiefs are known to have done this also.

The economics of the potlatch are not particularly complex. A chief announced his plans to his lineage or extended family mates some time in advance. He would normally expect them to contribute wealth goods to the extent of their ability. The low-ranking members of the group gave furs, blankets, or money for a variety of reasons: to gratify their personal sense of participation in the group performance, to assure the esteem of their chief and fellow group members, or to ensure public recognition for themselves or their children at the time of the potlatch by being given names or being included in some ceremonial in at least a minor capacity.

This concept of participation on the basis of familial ties is most obvious among the northern groups, where, in theory, a potlatch was supposed to be given by a chief (and his lineage) to lineages of the opposite moiety. For instance, among the

Haida, recent studies have made clear that certain types of potlatch given in honor of the children of a chief were actually given by the chief's wife and her lineage—the same lineage, of course, that the children belonged to—to the lineage of the husband and sometimes others of his moiety. Nonetheless, the husband and his close relatives contributed substantially to the accumulation of valuables to be distributed in honor of the children. Similarly, a Tlingit chief could count on his wife's brothers' contributing handsomely to his store of wealth intended for a potlatch given in the name of his lineage, even though the brothers-in-law were in the opposite moiety and would be among the guests at the affair. Such gifts were outright donations; no return was expected other than the sort of eventual turn-about-is-fair-play reciprocity we ourselves expect in connection with Christmas cards and dinner invitations. The presents the brothers-in-law received at the potlatch bore no relation to any such donations they might have made, but were scaled to each one's individual rank. The important compensation, in native eyes, was that at the potlatch the chief honored his own children and their lineage mates—members of the lineage of his wife's brothers —by formally presenting them, announcing their assumption of hereditary names and titles (of their own lineage), and arranging to have their ears pierced, or to have them tattooed. In other words, the potlatch was an occasion for the emphasis of unity of a group of relatives even where kinship was ostensibly broken by the unilateral structure of society.

The amount of property that the chief set as an objective depended on the size of the group or

groups he intended to invite and the elaborateness
of the spectacle he planned. Among the Kwakiutl
divisions and the more northerly tribes, he might,
if necessary, borrow blankets or funds to attain his
goal. Such loans were usually for a set period of
time—half a year or a year—and were ordinarily
repayable by a sum larger than the initial loan.
This loan, and its repayment, was a financial trans-
action entirely separate from and outside the potlatch and had no relation to potlatch payments or
gifts. When the time came for the big event and the
various genealogical claims had been announced
and the prerogatives and crests displayed, the gifts
were distributed. Among the northernmost tribes,
where the potlatch guests had performed certain
tasks such as the burial of the dead chief, the raising of a mortuary column, or the building or re-
building of the chief's house, etc., the chiefs to
whom these duties had been entrusted received
special gifts said to be payments for the work done.
The individual chiefs so honored were expected
later on to reward their own relatives and retainers
who had done the actual work. The same procedure
held true among the Haida, for example, when
certain chiefs were designated to tattoo crests on
noble children of the host group. These chiefs were
given "payments" for the tattooing, although they
themselves had not functioned as the artists. The
actual tattooers were paid by the recipients of these
payments. Eventually all these preliminaries were
completed. The main potlatch gifts were presented in amounts that varied according to the
rank of the recipient. (Of course the payments as
well as the gifts were distributed in the order of
rank.) On occasions when guests were invited from

various distant localities, as, for example, when a Tsimshian chief invited Haida and Tlingit guests, a tactful host would present gifts to the principal chiefs simultaneously.

A special class of objects, called "coppers" in English, was intimately associated with the potlatch. These large shield-like sheets were hammered out of placer copper found somewhere along the reaches of the Copper River in Alaska (Plates 27, 28). Of course in historic times many were made of sheet copper obtained from white traders. These coppers were traded southward as far as Southern Kwakiutl territory. Among the Tlingit, Haida, and Tsimshian, it was almost essential that one or two of them be used at the potlatch in honor of the dead chief, on the assumption of his place by his successor, and that they be broken and thrown on the fire or into the sea. To these people the coppers were valuable, but they were not nearly so highly regarded as they came to be among the Southern Kwakiutl, among whom the value of a copper was augmented each time it was given away, whether in a potlatch or in connection with bride price or dowry. Some coppers are known to have attained values of several thousands of dollars.

The northwest Californians—provincials from the areal point of view—staged performances that, like the potlatch, revolved about the wealth and status concepts. In these, however, the family wealth in material treasures was merely displayed, and was not distributed amongst the spectators. Rights and prerogatives such as existed in the north were lacking, so these folk contented themselves with an exposition of their valuables, then thriftily stowed them away for another year.

Marriage

Marriage was regarded as a social contract, not merely between the man and his wife, but between their respective families. The higher the rank of the couple, the greater the emphasis on this latter aspect. The concern of the individual's family revolved principally about the rule that a person should marry a spouse of corresponding social status. A chief, or heir to a chieftaincy, should marry the daughter of a chief, or at least the daughter of a man of high rank, closely related to a chief's line of descent. Throughout the area it was deemed essential for the groom's family to give a substantial quantity of valuables and goods—the "bride price" —to the girl's family. The higher the rank of the couple, the greater the amount of the bride price. In northwest California, where areal patterns were so often reduced to their bare essentials, a man's worth was gauged in terms of the amount of the bride price paid for his mother.

Two aspects of the bride price should be noted. First, it was not, outside of northwest California, a quantity arrived at through close bargaining by representatives of the two social units; it was rather as large an amount as the groom's group were capable of giving, given the status of the couple. Second, the woman's family did not, through the so-called "sale," lose all interest and rights in her, but continued to be concerned about her welfare. Their continuing interest was usually expressed by a return gift or series of gifts made to the man's family. The Southern Kwakiutl carried this concept to its logical conclusion by a series of return gifts from a

23. Wooden rattles. On the left, a design representing the Killer whale from the Haida; center, a human skull from the Kwakiutl; right, a form, from the Tlingit, representing a Hawk (about 10 inches high).

24. Various rattles for musical accompaniment. Upper left, puffin beaks from the Haida; upper right, teeth and amulets from the Tlingit (these two examples are 6 to 8 inches in diameter); center, pecten shells from the Tlingit but used more frequently by the Gulf of Georgia Salish (the shells are about 6 inches in diameter); bottom, deer hoofs on a stick from the Tlingit (about 18 inches long). The upper rattles are of a type widely used by the Western Eskimo.

25. Two examples of "chief's rattles." These were carved of two or more pieces of alder wood, hollowed out for the "sounders" of pebbles, and then fitted together. The top example is from the Haida and is a "raven rattle" used by northern chiefs and some shamans to accompany songs on state occasions. The principal figure is a raven with the stylized face of a hawk carved on the underside. On the raven's back is a shamanistic scene showing a spirit extracting disease from a sick person. The other is from the Tlingit; the main figure is a large water bird, perhaps a crane. The scene on his back is probably an episode in the origin myth of some clan and shows a person, apparently pursued by a wolf, escaping on the back of a friendly sea monster.

26. This "tambourine" drum, with the design painted on the inside so the drumming will not scuff the paint, is a type commonly found among the Tlingit, Haida, and Tsimshian. The straight drum stick below would have had a padded buckskin head to protect the rawhide drumhead and give a more sonorous tone.

27. An engraved "copper" from the Haida which was used in the potlatch ceremony. The coppers are generally about 2½ feet high.

28. *A Southern Kwakiutl princess of the 1890s. Note that a portion of the top of the copper she is holding has been cut away, probably in defiance of her father's potlatch rivals. Courtesy of the Smithsonian Institution.*

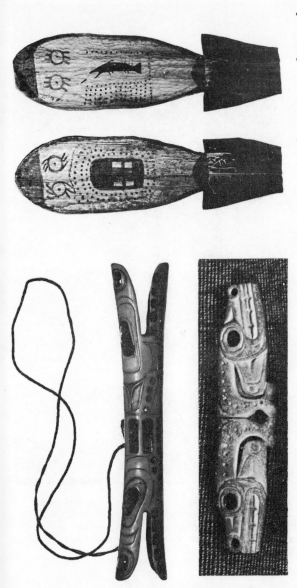

29. Two examples of carving, both in bone, are (top) a Tsimshian shaman's "soul-catcher," inlaid with abalone shell (about 7 inches long) and (bottom) a shaman's amulet from the Tlingit (about 5 inches long).

30. Typical spirit canoe boards, representing beings who assisted the shaman in his dramatized journey to recapture a lost soul. These are probably from the Salishan Duwamish or some nearby group of Puget Sound.

31. A shaman's rattle (about 20 inches high) from the Quinault, a Salish tribe of western Washington. Carved in the form of the shaman's guardian spirit with sounders of deer hoofs attached in the front, this specimen represents a distinctively Salish style.

32. This very old photograph shows the dramatis personae of a Southern Kwakiutl Shamans' Society performance. The crouching figures in the front, wearing masks with wide bird-like beaks, represent the Bakbakwalanusiwa, the monstrous man-eating bird who possesses and inspires the Cannibal-dancer. The house posts on either side in the background represent the Thunderbird, important in many Kwakiutl and Nootka family traditions. At the left of the picture can be seen part of a painted board screen; this is the front of the cubicle in which the principal performer was kept.

33. A Southern Kwakiutl changeable mask. The outer mask represents a Wolf Spirit. By manipulating strings the dancer can open the hinged halves to reveal a representation of a supernatural bird-being.

34. This jointed puppet represents the spirit presiding over the Kwakiutl Shamans' Society ceremonial (the dance series that includes the "Hamatsa," or Cannibal-dancer). Such puppets were displayed by chiefs giving the ceremonial and their principal guests. A simple sleight-of-hand trick made the objects appear to fly miraculously back and forth between host and guest, to symbolize the beginning of the performance. This specimen happens to be from the Haida, who used it with some of the performances they acquired from the Kwakiutl. Courtesy of the Smithsonian Institution.

man to his son-in-law, or the son-in-law's group, to
"buy back" his daughter. The completion of these
payments did not signify that the couple were
thereby separated, but it did permit her to remain
with her husband without pressure of obligation.

Since it was customary for the father-in-law to
include various crests and ceremonial privileges in
his gifts to his son-in-law, which of course were intended for the couple's children, acquisition of such
prerogatives through marriage came to be an end
in itself. Hence, during the period of population
shrinkage, or perhaps even before that time, the
Kwakiutl devised fictitious unions in which a young
chief was "married to" an arm, or leg, or the house
post, of another chief. The quantities of valuables
given by both parties, which were of course distributed by each recipient in potlatches, redounded
to the credit of both.

There were several varieties of preferred marriages. One of these, found among the northern
nations who reckoned descent matrilineally, was
cross-cousin marriage (that is, marriage to one's
mother's brother's daughter, or to one's father's sister's daughter). A young chief who married his
mother's brother's daughter was actually marrying
the daughter of the man whose position, house, and
properties he would eventually inherit, an obviously
convenient and practical arrangement. Among the
Kwakiutl groups, the Bella Coola, the Nootka, and
their nearest Salish neighbors, a chief or a chief's
son might seek to marry the daughter of some distant important personage to create useful alliances;
or he might marry a woman of approximately
equivalent rank from some extended family to
which he was already related, or, if the actual

blood kinship were not too close, from his own group.

The advantages of marrying into a related family, or to a woman from one's own extended family, were, according to the Kwakiutl, Bella Coola, and Nootka viewpoint, that one thereby regained crests and privileges that had been given away in previous marriages, in the one instance, or, in the other, retained such valuable possessions within the group. The Bella Coola are said to have arranged intragroup marriages quite often for their chiefs and chiefs' heirs in order to retain the family prerogatives. In fact, some early investigators interpreted this practical measure as a strict rule of endogamy (a term meaning a prohibition against marrying outside of a certain defined group), such as is found with a rigid caste system. However, this was not a correct interpretation, for many Bella Coola not only married outside their extended family units, but outside their nation as well, acquiring spouses among the Bella Bella and Wikeno in some numbers. Proof of this practice may be found in the number of crests and ritual prerogatives among the Bella Coola that they state were obtained from one or another Heiltsuk division "in marriage," that is, as part of the gifts made by the bride's father to his son-in-law, and in the various rights of similar type found among the Heiltsuk that are reported to be of Bella Coola origin.

The Coast Salish and Chinook—except for those living near and strongly influenced by Southern Kwakiutl and Nootka—having, as has been previously stated, a more rigid rule of patrilineal inheritance of their few prerogatives, did not transfer such rights to sons-in-law, and as they did not have a unilateral organization either, there was no particular advantage to their marrying relatives.

The Yurok and their immediate neighbors added a unique touch of their own to the areal patterns. Normally, a bride went to live in her husband's home. Occasionally, however, either to patch up an affair in which a man of few resources had become involved with a girl, or in a situation in which a man of importance had daughters but no sons and did not want to be without willing hands to serve him, a special arrangement was made, a "half marriage," as the Yurok translate their own name for the institution into English. In this type of marriage, slightly more than half the normal bride price was paid by the groom and his kin, and he went to live in his father-in-law's house, where, in effect, he worked out the balance of the bride price in services.

Wars and Feuds

The Nootkan and Kwakiutl tribes, and their neighbors to the northward, made war on occasion; those to the south carried on feuds. The distinction is much more than one of the scale of the military operation and number of people involved, although usually the feuds of the Salish, Chinook, and northwest Californians were carried on by a few individuals at a time. At times the northerners too had their feuds, in which the killing or injury of a kinsman was avenged by his relatives. But true warfare, aimed at driving out or exterminating another lineage or family in order to acquire its lands and goods, was a well-established practice in the north.

In the discussion of recent histories of the various

groups, some attention has been given to these northern wars of conquest. Some northern Tlingit lineage or lineages drove the Eskimo off Kayak Island; the Kaigani Haida forced some southern Tlingit to withdraw from part of Prince of Wales Island and established themselves there; the Tsimshian Kitkatla and Kitisu tribes, and apparently the Bella Bella as well, were doing their best to exterminate the Xaihais in order to take possession of their territory. Among the Nootka, bitter, long-drawn-out wars were carried on by various local groups and tribes for the express purpose of capturing the territory of their neighbors. In addition, the objective of frequent raids, some of them at quite long range, was to capture wealth goods and slaves. The Haida raids down into the Puget Sound area have been mentioned. Presumably the development of the concept of a war of conquest is to be attributed to the highly developed concepts of property right in lands and places of economic importance, and to a certain amount of actual population pressure in the north in aboriginal times.

The raid staged on the occasion of the death of an important person, whether or not he had died from natural causes, was a typically northern custom. The usually expressed purpose was that of "sending someone with the dead chief," or of "making other people mourn also." Such a party usually attacked and slew the first persons they met; sometimes even their own village mates were not exempted if the raiders encountered them offshore in a canoe.

After a successful attack the northern warriors beheaded their victims, brought the heads home, and usually set them up on tall poles in front of the village. Only the Tlingit scalped; they took the heads of fallen foe and removed the scalps on the way home.

Feuds were conducted in a different fashion among most of the Northwest Coast groups. After a slaying or an injury, the kin of the victim made an effort to retaliate, although sometimes the trouble could be smoothed over. In any case, whether or not revenge was taken, the customary method of settling the feud among almost all the groups, except the Kwakiutl and Nootka, was by payment of indemnities, or "weregild." When more than the initial offense had occurred, each injury to either side had to be paid for separately. Intermediaries were usually sent back and forth to negotiate agreements as to the proper amount of damages. It was at this time, in northwestern California, that the valuation put on a man according to the amount of bride price paid for his mother came into play. Elsewhere such neatly calibrated scales were not used; the aim was to demand enough compensation to embarrass and humble the opponents.

Sometimes, among the Tlingit and probably their immediate neighbors, in cases where no blood-money settlement could be agreed upon, a chief or noble of the slayer's lineage would take it on himself to resolve the matter. He, of course, had to be of a rank as nearly as possible equivalent to that of the slain person. He donned the finest ceremonial regalia of his lineage. Then he went out of the house, dancing one of the slow, stately hereditary dances of his lineage as he approached the waiting foe. The courteous gesture on their part was to allow him the dignity of approaching to within a few yards of them before they evened matters by killing him.

5 RELIGION

Native religious beliefs and practices on the Northwest Coast revolved about a series of patterns and concepts shared by all or nearly all of the groups participating in the areal culture. There was, of course, a good deal of variation in the detailed manifestations of these basic tenets, but from the broad point of view these differences are quite superficial. These fundamental principles that combined to give Northwest Coast religion its distinctive cast were: lack of systematization of beliefs on creation, cosmology, and deities; a rather vague notion of a remote, disinterested Supreme Being or Beings; a set of beliefs revolving about the immortality of certain economically important species of animals, combined with a series of ritual practices to ensure the return of those creatures; and, finally, the concept of the possibility of lifelong assistance by a personal guardian spirit.

It is worth stressing that among these people, as among other American Indians, religious belief played an important part in everyday life. The preparatory rites and observances at the time of a fishing or hunting expedition, or an appeal to one's guardian spirit, were equally important parts of getting ready as the preparation of the fishing or hunting gear. The same principle applied to preparations for a potlatch or a war party.

The absence of systematized beliefs about the cosmos, and about origins, and the failure to arrange the various deities and lesser supernatural beings in formal hierarchies, so characteristic of the religious thought of many, though not all, of the simpler American Indian cultures, strike us as somewhat inconsistent with a civilization like that of the Northwest Coast, where so many patterns were refined and enriched to an amazing degree. One may find, for example, that among the members of a single tribe, or in neighboring tribes of the same linguistic and cultural division, various individuals will give completely different accounts of the ancient beliefs as to how the world was supported, and whether the Land of the Dead was across some distant river, somewhere in the sky, or in an underworld. Likewise, a god or spirit regarded by one informant as of great importance will be described as a minor personage by another. Strangely enough, or so it appears at first, this anarchy of concept was most extreme among the more advanced groups from Vancouver Island northward. It may well be that their influence on areal patterns also affected their southern neighbors.

The real reason for this apparent disorganization of belief seems to have been that there was a very rich unwritten literature of myths and legends current in the area; in fact, several distinct cycles seem to have been represented, perhaps reflecting the diverse origins of the several distinct linguistic divisions on the coast. Each lineage or extended family took over some myth or mythical episode, incorporating it into the official family tradition to explain the origin of the kin group. Hence each of these social units had its own official version of

creation and the like. An early investigator among
the Bella Coola was told, for example, of a series of
superimposed heavens, in the highest of which the
gods dwelt in a single vast house. Just like the Indians who occupied a house in this world, the gods
were ranked in a series of statuses from the highest
to the lowest. As previously remarked, hierarchical
structures of this sort were not typical of the coastal
culture. The Bella Coola were therefore regarded
as exceptional in the area for their systematization
of religious thought. More recent studies, however,
have revealed that this concept was part of the origin tradition of a single Bella Coola family line.
Other Bella Coola were not familiar with the details of the story, nor did they accept it as true at
points where it contradicted their own extended
family traditions. Similarly, most Haida conceived
of the sky as a bowl-like firmament over the earth
and believed that on the upper side of the bowl was
a Sky-World inhabited by certain supernatural beings. However, one tradition, presumably the possession of some lineage and related to its legendary
origin, describes a series of five Sky-Worlds, one
over the other.

Beliefs in a Supreme Being were common to
many of the Indian groups of our area. Typically,
this deity was remote from the affairs of men and
the world. He may formerly have taken a more active role. According to some myth cycles he was the
Creator; in others, he was a Transformer (a being
who went about in an existing but incomplete
world, setting things in order). Nonetheless—and
somewhat inconsistently—he was often addressed in
prayer by the Indians. This was equally true of the
Tlingit deity "Raven-at-the-head-of-the-Nass," the

Haida "Power-of-the-Shining-Heavens," the Tsimshian "Laxha." The Nootka varied the pattern
slightly by referring to and praying to the four
"Great Chiefs," each of whom ruled a segment of
the universe. In certain of their manifestations,
Kwakiutl and Bella Coola Supreme Deities were
closely associated with the sun. The Coast Salish
(other than the Bella Coola) and Chinook seem to
have been atypical, and apparently lacked any such
concept. Farther south the data are less clear, because of the early shattering of the native culture,
but the Athapascan-speaking tribelets on both sides
of the California-Oregon border prayed regularly to
a deity who had created their world.

A set of beliefs relating to the immortality of certain animal species was universal throughout the
Northwest Coast. It seems fairly clear that in most
cases the original concept, regardless of the group
or groups of its origin, probably referred specifically
to salmon. When one considers the spectacular phenomenon of the annual salmon runs, such a belief
seems reasonable enough, especially to primitive
people. At the same season every year, the same
one of the five varieties of salmon would appear in
great numbers in the bay or cove at the mouth of
some stream, and after a short time would start upriver. A relatively small number, of course, were
harpooned, netted, or trapped, but the majority proceeded to the spawning grounds far upstream,
spawned, and died. Their lean, battered bodies
lined the river banks and drifted back to the sea. It
is doubtful whether the Indians understood the life
cycle of these fish, or connected the spawning with
the tiny new-hatched parr, or these with the adult
salmon. Yet the following year the species appeared

again. Hence, what could be more logical than the concept that the salmon ascended the streams to benefit mankind, died, and then returned to life? The general belief was that the salmon were a race of supernatural beings who dwelt in a great house under the sea. There they went about in human form, feasting and dancing like people. When the time came for the "run," the Salmon-people dressed in garments of salmon flesh, that is, assumed the form of fish to sacrifice themselves. Once dead, the spirit of each fish returned to the house beneath the sea. If the bones returned to the water, the being resumed his (human-like) form with no discomfort, and could repeat the trip next season. Since the Salmon-people's migration was considered to be voluntarily undertaken, it followed that it behooved human beings to take pains not to offend their benefactors. To return all the salmon bones to the water was one of the procedures believed to be essential. If some bones were thrown away on land, on resurrection the Salmon-person might lack an arm or a leg, or some other part, and he and his tribe would become angry and refuse to run again in the stream in which they had been so unappreciatively treated. All the Northwest Coast groups had long lists of regulations and prohibitions referring to the Salmon-people in order to continue to maintain good relations with these important beings.

This concept was extended to many other species. Herring and olachen, also seasonal species, were widely believed to have their own house under the sea (or to share the Salmon-people's house) and to behave the same way. The Nootka believed that whales, hair seal, and, on land, the wolves (not of economic, but of ritual importance) likewise had their houses, and emerged wearing their animal form like a replaceable garment. Even creatures who were not believed to live in "tribal" houses were considered immortal. Among the Yurok, and probably their neighbors as well, deer were thought to be resurrected in the same fashion, and it was believed that they deliberately entered the snares or exposed themselves to the fire of hunters who meticulously observed the rites that the Deer-people considered pleasing.

It was not only the beliefs themselves that unified a great part of the areal religious patterns, but also the rites and observances developed out of them. For example, a First Salmon ceremony was held over the first catch from each important stream or area, the purpose of which was to honor and to welcome the first of the species. Usually the fish was addressed as though it were a visiting chief of high rank; it was handled in a ceremonious way, and was frequently given offerings such as the sacred eagle down of the northern groups; it was cooked and eaten in a formal fashion. This type of rite, except for details of performance, was almost uniform everywhere, except at the very extremes of the area. Tlingit and Haida attached less importance to it, and performed it in more attenuated fashion than did their neighbors to the south. In northwestern California the ritual was integrated with a First Fruits rite (and, among the Karok, with a New Fire ceremony) and, as well, with the Wealth Display performances, into a cult-system that has been designated a World-Renewal cycle. Nevertheless, the First Salmon ceremony was performed in some form by all the groups of the coast, and even by a few of their peripheral and ruder neighbors of the interior.

By analogy, similar rituals were performed to honor other species, such as herring and olachen in the north, and smelt (or "surf fish") along the Oregon and northern California coasts. Other game, including sea and land mammals, was treated ceremoniously when killed, so that the spirit would be placated and would return to the hunter wearing a new body whose flesh and fur the hunter might take.

The significance of these rituals in honor of important animals led to the development of a priesthood, another distinctive trait of Northwest Coast culture. The procedure for handling the first of the season's salmon catch became so complicated, and the prayers addressed to the Salmon-spirits became so lengthy, that a specialist had to take charge. Rites of limited importance, like those of the bear hunter or mountain-goat hunter, became individual possessions and were transmitted from generation to generation as valuable secret techniques for securing game. Rituals for species that affected the general welfare, like salmon, likewise became private possessions, to be performed in the public interest. The Yurok ritualist had to be paid by public collection to recite his incredibly long formulaic prayers to the salmon and acorns; the Nootka or Kwakiutl chief ritually cleansed himself and performed his ceremony as part of his duty toward his people. It is particularly interesting that Nootka and a few Southern Kwakiutl ritualists made use of human bones and corpses in their rites, just like the Aleut whale-lancers, in the belief that the dead had great power over game.

It was generally accepted that an individual's control over his destiny—his good or bad fortune—depended on the intercession of a spiritual helper. The favor of such a being was won only after an arduous search, in which one cleansed one's self of taints offensive to supernatural beings by fasting, bathing in icy pools, scrubbing away the clinging aura of human sensuality with harsh flesh-mortifying bundles of twigs or nettles.

Among the Tlingit, Haida, and perhaps the Tsimshian, there was a tendency toward a sort of inheritance of spirit helpers. That is, an individual went through the usual quest, but encountered a particular spirit or spirits that "belonged," as it were, to his maternal lineage. Simply performing these rites contributed to one's success, but in addition one might encounter a spirit who allowed himself to be subjugated if the quester were properly purified, and thenceforth served like Aladdin's djinni. Such a "guardian spirit" might confer power to cure the sick, to become a great warrior, to acquire wealth, or, among the tribes north of Puget Sound, might bestow the right to display some ceremonial performance representing the being himself. As a matter of fact, all the prized crests of the northerners were supposed to have been obtained originally through just this kind of supermundane authorization. The clan ancestor, among the northernmost groups, or the benefactor of the lineage among Kwakiutl and Nootka, appeared and conferred the right on all ensuing generations to use masks or symbols representing himself.

From the individual point of view, one of the maximum gifts a spirit could bestow was one that could be utilized to affect the fortunes of one's friends and neighbors. The best way to achieve that was to be granted the power to cure or cause illnesses. The "medicineman," or "shaman" as he is called in the literature, was a power in the community. Many commoners who possessed no high social rank to bring them into the public eye found a compensatory prestige in shamanistic power. Everywhere the popular phrasing was that to be a shaman sent an individual on the road to wealth. Actually, the medicineman, although often well paid for curing the sick, could never accumulate enough valuables to offer serious competition to the chief, who, as lineage head, inherited not only economic rights and properties, but also the right to call on the produce of all the members of the family. What the shaman actually obtained was public recognition, either esteem or fear or a blend of both, far beyond that to which his modest birth would have entitled him. By performing the arduous cleansing rites and encountering a spirit who granted curing power one became a public figure, the cynosure of all eyes when the whole village congregated to watch the treatment of a patient.

Illness was generally believed to be caused either by intrusion of small semi-animate objects that drove bullet-like into one's body, or by witchcraft, either of the contagious variety in which some enemy cast spells over bits of one's clothing, hair combings, etc., or of the type in which a wizard "sent" or "threw" disease-causing objects into one. From the Oregon coast northward the belief was held that one's soul might be lost, either stolen or just gone astray. Another possible cause of disease was a sort of contamination by a ghost or spirit, particularly if one were not ritually clean at the time of the encounter. The shaman's task consisted in summoning his spirit helper or helpers, usually by singing their songs and dancing, until the supernatural assistant bestowed the power to extract the disease object, find the strayed soul, or remove the contamination. Among some Salish groups, especially in the Puget Sound area, a dramatization of the journey in a spirit canoe in quest of the lost soul was a most spectacular performance.

The shamanistic regalia and gear varied. The Tlingit and Haida shaman allowed his hair to grow, and never combed it; the shaggy tangle was his badge of office. Among both these divisions he typically wore elaborately carved necklaces of bone, and had a special bone tube (Plate 29) to blow sickness away and to catch souls. Haida medicinemen usually accompanied their songs with carved globular rattles; some Tlingit and Tsimshian used "chief's rattles," carved with figures of the raven and the frog; others used rattles of puffin beaks or deer hoofs (Plates 23, 24, 25). The Tlingit shaman usually owned a variety of masks representing his familiars, and wore them as he danced when beginning a cure. Kwakiutl, Nootka, and Bella Coola donned turban-like headbands and neck-rings of shredded and dyed red cedarbark as insignia of their professions. Some Salish shamans had peculiarly shaped boards painted with crude designs referring to their spirit helpers; others carved representations of those beings (Plates 30, 31).

The northwestern Californians varied the general shamanistic pattern of the area somewhat. Among these groups most shamans were women, in contrast to the north where the profession was predominantly, though not exclusively, a male one. The guardian spirit concept was played down. And although a Yurok, Karok, or Hupa shaman had some sort of supernatural mentor, she acquired her power principally through capturing, swallowing, and learning to control the semi-animate objects believed to cause illness. She made considerable use of a tobacco pipe and of smoking in connection with her cures, and—whispered gossips—in causing people to become ill so that she might be paid for curing them.

On the Northwest Coast there were two principal centers of development of ceremonialism. One of these was among the Kwakiutl and Nootka, the other in northwestern California, where the Yurok, Karok, and Hupa interwove a series of rituals into the elaborate World-Renewal ceremonial cycle. The performances of the Wakashan-speaking groups were both unique and spectacular (Plate 32). Essentially they were cycles of dramas revolving around a single theme: the protagonist's encounter with a spirit who kidnaps him, bestows supernatural powers upon him, then returns him to his village, repeating the experience of the ancestor from whom the performer inherited the right to the performance. If this sounds as threadbare and monotonous as a much-repeated plot, it should be pointed out that the Indian dramatists were able to elaborate as many variations and new twists with it as our playwrights do with our standardized boy-meets-girl theme.

The Kwakiutl hero, depending on the particular version to which he was hereditarily entitled, might enact his kidnaping by slipping quietly away from the village, or he might pretend to be struck dead by the power of the spirit, then to be resurrected by public ritual. Or he might be pounced on by men wearing monstrous disguises who would carry him off bodily to the woods. After the proper period of hiding, during which he was supposed to be at the home of the spirit, he returned, or was escorted back, and had to be captured by his fellow villagers because he was so imbued with supernatural power that he was in a state of frenzy; and, finally, he demonstrated the powers with which the spirits had endowed him. These powers might consist of the right to display some sleight-of-hand tricks, or might involve the ability to transform himself into the spirit (or cause the spirit to appear). Some of the representations of spirits were in the form of stately dances by masked performers; others, portraying savage and war-like spirits according to the fiction of the particular rites, had to be forcibly restrained from wreaking violent acts, or performed horrendous deeds and then were ritually calmed down by their attendants.

The skill of these Indians in elaborating sensational stage effects was unsurpassed among the natives of North America. Many of the masks have movable parts, or are arranged to change their form (Plate 33); in the houses, tunnels and trap doors were prepared so that actors could "miraculously" appear and disappear; lines of hollow kelp stems concealed under the floor were used as speaking tubes, causing performers' voices to come from unexpected places, such as under the fireplace. Puppets and monsters flew across the house, over the "spirit room"; these were wooden figures strung from ropes (Plate 34). It must be noted that these climactic displays occurred at night. In the huge houses lighted only by a blazing fire in the central hearth, such stage props as ropes from which figures were suspended and the strings that operated the movable parts of the masks were not easily seen.

In one of the dance cycles, the personage of highest rank was supposed to have been carried off, and on his return inspired by a Cannibal Spirit. According to the plot, the dancer periodically became frenzied. To prevent him from killing and eating his fellows, he was fed specially prepared human corpses. It is highly improbable that corpses were actually used; as remarked previously, the Kwakiutl were past masters at producing realistic tricks for stage effects. The smoked carcass of a small black bear, for example, fitted with a carved head, would look convincingly like a well-dried human body at a little distance, and by firelight into the bargain. After his grisly meal the *Tanis* (or *Hamatsa* as the Southern Kwakiutl called him), that is, the personage inspired by the Cannibal Spirit, was ritually pacified by his attendants, and then he would dance quietly. After a while he might become excited again and, escaping from his attendants, might run among the audience where he seized certain persons by the arm and bit off large circular pieces of skin. This was not a trick, although it is said that usually the dancer actually cut off the piece of skin with a sharp knife concealed in his hand. The persons to whom this was done were not selected at random—it was arranged beforehand that they were to allow themselves to be bitten, and they were subsequently rewarded with special gifts. Finally, after a long period devoted to dances, temporary escapes, and ghoulish feasts, the dancer was sufficiently pacified so that he might safely be permitted to return to normal life.

Other spirits represented in the same cycle were

War Spirits, Destroyers-of-Goods, Fire-throwers, and the like. Normally there was more than one dancer, or novice, since the younger relatives of the principal dancer were supposed to be abducted and inspired by less important spirits. As good dramatists, the Kwakiutl heightened the effect of the violent and frightening scenes by alternating them either with quiet, stately dances or with periods of clowning and horseplay during which any sort of practical joking was permissible, and at which no one might take offense.

The various dances have been compared to "secret societies" into which a person was initiated by public performance of the rite. Actually it was not the individual dance or performance that constituted the "society," but a series of them, ranked in order of importance in what the Indians refer to as a single "dance house." For example, among all the Northern Kwakiutl groups—the Wikeno, the Bella Bella, Xaihais, and Haisla—the Cannibal Dancer (*Tanis*) was the highest-ranking of a series that formed a single society or dance house, called by the Heiltsuk word for "shamans" (*tsitsiqa*). Among the Wikeno there were eight higher orders in the Shamans' Society:

1. The Cannibal Dancer
2. The Fire-throwing Dancer
3. The Grizzly Bear Dancer
4. The Rat Spirit Dancer
5. The Chewing Spirit, or Destroying Spirit Dancer
6. The Scalped Spirit Dancer
7. The Woods Spirit Dancer
8. The Ghost Dancer

Of lesser importance were a host of minor representations that may be performed by women and by men of low rank (the rights to use the individual performances were, of course, hereditary property).

Persons who were active participants in the Shamans' Society—and most of the higher orders had to be repeated annually for four years—were barred from attending the performances of the other principal society whose name in Heiltsuk means something like "The-Ones-Returned-from-Heaven" (*Dluwulaxa;* sometimes the word *"Mitla,"* which also seems to refer to descending from above, is used). The highest-ranking dances of this society are as highly esteemed as those of the Shamans. The principal differences between the two societies lie in that performances are held at different times of the year (the Shamans usually perform in the fall, The-Ones-Returned-from-Heaven in the spring); the novices in the latter series are supposed to be taken up into the sky; and there is usually only a single order among The-Ones-Returned-from-Heaven who performs violent acts.

Another society among these groups, the Nutlam (*Nułam*), was again separate and distinct. The name is apparently not translatable. It may be an archaic word, long gone out of ordinary use. The origin traditions of the ceremony relate that originally Wolf Spirits abducted ancestors of certain extended families, who, on their return, behaved like wolves, killing and eating dogs when frenzied. This was the characteristic act of the Nutlam novices. There does not seem to have been a ranked series of orders in this society. It seems likely that this may have been the most ancient of all these performances, for the now meaningless term "Nutlam," which is associated with Wolf Spirits in one way or another—usually with the act of dog eating, and, of course, with an initiatory performance into an exclusive society—is found as an obvious borrowing among many neighbors of the Northern Kwakiutl.

Most of the Southern Kwakiutl groups had a single secret society that includes a hodgepodge of all the performances of the Shamans' Society, The-Ones-Returned-from-Heaven, and the Nutlam. At least one division, however—the Koskimo and neighboring tribes of Quatsino Sound—had a separate ceremony called the "Nutlam," in which the initiates were supposed to be carried off by Wolf Spirits who gave them various dances and display privileges to use on their return. This was the same as the major ceremony of the neighboring Nootka, except that the Nootka called their ritual by the word for "The Shamans," and relegated the term "Nutlam" to a minor performance during the ceremonial. Dog eating was not practiced by either the Koskimo tribes or the Nootka in recent times, but may have been at one time, since a few Salish and Quileute groups of northwest Washington state, in their obvious borrowings of the Nootka version of the ceremonial, included the macabre act in their rituals.

Northward, the various Tsimshian tribes possessed both The-Ones-Returned-from-Heaven Society and the Nutlam. Many of the individual dances or orders of the former were known by their Heiltsuk names, indicating the source of the complex. A few Coast Tsimshian chiefs, through either marriage dowries or capture of the masks and other ceremonial regalia in war—a legitimate mode of acquisition—had acquired the right to perform various

dances of the Shamans' Society, for which, once
again, they used the Heiltsuk names. (They must,
of course, have captured prisoners who were made
to teach them the rituals.) Tlingit and Haida seem
to have been in the process of acquiring the performances during the historic period, and were just
beginning to integrate them into the system of lineage crest-display dances.

Aside from a few Gulf of Georgia Salish who had
obtained Southern Kwakiutl masks and dances, and
the Olympic Peninsula groups who imitated the
Nootka Shamans' Dance, the prevailing Salish
ceremonial pattern consisted of semi-competitive
"guardian-spirit singings," in which various individuals, not only shamans but men with hunting or
war power, sang the songs taught them by their
tutelary spirits, while friends and neighbors formed
a chorus. The lack of variety in these performances
was apparently compensated by the enthusiasm
with which they were carried on. The same guardian-spirit singing was known on the lower Columbia,
and along a good part of the Oregon coast.

The Yurok, and their Karok and Hupa neighbors
also, performed a cycle of rituals in spring and fall
with the avowed purpose of "renewing the world,"
ensuring an abundance of wild crops and salmon,
and preventing disasters like floods and famine. A
great part of this procedure was carried out by a
priest at each place—for the rites were inseparably
linked with certain localities to which the performance was restricted. The priest, with one or more
assistants, performed a series of ritual acts, proceed-
ing from one sacred spot to another, reciting a
tremendously long formula that was actually a narrative relating how the ceremony had been estab-

lished by an ancient race of supernatural beings. At or near the end of this long recitative, dances that were more or less frankly entertainment and for display of the wealth and treasures of important men were held. Normally there was a competitive element about the dances. Groups of men performed in turn, each group representing one of the nearby villages, and each group was equipped with valuables by the rich man of that place. There was a definite attempt to develop a climactic effect: at first the dances were brief, with few performers and valuables of small moment. As the days passed, more dancers participated; the performances themselves were longer; and each rich man brought out more and better treasures for his dancers' use. On the final day the greatest treasures—the crown jewels, so to speak—were displayed.

There were two types of these dances, called in English the "White Deerskin" and the "Jumping" dances. Each had its own special regalia and valuables. In the former, the dancers carried skins of albino or oddly colored deer, the heads stuffed and adorned with bright-red woodpecker scalps. Two, or sometimes four, men carried the highly prized large obsidian blades instead of skins, and danced back and forth in front of the line. In the Jumping Dance the performers marched in a line from the village to one of the sacred spots that had been renewed and cleansed by the priest, and at certain places in each song gave a series of leaps. The principal ornaments consisted of wide buckskin bands, tied across the forehead with the ends flapping loose, each decorated with a sort of feather mosaic made out of fifty bright-red scalps of the pileated woodpecker, bordered by other feathers and white fur. At the end of the ceremony, each rich man retrieved his treasures from the dancers and took them home.

7 THE CYCLE OF LIFE

The Northwest Coast people, like all others—ourselves included—considered that there were certain critical periods in the life of the individual, points of transition from one status to another, that required special care and attention. In their view, his behavior at that time determined the course of his subsequent life. There was also the feeling that the individual, at certain of these periods, might be dangerous to others. Therefore various procedures were carried out to ensure the well-being of the individual and his relatives and friends as well.

The occasions regarded as particularly significant by all these tribes were: birth, a girl's puberty, and death. There were, of course, numerous minor rites practiced by the several groups under consideration, such as specified ways of disposing of the first baby tooth—or all of the baby teeth—that a child shed, some kind of formalities connected with the first game a boy killed, or the first basketful of roots or berries a girl collected unaided, and so on. Marriage was an occasion for formalities and festivity, particularly if the couple were of high rank, but it was not considered to have the crisis aspect of the other life stages.

It would be out of place in a summary of this kind to relate in detail the multitude of observances of all the groups of the area. A few generalized statements must suffice. Procedures for ensuring the individual's well-being were most emphasized at birth, of course. Commonly, there were privately owned magical techniques to ensure long life, success in some particular career such as canoe making, gambling, and the like, as well as rites that were common knowledge, such as methods of disposing of the end of the umbilical cord when it had been detached. The infant's mother was usually secluded for a varying number of days, during which she was kept on a restricted diet, being permitted no (or few) fresh foods, and being universally enjoined against eating fresh salmon. At the end of the set period she was ceremoniously restored to normal life, usually by a ritual bathing.

Among some of the groups, the father's diet and activities were somewhat restricted during his wife's lying-in. Most of the northern nations, believing that twins were mysteriously related to the Salmon Spirits, required parents of twins to camp far from salmon streams and to subsist on a diet of dried foods for a long time, lest the Salmon Spirits be offended. Among these groups a twin, when grown, was believed to have special power to cause bountiful runs of salmon.

At the onset of a girl's puberty she was invariably secluded. Her presence was believed to be offensive to the spirits of salmon and other game; therefore she was prohibited from approaching the river and from eating fresh fish or meat. The northwestern Californian pubescent was restricted to a diet of very thin acorn mush. All the groups believed that by doing certain types of work, performing certain magical procedures, and, of course, by faithful obedience to the taboos, the girl would become an industrious woman, would bear many healthy children, and would live long. By remaining in seclusion at the proper times, by observing all the rules and so avoiding the offending of salmon and other important fish and game, she protected the food supply of her family and did not, by her contaminating presence, endanger the luck of any fisherman or hunter. Bathing rituals normally occurred during the period of seclusion or at its termination.

When a person died his kin were torn between grief at the loss and fear of the ghost. Among the southern divisions, the body was removed from the house as soon after death as possible. Wakes, at which family dirges were sung, were held by the northern groups, as far south as the Gulf of Georgia. When a chief died, a wake might last several nights. Removal of the body through a hole in the wall was almost universally practiced, so that the living would not have to follow the path of the dead as they passed in and out through the door. The method of disposal of the body varied. The Tlingit, Tsimshian, and Haisla cremated their dead. The body of a shaman, however, was put in a little grave-house on a point overlooking the sea. The body of a Haida was also placed in a grave-house. A mortuary pole would eventually be carved and set up for a Haida chief, and his remains transferred to a niche in the back of the pole, or to a box placed on top. A Haida who died far from home was cremated, however, and only the charred bones and ashes were brought home. Bella Coola traditions indicate that long ago their forefathers used to practice cremation. In more recent times they, like their Heiltsuk, Southern Kwakiutl, and Nootka neighbors, wrapped the dead in cedarbark mats, then placed them in wooden boxes, which they lashed high in the branches of a tree, or stowed away in a cave, or, more recently, buried in the ground. Some of the Gulf of Georgia Salish followed the same custom; others, that of their kin of Puget Sound and western Washington, and of the Chinook groups, who placed the body in a canoe, usually raised off the ground on a sort of scaffolding. The northwest Californians interred their dead.

Everywhere the personal possessions of the deceased were buried with him, burned, or deposited at the grave. In the north a potlatch was held during which most of the wealth of a dead chief and his family was given away to the members of the "opposite" moiety or clan who had done the burying, carved and erected the mortuary or memorial column, and rebuilt the house of the chief's successor. The mortuary potlatch given in honor of a chief was indubitably the most important affair of this type among Tlingit, Haida, and Tsimshian.

Almost everywhere along the coast, both male and female mourners (the immediate family, had the deceased been a man of little consequence; the entire group, had he been a chief) cut their hair short in sign of mourning. Among some groups women also scratched their faces to indicate mourning. Usually both the principal mourners and the pallbearers had to be ceremonially bathed or otherwise purified to remove the contaminating influence of the dead, or actually of the ghost, before they could resume their normal lives.

8 ART

Art, particularly carving in relief or in the round, was highly developed on the Northwest Coast. This applies to the region from the lower Columbia northward; the northwestern Californians and their neighbors did not participate in this artistic tradition, although they did decorate some of their small utensils with neat, if simple, geometric patterns. It was among the more northerly nations that the famous sculptural art, one of the finest in aboriginal America, came into full bloom.

There were two major stylistic divisions of this art, as well as several minor derived ones. The two principal strains, which were probably originally related, differed primarily in that one stressed applied design and formalization of representation, while the other was more fully sculptural and three-dimensional, combining realism with an impressionistic suppression of non-essential detail. In the north, the Haida, Tsimshian (including all the Tsimshian subdivisions: Coast, Gitksan, and Niska), and, to a slightly lesser degree, the Tlingit, developed a highly standardized style in which conventionalized forms were used to decorate innumerable objects. Symmetry and rhythmic repetition were accentuated. The Wakashan-speaking groups just to the south developed a simpler but more truly sculptural and vigorous style, which stressed mass and

movement rather than conventionalization. It must
be noted, however, that the northern carvers, when
they wished, could produce restrained, highly realistic works of great merit, as, for example, portrait
masks and helmets (Plate 36). In relatively late historic times, the northern artists began to incorporate some of its conceptual principles into their
work. They managed to retain, however, the vigor
of their old style, and the old sculptural quality, so
that their carvings can always be distinguished.

The Coast Salish imitated the older Kwakiutl and
Nootka carving. Much of their work was a simplifi-
cation of an already boldly simplified style, so that
it seems crude in comparison with its prototype.
There were several minor local patterns among the
Salish and Chinook that appear to reflect minor differences in sources of inspiration—that is, whether
the group in question had closer cultural contacts
with the Southern Kwakiutl or with the Nootka,
and also, the distance from these sources. As far
south as the Columbia River, traces of Wakashan
stylistic influence may be seen, although the original three-dimensional treatment was crudely reduced to two dimensions, and a few purely local
touches were added, perhaps because of influences
from the interior.

The origins of the styles are unknown. Most authorities, however, agree that their perfection and
standardization indicate a lengthy developmental
history. The first European explorers in the area,
Cook and Dixon, saw and collected objects at
Nootka Sound and on the Queen Charlotte Islands
stylistically identical with those made a century
and more later. There is no evidence of any important modification of stylistic patterns during the his-

toric period other than their gradual deterioration through disuse toward the end of the last century and the early decades of the present one. This decline resulted from loss of interest due to the rapidly accelerated acculturation of the Indians and to their nearly complete missionization, which was accompanied by pressure brought to bear by missionaries in favor of the abandonment of all pagan customs. The impairment of the art style was also affected to some extent by the legal prohibition of certain customs, like the potlatch, with which much of the art was associated. At the present time this great art is virtually extinct.

Such earlier developments as can be reasonably well documented during the nineteenth century point to its strength and vigor prior to the historical deteriorations just mentioned. For example, some time quite early in the nineteenth century, or perhaps in the closing years of the eighteenth, the Haida began to mine a soft black slate that occurs in one locality in the Queen Charlottes, and to carve it into pipes and pipestems for sale to whites. A number of reasons lead us to believe that this work began under white stimulus. First, the earliest explorers and fur traders who visited the Haida do not mention any articles of slate. Second, pipes were not known to the Haida or their neighbors of the north until smoking was introduced by whites. Finally, the pipes seem to have been made purely for sale or barter, not for native use. By the time the United States Exploring Expedition, under Lieutenant Wilkes, U.S.N., visited the Oregon Territory in 1841, where they were given quantities of specimens from the Queen Charlotte Islands by the Hudson's Bay Company personnel at Fort Vancouver

(Plate 37), the Haida were turning out considerable numbers of elaborate and ornate—and most certainly unsmokable—slate pipes, most of them obviously poor imitations of white seafarers' scrimshaw work. Some of these objects show considerable technical skill, but artistically are pretty sad. During the next two or three decades, however, the aboriginal art style, latent in the consciousness of the carvers, began to come to the fore, submerging the clumsy copying of alien patterns. Some of the "pipes" were still made, but came to be decorated with native motifs. Even during the "scrimshaw" period, carvers occasionally utilized aboriginal themes, though in a stiff awkward manner (Plate 37). The Haida artists began to carve models of "totem poles," decorated boxes, and feast dishes, in slate, and by the 1880s the ancient style dominated the slate carving to the point where the specimens of purely classic type and of considerable artistic merit were being produced (Plate 38). In other words, the basic tenets of the style were strong enough to dominate the introduced complex, in which a new material was first used to copy new forms (pipes and scrimshaw work) for a new purpose (for sale as curios), suggesting that the native art was firmly rooted in, and thoroughly harmonious with, the native culture.

This whole art, both among the three northernmost nations and the Kwakiutl and Nootka (and the Bella Coola), was aimed at the depiction of the supernatural beings, in animal, monster, or human form, who according to lineage or clan traditions had appeared to some ancestor, or, in some instances, had transformed itself to human form and become an ancestor. In either case the descendants of that ancestor, in the proper line, inherited the right to display symbols of the supernatural being to demonstrate their noble descent. Whether painted or carved, the motifs are often referred to as "crests," and were much like the heraldic emblazonments of European nobility. Similarly the masks and other appurtenances of the dancing societies were hereditary lineage property (although they, and the rituals they represented, could be formally bestowed outside the family line under certain conditions, or captured in war). Thus the art style itself, through the objects made according to its dictates, was intimately linked with the social organization, rank, and status, as well as the ceremonial patterns, of the northern groups.

Perusal of the illustrations in this volume showing Tlingit, Haida, and Tsimshian objects will make the special features of the northern art style clear, and will demonstrate its aesthetic value. For orientation, its major characteristics are listed below.

1. Whether two-dimensional (painting or low, flat relief) or three-dimensional (carving in high relief or full round), it was essentially an *applied* art. Thus its forms were typically adapted primarily to the shape of the object decorated. This was true even of the figures carved in high relief, like those on "totem poles" and spoon handles of mountain-goat horn, in which they appear to be contained within the mass of the material. Masks, because of their specialized function, formed the only important exception to this rule.

2. Conventionalization of form was carried to an extreme degree. However, this did not take place in a random manner, in one way in one specimen and differently in another, but according to certain

principles. The first of these resulted from adaptation to the object decorated, as just mentioned. The second was based on what amounted to a passion for symmetry and balanced design. This may be observed most clearly in two-dimensional design, where, for balance, the figure was treated as though it had been split lengthwise and spread out flat, as it were, on the level surfaces, or wrapped around the sides of the whole object (Fig. 24). There were many ways of accomplishing this. One was by "splitting" the figure into two separate halves, each half then being shown in profile, head to head, tail to tail, or back to back. Another slightly more complex mode of representation was to "split" the subject from the neck back, showing the head and face in front view, with the two halves of the body spread out on either side. Third, the artists emphasized certain areas in which they were interested, such as the head and face, and sometimes the paws or tail, and minimized or suppressed other parts. This trend was related to the fourth factor in conventionalization: the exaggeration and standardization of certain details for identification of the being represented. As already remarked, the objective of the art was to depict definite symbols, the property of the clans and lineages. To render these symbols recognizable, certain distinctive features were selected, and consistently used. The following list enumerates a few of these typical keys to identification:

Bear: Short snout, large teeth, protruding tongue, large paws and claws

Wolf: Long snout, large teeth

Beaver: Prominent incisors, holding stick in forepaws (forepaws sometimes raised to this posi-

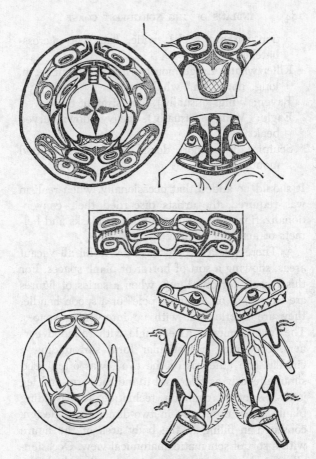

Fig. 24. *Northern designs illustrating the method of two-dimensional application of three-dimensional concepts. The figures are portrayed as if they had been split and spread out flat (see detail of hat, top right). These examples are Haida, but Tlingit and Tsimshian artists used this technique, too. Top left, a Beaver design from a basketry hat; center, a sea monster painted on a screen; lower left, carving on a wooden hat (seen from above) representing a sculpin; lower right, a tattoo design representing a "wasgo," a being which combined characteristics of the whale and the wolf.*

tion without stick), wide, flat, scaly (cross-
hatched) tail
Killer whale: Large mouth with prominent teeth,
long "dorsal fin," whale flukes
Raven: Wings (usually), long straight beak
Eagle: Wings (usually), heavy down-curved
beak
Sculpin: Two short dorsal fins, spines around
mouth

It should be added that occasionally, when realism
was required, the artists discarded their conven-
tionalizations and produced portrait masks and helmets of amazing fidelity.

3. There was a strong tendency to fill all vacant
areas, showing a sort of horror of blank spaces. For
this reason, for one thing, when a series of figures
are carved, as on a "totem pole" or a spoon handle,
they are interlocked, with no intervening spaces.
The "eye element," a rectangle with rounded corners, containing a lenticular form surrounding a
circular one (the iris of the eye), was often used
simultaneously as filler and to indicate arm and leg
joints. Another common technique for avoiding
blank space, especially in two-dimensional design,
consisted in filling in the body area of the figure
with a sort of schematic anatomical view. Occasionally this had a purpose, as in cases in which the
being had eaten someone or something in the legendary episode in which he appeared. Even where
such "X-ray" views or anatomical sections had no
bearing on the myth, however, the device was frequently used.

4. Movement in the artistic sense—that assists in
carrying the viewer's eye from one part of the com-

35. *Hupa White Deerskin dance. The two dancers in the foreground carry large obsidian blades, an important type of treasure on the lower Klamath River. A. L. Kroeber photograph.*

36. *These Haida portrait masks were made to represent real persons, probably in connection with a performance involving representation of the killing and miraculous resuscitation of the person concerned.*

37. Two kinds of tobacco pipes. Top, Tlingit pipes carved of wood with metal bowls from the late nineteenth century. Below, a pipe carved by the Haida from slate and collected from Hudson's Bay Company personnel on the lower Columbia River in 1841. (Bottom photograph courtesy of the Smithsonian Institution.)

38. Slate carving comes of age. Traditional figures, model totem poles, and carved boxes were made by Haida artists in the latter half of the nineteenth century. This particular box measures approximately 8 inches by 11½ inches. The figure in the upper right hand corner of the lower illustration is a representation of the famous "Bear-mother" tale, a part of the origin tradition of certain important clans. It stands about 8 inches high.

39. A Southern Kwakiutl mask representing the Thunderbird, and a Nootkan mask (below, about 25 inches high) portraying the spirit of a minor ceremonial.

40. A Nootkan headdress mask, representing a supernatural wolf and (below, about 22 inches in diameter) a Bella Coola mask. The Bella Coola had a number of masks of this type, with a corolla around the central face, and they also borrowed extensively from their Kwakiutl neighbors.

41. Tlingit shamanistic figurines, about 6 inches high, which were attached to the shamans' headdresses. They may have represented intended victims of black magic. This type of simplified but vigorous art is probably a holdover of a very old Northwest Coast art style, preserved by the Nootka and Kwakiutl and imitated in a crude way by the Coast Salish.

42. Coast Salish "sxwaihwai" mask. This mask represents one of a special group of supernatural beings connected with bird-spirits, developed on the lower Fraser River and elaborated in the Straits of Georgia region.

43. Haida "totem" and mortuary poles on Anthony Island at the southern end of the Queen Charlotte Islands.

44. Some poles and houses at the Haida village of Skidegate.
This photograph was taken by the noted British Columbia
photographer Maynard about 1885.

position to another—was achieved in several ways. The interlocking of a series of figures, mentioned above, contributed to that effect, particularly when the large principal figures were alternated with smaller ones in a rhythmic sequence. This device was used frequently, though not exclusively, by Tsimshian totem-pole carvers. Painted lines typically vary in width, being thicker at the centers and tapering toward the ends. (In self-enclosing elements, like the "eye" design unit, the upper and lower margins usually taper toward the sides.) Movement as well as accentuation was frequently given to carvings by flowing painted lines.

Two-dimensional design—either painting in red and black, other than that used for accent and embellishment of high relief carving, or incised or very low relief carving—was applied to a great variety of objects: storage boxes, "settees" or chiefs' backrests, cradles, globular wooden rattles, canoe hulls and paddle blades, house fronts, the highly valued shield-like "coppers," "oil cups" of wood or mountain-sheep horn, shamans' charms and "soul catchers" of bone, horn, or ivory, and as well to buckskin, elkskin, or caribou-skin robes. In the field of textiles twined-woven spruce-root hats were painted with crest decorations, and a few plain woven Chilkat blankets have been collected that have designs painted on them. It is not known whether this was an older practice than weaving designs in panels. It may have been, and persisted into historic times.

An early historic reference to robes "with designs in blue, yellow, black, and white" can refer only to the usual type of Chilkat blankets that we know from historic times. Incidentally, the typical Chilkat blanket and "dance shirts" with patterns woven in, and the older dance aprons and leggings, are the only objects we know that were regularly made by women in the classic northern art style. It is not that there was a specific taboo involved, but the motifs did not ordinarily lend themselves to the geometricity of basketry decoration. Hence, women did not learn the working principles of the art as did the men interested in painting and carving. (It should be noted that only certain men—not all—learned the principles of the art style and applied them to painting and carving.) There are a very few—and they are few indeed—Tlingit and Haida baskets that bear woven crest designs rather than the usual geometric patterns. As a matter of fact, in the manufacture of Chilkat blankets, male artists made pattern boards that the women weavers, technicians but not artists, carefully and methodically followed. The only other woven representative designs made by women in the area were the whaling scenes, schematic but with a certain verve, imbricated on the spruce-root hats of the Nootka. These, like the male-made Nootkan art products, vary from the northern pattern in their angularity, detail-less motifs, and extensive open areas.

Carving was done in high relief or the full round, in the classic tradition, in diverse materials and applied to a variety of objects. Most authorities are agreed, however, that this type of work was originally developed around a complex of woodworking, and then secondarily extended to horn, bone, ivory (traded from some Eskimo source), and even an occasional piece of stone. The handles of mountain-goat horn spoons, many feast dishes in their entirety, sealing and halibut clubs, figures mounted on canoe prows, "totem poles," the shanks of halibut hooks, speakers' staffs, and a host of other artifacts, were executed in high relief.

The Wakashan version of this art, as was remarked before, differed in a number of ways from that of the northernmost nations. Basically, it was more frankly sculptural, and less an applied art. Whereas even in full-round carving the work of the northerners gives the impression of being contained within the original volume of the log, horn, or bone on which the carving was done, Kwakiutl and Nootka artists did away with the confines of their material, cutting it away into new planes, and expanding beyond it by adding appendages—for example, the outstretched wings of a Thunderbird, or the prominent "dorsal fin" of the killer whale (occasionally northern artists added pieces to carvings, especially long beaks of certain birds carved on "totem poles," but this was not characteristic of their work). The Wakashan carving was less often applied to objects of utilitarian use, and hence was freer of the restraints of an applied art. The themes depicted were much less rigidly conventionalized; instead, there was a stress on realism of significant areas. At the same time large open areas were tolerated, and minor details were suppressed, so that the sweeping lines lead directly to the key areas and the eye is not distracted by secondary space-filling motifs. All these features of the Wakashan style combine to give great strength and force. Its impressionistic simplicity gives it a certain "primitive" cast, but also boldness and vigor (Fig. 25, Plates 39, 40). It is interesting to note that where Tlingit art differed from that of the neighboring Haida and Tsimshian, it was in the same direction, toward a simplified realism. Some Tlingit work is

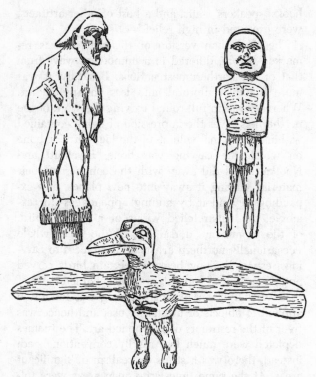

Fig. 25.   These old Southern Kwakiutl wooden sculptures represent: upper left, the Chief Speaker, used in the pot-latch; upper right, a counter of blankets holding a copper; and below, a grave monument.

very similar to Wakashan art in treatment and force-fulness (Plate 41). It may be that such carving is closer to the original style from which Haida and Tsimshian (and some Tlingit) art was evolved.

Archaeological materials, chiefly from the lower Fraser, reveal an old art style that contrasts mark-edly with the classic northern pattern. Yet these ancient objects fit the artistic traditions which the historic Coast Salish derived from their Kwakiutl and Nootka neighbors (Fig. 26, Plate 42). This archaeological material thus fits the hypothesis just suggested: that the Wakashan style, and its Salish derivatives, may have been the old form. Gradually the ancestors of the historic Tlingit, Haida, and Tsimshian modified that basic pattern into the subtle, more symmetrical, and also more static and more rigidly standardized style that was in use at the time of early historic contacts and was continued with no essential change till the closing decades of the nineteenth century.

Fig. 26.   A Salish stone mortar carved in the form of a human head, the bowl being in the top of the head. The original is in the Provincial Museum, Victoria, British Columbia.

Totem Poles

No discussion of classic Northwest Coast art can be complete without a mention of the famous "totem poles." The term is quoted because it is something of a misnomer. Strictly speaking, a totem among primitive peoples the world over is a creature or object associated with one's ancestral traditions, *toward which one is taught to feel respect and reverence*—true totemism involves a basic attitude of religious awe. The Australian aborigines, like many other totemic peoples, do not kill their totem animals for food, even in times of hardship. Other groups have rituals to propitiate their totemic species. Not so the Northwest Coast Indians. There a person with an Eagle, Raven, Bear, or other crest had no particular regard for creatures of that species. It was not the biologic species in general that was of importance in his clan or lineage tradition, but a single specific supernatural being who had used the form of an eagle, raven, or bear. The Indian had no compunctions whatsoever about killing contemporary representatives of these species. In discussing pride in one's ancestry, we have already drawn the comparison between the crests and European heraldic quarterings. From the point of view of use, the crests can be compared to a cattle brand that the modern Western cowman burns not only on his animals to establish legal ownership, but on the gatepost of the corral, on the wings of his chaps, on the doorjamb of his house, and all sorts of places, because it is his brand and he likes it. Similarly, the northern nations along the coast took pride in their crests and sought to display them as often and in as many ways as possible.

Several varieties of totem poles (we may dispense with the quotes now and use the popular term) with varying functions were set up. The first was the memorial pole, erected by a deceased chief's heir as part of the process of assuming his predecessor's title and prerogatives. Such poles were erected along the beach in front of the village. Among the Southern Tlingit and the various Tsimshian divisions this was the principal kind in use in historic times. Another type, the mortuary pole, was set up alongside the grave of the deceased chief. Sometimes it actually constituted the grave, since the box containing the remains might be placed in a niche in the back of the pole, or was supported on top of it. The house-portal poles were a third type. They were built onto the front of the house and rose high above it, with a large opening, forming the doorway, at or near the base. Carved structural members of the houses, posts, and sometimes the beams, form another category. Finally, some poles symbolized some special privilege. Among the Southern Kwakiutl and Nootka, the tall slender poles surmounted by a bird-like figure marked the house of the Beach-Owner—the chief who had inherited the prerogative of being the first to invite important visitors to the village to a feast. Some authorities have disagreed as to which of these types are and which are not to be considered totem poles. The only reasonable solution is that *all* are, since they all consist of symbols which belonged to a particular lineage or family and referred to events in the lineage tradition giving the right to display such a symbol, and which could be displayed by the head of that lineage. Of course the crests used on either a memorial or mortuary pole were part of the lineage property, which both the deceased chief and his successor (who had the pole carved and set up) were entitled to use. The only variation to this consistent lineage-right pattern was a specialized type of Haida pole associated with house building that sometimes included crests of both husband's and wife's lineages (Plates 43, 44).

It was stated above that the crests displayed on

totem poles and elsewhere represented encounters by clan or lineage ancestors with supernatural beings. In its broadest terms, the phrasing should have been that the crests represented important events in the family history, for the Indians believed the legendary encounters with spirits and monsters to have been actual historical events. By accepting the native viewpoint, we can account for two specialized types of carvings, used chiefly by Southern Tlingit and Kaigani Haida. In one of these, figures of white men and European sailing vessels were carved. On one famous pole in the Alaskan Haida village of Old Kasaan, several personages who obviously represent nineteenth-century Russian priests are to be seen. The significance of these figures is that Chief Skowl, for whom the pole was carved and set up, was inordinately proud of the fact that he had successfully resisted the attempts of the Russian priests to convert him and his people to their faith. This he regarded as an important phase of his life, and so the figures of the priests were carved to symbolize it. In addition, according to the Indian concept, by thus publicly referring to the "defeat" of the foreign priests by the chief, they were ridiculed. This brings out another use of the totem pole: to refer to success over a rival, and in this way to humiliate him. When, after an altercation, a chief managed to humiliate another publicly, that event was important enough to be recorded either contemporaneously or on the victor's memorial pole. Under these circumstances the successful chief and his lineage had to be certain enough of their own strength to have no fear of desperate attempts at revenge by the chief and lineage whose disgrace was thus advertised.

The few old poles still standing in their original positions give an impression of great age, with their surfaces weathered to a silvery gray, and bits of moss growing here and there in cracks and crevices. It therefore comes as a surprise to many people to discover that few of the individual poles are even a hundred years old. After all, the wet climate must destroy even the durable red cedar, or at least the base of a pole set in soggy ground, in less than a century. In reaction to this really not very surprising discovery, a few persons have interpreted this to mean that the custom of carving and setting up totem poles was of recent origin, a conclusion completely incompatible with the facts.

First of all, the earliest European explorers to visit the permanent (winter) villages saw various kinds of poles. Meares (1788) and Boit (1799) describe elaborately carved portal poles at the Nootka village of Clayoquot. Among other early voyagers, Marchand (1791) describes both portal and mortuary poles at the Haida village of Kiusta. In 1793 the Malaspina Expedition observed a tremendous Bear mortuary post set up at a chief's grave at Lituya Bay in Huna Tlingit territory. The second point of importance is that the most common functions of the totem pole—aside from such specialized variants as the Haida combinations of husband's and wife's crests (not well understood by ethnologists) and the Southern Kwakiutl-Nootka Beach-Owner posts—are related to mortuary rites and/or memorials to the dead.

It has been demonstrated that the northern Northwest Coast is only part of a larger area of distribution in which some kind of pole or post, painted, plain, or with attached ornaments, was erected at or near a grave in memory of and in honor of the dead. This practice prevailed over a wide area in northeastern Siberia, among the Western Eskimo in Alaska, and southward through the interior of northwest North America at least as far south as the Columbia Basin, where we have archaeological records of cedar posts set up at the head of prehistoric graves. On the coast this widespread ancient custom was elaborated until, long before first European contacts, the totem-pole complex was evolved.

9 SUBAREAS AND CULTURAL RELATIONSHIPS

The foregoing pages have summarized, in a very condensed fashion, the salient features of the culture area that fringed the Pacific Coast of North America from Yakutat Bay to Trinidad Bay. The aim thus far has been to point out the principal patterns that distinguished the areal civilization and combined to set it off as an entity distinct from other aboriginal American cultures. We have discussed most of the outstanding patterns: emphasis on woodworking; rectangular plank houses; specialized varieties of dugout canoes and emphasis on water transportation; untailored (wrap-around or slipover) garments principally of plant fiber; barefootedness; an economy built around fishing, with an elaborate series of types of fish traps, angling devices, and harpoons; sea-mammal hunting, important both as food source and for prestige; relatively slight use of vegetal foods; lineage-local group basic sociological unit; rank-wealth correlation defining status, and emphasis on individual status in social affairs; slavery; elaboration of ceremonialism (potlatch, dancing societies, wealth displays); and First Salmon and related types of ceremonies deriving from belief in immortality of game. At the same time, our hasty survey has touched on local variations of these primary patterns and specialized local developments. It will be worthwhile to review these traits and complexes of limited distribution, to define the subareas, or provinces, within the Northwest Coast area, to determine the inferences to be gleaned from indications of relationships between these subdivisions and between them and the neighboring culture areas.

Beginning in the north, it is fairly clear that the Tlingit, Haida, the Tsimshian formed a sub-unit, or province, of areal culture, in which the northern divisions of the Kwakiutl, particularly the Haisla, participated in a marginal fashion—that is, these latter peoples shared some, but not all, of the distinctive traits. Some of the chief features of this Northern Province were:

"Joined" house construction (plates slotted to receive planking)

Rod-and-slat armor (rod armor in northwest California also)

Porcupine-quill embroidery (infrequent)

"Elbow" adze

One-piece barbed harpoon points

Hafted stone mauls (also Heiltsuk and Bella Coola)

V-shaped halibut hook

Woman's labret (also Haisla and Heiltsuk)

Man's breechclout

Leggings (ceremonial)

Blankets in twilled twining (if true that Tsimshian formerly wove articles of "Chilkat blanket" technique)

Tobacco chewing with lime

Matrilineal social organization with crests (also Haisla; Bella Bella in imperfect form)

Crest displays principal ceremonial

Cremation (Haida only rarely)

Highly stylized representative art (also Haisla and Heiltsuk)

Several of these traits immediately suggest Eskimo-Aleut parallels: the elbow adze, the hafted stone maul, one-piece barbed harpoon heads (nontoggling), labrets (although the form varied), and rod-and-slat armor. When we add to this list a few sporadic but specific items such as Aleut-style atlatls (with unmistakable Tlingit carved decoration) collected at Cross Sound by the explorer Vancouver, the umiak seen by La Pérouse at Lituya Bay, and the occurrence of sinew-backed and compound bows among the Tlingit, the existence of Eskimo-Aleut influence cannot be overlooked. It is of no great consequence whether the material objects were captured in Tlingit raids or acquired through trade. There has been a tendency on the part of some students to attribute all Northwest Coast-Eskimo (and Aleut) parallels as representing cultural borrowings by the latter groups, but it is more reasonable to assume that the interchange flowed in both directions.

Another line of influence in the Northern Province is indicated by such items as the man's breech-clout, leggings, the occasional use of porcupine-quill embroidery, sinew-backed bows, bows with string guard, and cremation, all of which point to the Athapascans of the interior as their source. We know that certain Tlingit and Tsimshian groups—the Chilkat, the Stikine, and the Niska particularly—carried on considerable trade with the interior people, and were in a position to acquire not only furs and placer copper, but manufactured objects and techniques as well. Although it is often assumed that the matrilineal organization of the Athapascans of the interior (Ten'a, Tanaina, Atna, Loucheux, Tsetsaut, Tahltan, Western Nahane, Babine, Chilcotin, Carrier), and of the Eyak, represented coastal influence, the opposite may be true.

Southward, the next province to set itself apart is that of the Wakashan-speaking (Kwakiutl and Nootka) groups. The isolated northernmost Salish, the Bella Coola, belong with this subarea culturally, at least on the basis of data from the early historic and ethnographic horizons, although they retained a few traits reminiscent of the patterns of their southern kinsmen. Some of the unique traits and complexes of this cultural subdivision are:

"D" adze (adjacent Coast Salish also)

Curved halibut hook (adjacent Coast Salish also)

End-thrown sealing harpoons with finger rests or finger holes

Sealskin floats for sea-mammal hunting

Harpoon rest on canoe

Whaling with lines and floats (Nootka only)

Ritual use of human corpses and skeletons

Lineage-local group organization with bilateral bias

Dancing societies (borrowed in Northern Province, and correlated with crests; borrowed by Salish to some extent)

Movable masks, puppets and similar mechanical devices in ritual

Despite the geographical distance separating the two regions, this list includes a lengthier series of features reminiscent of Eskimo-Aleut culture than the preceding. As Boas pointed out long ago, the end-thrown sealing harpoon with finger rests or finger holes is very probably a form related to the use of the atlatl. The use of sealskin floats, the harpoon rest, the whole Nootkan whaling complex, the ritual use of human remains, and the use of mechanically operated masks and puppets and the like are all Eskimo-Aleut traits, and some of them, like whaling, are demonstrably old in Eskimo culture, according to archaeological evidence.

We may note, too, that for the most part these traits are of a different order from the Eskimo-Aleut elements of the Northern Province. Anyone might find a hafted stone maul, or an umiak, at an abandoned or massacred Eskimo camp, and, impressed by the object's obvious practicality, take it home to use and eventually even copy it. However, the complicated techniques and rituals of the whaling complex are obviously of a different order. They could only be learned and adopted after a long period of intimate contact. This is even more understandable when one considers that the whaling rituals were jealously guarded secrets among both the Nootka and the Eskimo. Another point of interest, although its significance is not entirely clear, is that the Nootka actually practiced two different kinds of whaling: one, actual whale hunting with harpoons and floats, identical in technique to that of the Eskimo of the Bering Sea and parts of the Arctic coasts, and second, a ritual procedure corresponding closely to that associated with the lance hunting of the Aleut.

The absence of the whaling complex among most of the Kwakiutl (except for certain groups in Quatsino Sound) can only be attributed to its abandonment, because it is inconceivable that these people, so closely related culturally and linguistically to the Nootka, should not have practiced this art at one time. Furthermore, it is precisely the Kwakiutl who have retained the Eskimo-type harpoon rest on their hunting canoes. They also used sealskin and seal-bladder floats when harpooning smaller sea mammals. Human remains played a part in magical rituals as well as in certain of their dancing society performances.

In brief, then, we have a very definite indication that the Nootka, and undoubtedly their Kwakiutl relatives also, were at one time in close contact with people who participated in a considerable number of Eskimo and Aleut activities. The absence of these particular Eskimoid complexes among the Tlingit, Haida, and Tsimshian suggests that these last-named three nations may have intruded on and disrupted a former very active route of communication and cultural influence. It is also interesting to note that there are no cultural features distinctive of the Wakashan province that suggest influences from the adjacent interior, with the unimportant exception of coiled basketry. We know that the latter was introduced among some Nootka groups within historical times as a result of contact with the Salish in the Fraser River canneries and the Puget Sound hop fields.

A number of complexes shared by the northern and the Wakashan provinces are not found elsewhere in the area. These include the following:

Sporadic use of pile dwellings
Canoe type (except Nootka)
Suspended-warp loom (adjacent Salish also)

Twined robe of vegetal fibers with three straight
    sides and curved lower edge

Urine used as detergent

Extreme rigidity of social ranking

Kerfed, bent, and sewn (or pegged) wooden
    boxes

Pre-European use of iron (in small quantities)

The significance of the foregoing complexes
varies. Construction of pile dwellings, for example,
may reflect both superior engineering skill and the
fact that in the rugged terrain of the northern
coasts, extensive areas suitable for habitation were
scarce. The type of loom and the form of robe
woven on it apparently represented the basic pattern from which the highly specialized Chilkat
blanket was developed. A number of Salish neighbors of the Kwakiutl and Nootka are reported to
have made the kerfed and bent boxes. In all prob-
ability, however, most of the boxes of this type that
they possessed—like most of their Nootka-style canoes—were articles received in trade. The use of
urine as a detergent, especially in view of its ceremonial associations, is unquestionably related to
Eskimo-Aleut practices. The pre-European use of
iron points in the same direction, although rather
than representing diffusion of a cultural concept,
it indicates trade connections with Asia through
Eskimo and Aleut. Iron, in small quantities, used
for cutting tools first appears in Eskimo culture in
the horizon designated "Punuk," after the St. Lawrence Island site where it was first identified, dated
at about 1000 A.D. The iron tools that the first European explorers like Captain Cook observed on the
Northwest Coast, and the obvious familiarity with

the material that led to its demand by the natives in exchange for their furs, mean that the trade connections continued up to the historic period. The significance of established trade channels is that such contacts between peoples facilitate transmission of culture traits along with or in addition to the material objects bartered.

Adjoining the Wakashan province on the east and south, we find that the Coast Salish, the Chinook, and the small enclaves of miscellaneous linguistic affiliation such as the Quileute-Chemakum, probably the Klatskanie, and the small tribelets of the central Oregon coast, formed a subdivision by virtue of sharing a series of distinctive modifications of general Northwest Coast pattern. Not all of the provincially distinctive traits were shared by all of the groups, but there is a sufficiently high degree of correlation to link them all together. The Salish-Chinook province is distinguished by the following:

Mat-lodge temporary dwellings
Coiled basketry (recent among some Nootka)
Woman's basketry cap (truncated conical form)
Dog-wool blankets and the double-bar loom (Gulf of Georgia and Straits of Juan de Fuca only)
Closely twined wool blankets ("nobility blankets")
Chinook-type head deformation
Loosely defined system of social rank
Spirit-canoe ceremony
Guardian spirit singing
Abbreviated version of Nootka dancing society, with dog-eating
Small steam sweatlodge

Most of the items in the foregoing list are obviously interior traits and complexes. The fact that there are so many may reasonably be interpreted to indicate that the Coast Salish and perhaps the Chinook retained a great deal of their ancient cultural heritage after they entered the coastal region. The mat lodge that they used as a temporary shelter at fishing camps and the like, was, of course, one of the very common house types east of the Cascades. Steam sweating has an extensive inland distribution. Coiled basketry, again, was widespread in the Plateau region, and extended through the Great Basin into central California. The type of woman's basketry cap had a widespread distribution in the Plateau. Even though the dog-hair blanket and the double-bar loom on which it was woven had a limited distribution in the province, it appears to be a significant feature, because the blanket itself was woven in the same checkerwork technique as the rabbitskin robe so common throughout the Plateau and the Great Basin. It is even possible, as was suggested in an interesting paper published some years ago, that this Salish weaving complex may ultimately be derived via the Plains and Southwest from a Mesoamerican center of origin, presumably with the rabbitskin robe as the connecting link.

Both the loosely organized social structure that conforms only superficially to the basic Northwest Coast pattern of graded social status and the comparatively simple and unelaborate ceremonial patterns, are reminiscent of Plateau and Great Basin cultures. Here, of course, appraisals must be made on the basis of degree rather than presence or absence of specific concrete elements, but nonetheless, it seems quite clear that insofar as Salish-Chinook society and ritualism vary from coastal standards of rigidity and elaboration, they resemble patterns more at home east of the Cascades. Incidentally, it is worth noting that the heritage, or borrowing, of interior features in almost every instance indicates linkages with the Interior Salish and Sahaptin groups, and in this respect differs from the suggestions of interior influence on the three northernmost nations whose cultural ties appear to be with the Northern Athapascan divisions.

There are very few traits and complexes peculiar to this culture province and that of the Wakashan-speaking peoples aside from those attributable to distribution of material objects through trade, such as canoes and wooden boxes made by Nootka and Kwakiutl, and Nootkan hats, and a few complexes like Nootkan whaling with all its ritual accompaniments and certain ceremonial patterns. The principal inter-province parallel is one connected with house construction, in which the framework of the house was structurally separate from the horizontal removable planking of the walls. It appears to have been only the Coast Salish and Chemakum-Quileute in their areal subdivisions who used this type of structure. The Chinook and the central Oregon coast groups apparently did not.

The potlatch is the principal complex shared by all three provinces just described, but lacking in the remainder of the area.

Northwestern California, that is to say, the focus of culture along the lower Klamath, together with the culturally marginal Athapascan groups of southwest Oregon and the adjoining northwest corner of California, formed the fourth distinctive subdivision of Northwest Coast culture. While we have seen that basically Northwest Coast patterns underlie the civilization of the lower Klamath, the developments there were in many respects the most aberrant of the entire area. Some specific traits patently reflect central California influences. Others are more difficult to identify as to source. We may list the outstanding distinctive features:

Men's house-sweathouse complex with direct fire sweating

Wooden pillow and stool

Plank dwelling with three-pitch roof and central pit

Specialized canoe type

Woman's basketry cap

Straight adze

Grinding and leaching of acorns

Featherwork decoration (woodpecker scalps, etc.)

Wealth-display ceremonials and World Renewal rites

The first two items mentioned as regional peculiarities have a most remarkable distribution, the significance of which cannot be interpreted at present. The entire complex associated with the construction of a large sweathouse, direct fire sweating, draft-exit tunnel, and use as a men's house is strongly reminiscent of the Western Eskimo *kashim*. The complex likewise has a number of similarities to the Southwestern *kiva*. It is impossible to determine as yet whether or not these three institutions actually have any genetic relationship.

The second item—the use of wooden pillows and stools—is again reminiscent of Eskimo culture, although the specific forms are not identical. If more regional elements had an identical distribution, we might be justified in regarding them as representing tag ends, as it were, of influence from the north. The canoe type characteristic of this province seems to be the local elaboration of the so-called "shovel-nose canoe," widely, if sporadically, distributed over the coastal area wherever river travel was frequent. The type of woman's basketry cap, the entire acorn complex and its economic importance, featherwork decoration, tobacco smoking in the tubular pipe were all widespread in aboriginal central California.

Our hurried analysis of regional specializations within the Northwest Coast area has emphasized the fact that four fairly clearly defined provinces existed—three of these, it appears, reveal cultural relationships of at least moderate strength with the non-coastal cultures of the adjacent regions. The Northern Province also shows traces of superficial influence from southwestern Alaska. At first glance this situation is not particularly noteworthy; after all, it is what one normally expects to find. People acquire new traits and complexes from groups with whom they have the most contact. The principal significance arises in the first place from the fact that the Wakashan subarea has been demonstrated to have few or no traces of direct interior influence, and second, it includes a series of features that very strongly suggest close cultural linkages to Eskimo-Aleut, from whom the groups in this area are now separated by several hundreds of miles and a number of alien nations.

The most logical inference to be drawn from this situation is that the earliest inhabitants of the northern coasts—the people with whom the ancestors of the modern Kwakiutl and Nootka came into contact (or who may have been the ancestors of the Kwakiutl and Nootka)—possessed a culture, if not specifically Eskimo, at least Eskimoid in its essential features. Theirs must have been the southernmost extension of the highly specialized and ancient circumpolar tradition. That is, the ancestral culture of the Northwest Coast, whether it was specifically "Eskimo" with all the cultural and ethnic connotations of the term, or, as may have been the case, was a slightly watered-down derived version, nonetheless was based on the essential patterns of ancient Western Eskimo civilization: it was a culture oriented toward the sea, with an emphasis on navigation and the hunting of sea mammals, and a tradition of neat craftsmanship in working wood and bone. The recent discoveries of an archaeologically early pattern in the lower Fraser region that is distinguished from the successive later levels precisely by possession of articles definitely Eskimo in type, such as one-piece toggling harpoon heads, bone foreshafts, an abundance of ground slate implements, as well as definitely Eskimo-type labrets, seems to corroborate this hypothesis. If the Eskimoid type of the original Northwest Coast culture is eventually proved, it will go a long way toward explaining the uniqueness of the Northwest Coast in relation to aboriginal cultures of ethnographic times in western North America.

An older interpretation of Northwest Coast culture as essentially an extension of that of northeast Asia, contacts with which were disrupted by "the intrusion of the Eskimo into western Alaska" no longer can be sustained. Investigations of recent years in Eskimo and Aleut archaeology demonstrate

that those people have occupied the shores of Bering Strait, southwest Alaska, and the Aleutian Islands continuously since before the birth of Christ.
The Asiatic influences that reached the Northwest
Coast must have been transmitted by Eskimo and
Aleut, or else formed a part of the ancestral sea-
hunting culture. In fine, all the light of modern
evidence fits the hypothesis that the source of the
Northwest Coast civilization, as we know it from
modern ethnography, was a derivation of that of
the ancient Eskimo. Those old patterns were modified and adapted to the richer and milder environment in the course of time, and further modified,
and eventually enriched and elaborated to new
heights by the ancestors of the Tlingit, Haida, and
Tsimshian, and Salishan-speaking peoples as well,
who worked their way down to the coast from the
interior.

BIBLIOGRAPHY

The literature on the aboriginal cultures of the Northwest Coast is both abundant and widely scattered. For convenience of reference, it may be broken down into two principal categories: early historic accounts, that is, descriptions of natives made by early explorers and fur traders; the second, recent studies made by ethnologists. The early records, although for the most part limited to observations (since with rare exceptions the writers could not converse with the natives at any length but reported only what they could see), are often lively and vivid. The recent descriptions, based on questioning Indian informants about customs, many of which have been discarded and must be reconstructed from memory, are more complete, but lack the vitality of firsthand observations. Some of the best-known and more accessible of the early historic accounts are:

Cook, James, and James King, *A voyage to the Pacific Ocean, undertaken by the command of His Majesty, for making discoveries in the Northern Hemisphere . . . in the years 1776 to 1780.* 3 vols. Various editions.
    First description of the Nootka.
Dixon, George, *A voyage round the world, but more particularly to the North-West Coast of America; performed in 1785–1788, in the "King George" and "Queen Charlotte,"* [by] *Captain Portlock and Dixon,* London, 1789.
    First description of the Haida.
Howay, F. W. (ed.), *Voyages of the "Columbia" to the Northwest Coast 1787–1790 and 1790–1793,* Massachusetts Historical Society, Collections, Boston, Massachusetts, vol. 79, 1941.
Jewitt, John R., *A narrative of the adventures and sufferings of John R. Jewitt; . . . during a captivity of nearly three years among the Savages of Nootka Sound; with an ac-*

count of the manners, mode of living, and religious opinions of the natives. Many editions. Middletown, Connecticut, 1815.

A very detailed description of native life, and livelier reading than many novels!

Mackenzie, Alexander, *Voyages from Montreal, on the River St. Lawrence through the Continent of North America, to the Frozen and Pacific Oceans; in the years 1789 and 1793. With a preliminary account of the rise, progress, and present state of the fur trade of that country,* London, 1801.

Mackenzie crossed the Rockies and the Cascades in 1793, coming down the Bella Coola River. His is the first detailed description of the Bella Coola, although Vancouver had surveyed Dean and Burke channels the same year.

Meares, John, *Voyages made in the years 1788 and 1789, from China to the North West Coast of America, to which are prefixed an introductory narrative of a voyage performed in 1786, from Bengal, in the ship Nootka; Observations on the probable existence of a North West passage, etc.,* 2 vols., London, 1791.

Vancouver, George, *A voyage of discovery to the North Pacific ocean and round the world, performed in the years 1790–1795,* 3 vols. Various editions.

Descriptions of Nootka, and brief descriptions of various other groups: Coast Salish, Kwakiutl, etc.

Aside from a few works on Northwest Coast art style, two of which are cited below, there are no general popular works on the area, nor, strange to say, is there anything like the number of popular books describing the cultures of the individual groups such as there are on tribes of the Plains or the Southwest. The principal honorable exception to this statement is found in a series of brief but good descriptive accounts prepared for school use by the Department of Education of British Columbia (Victoria, B.C.): the "British Columbia Heritage Series: Our Native Peoples" (vol. 1, Introduction to our Native Peoples; vol. 2, Coast Salish; vol. 4, Haida; vol. 5, Nootka; vol. 6, Tsimshian; vol. 7, Kwakiutl; vol. 10, Bella Coola [other volumes in the series treat of groups of the interior]). There is a very extensive professional literature in anthropological journals and series, but even there most of the works deal with some particular trait or complex—houses, weaving, potlatches, and the like; there are relatively few reasonably complete descriptions of any single native nation. A list of books and monographs, most of which should be available in any large public library, follows:

Boas, Franz, The social organization and secret societies of the Kwakiutl Indians, based on personal observations and on notes made by George Hunt, *U.S. National Museum Report for 1895*, Washington, D.C., 1897.

Davis, Robert Taylor, William Reagh, and Alvin Lustig, Native Arts of the Pacific Northwest, *Stanford Art Series*, Stanford, California, 1949.

Drucker, Philip, The Northern and Central Nootkan Tribes, *Bureau of American Ethnology*, Bulletin 144, Washington, D.C., 1951.

Garfield, Viola E., Tsimshian Clan and Society, *University of Washington Publications in Anthropology*, vol. 7, no. 3, Seattle, Washington, 1939.

Gunther, Erna, Klallam ethnography, *University of Washington Publications in Anthropology*, vol. 1, no. 5, Seattle, Washington, 1927.

Halliday, William, *Potlatch and totem*, Toronto, 1935.
    An interesting but somewhat administratively slanted account by a man who was Indian Agent for the Southern Kwakiutl for many years.

Hill-Tout, Charles, *British North America: The Far West. The Home of the Salish and Déné*, London, 1907.

Inverarity, Robert Bruce, *Art of the Northwest Coast Indians*, Berkeley and Los Angeles, California, 1950.

Kroeber, A. L., Handbook of the Indians of California, *Bureau of American Ethnology*, Bulletin 78, Washington, D.C., 1925. (Chapters on Yurok, Karok, and Hupa Indians.)

McIlwraith, T. F., *The Bella Coola Indians*. 2 vols., Toronto, 1948.

Niblack, Albert P., The Coast Indians of southern Alaska and northern British Columbia, *U.S. National Museum Report for 1888*, pp. 225–386, Washington, D.C., 1890.

Olson, Ronald L., The Quinault Indians, *University of Washington Publications in Anthropology*, vol. 6, no. 1, Seattle, Washington, 1936.

Ray, Verne F., Lower Chinook ethnographic notes, *University of Washington Publications in Anthropology*, vol. 7, no. 2, Seattle, Washington, 1938.

Smith, Marion W., The Puyallup-Nisqually, *Columbia University Contributions to Anthropology*, vol. 32, New York, 1940.

Swan, James G., *The Northwest Coast, or Three Years' Residence in Washington Territory*, New York, 1857.

For those interested in ethnological monographs, many, on individual tribes, will be found in the following institutional series:

American Museum of Natural History, especially in the Memoirs series, reporting the results of the Jesup North Pacific Expedition (chiefly on Tlingit, Haida, and Southern Kwakiutl).

Bureau of American Ethnology (on Tlingit, Tsimshian, Southern Kwakiutl, Nootka, northwestern California groups).

University of California (northwestern California groups, Coast Salish, Northern Kwakiutl [Haisla and Wikeno]).

University of Washington (Coast Salish, Chinook, Nootka [Makah]).

National Museum of Canada (Tsimshian).

Most monographs in the foregoing series give bibliographies in which additional references may be found. In addition, a very useful compendium, the *Ethnographic Bibliography of North America*, by G. P. Murdock (third edition), Human Relations Area Files, New Haven, Connecticut, 1960, lists a great many books, short papers, etc., on the areal cultures.

INDEX

INDIANS OF THE PLAINS

About the Author

DR. ROBERT H. LOWIE, one of the most distinguished anthropologists in America, spent the greater part of his teaching career at the University of California, Berkeley, where he was visiting associate professor of anthropology from 1917 to 1918, associate professor from 1921 to 1925, professor from 1925 to 1950, and, subsequently, professor emeritus.

Dr. Lowie came to America at the age of ten, received his A.B. degree from the College of the City of New York in 1901 and his Ph.D. from Columbia University in 1908, where he studied anthropology under Franz Boas. From 1907 to 1921 he was a member of the staff of The American Museum of Natural History, where he worked closely with Dr. Clark Wissler.

A summary of part of Dr. Lowie's work among the Indians was first published in 1935 under the title, *The Crow Indians*. He also did a considerable amount of work among the Indians of the Great Basin and the Southwest.

In 1948 Dr. Lowie delivered the Thomas H. Huxley Memorial Lecture before the Royal Anthropological Institute in England and was awarded the Huxley Memorial Medal. He was a member of the National Academy of Sciences and the American Philosophical Society. He received the degree of Sc.D. (*hon. causa*) at the University of Chicago in 1941 and the Wenner-Gren Medal and $1000 award in 1947.

INDIANS OF THE
PLAINS

Robert H. Lowie

ORIGINALLY PUBLISHED AS AN
ANTHROPOLOGICAL HANDBOOK BY
THE AMERICAN MUSEUM OF NATURAL HISTORY

AMERICAN MUSEUM SCIENCE BOOKS
Published for The American Museum of Natural
History

The Natural History Press
GARDEN CITY, NEW YORK

The line illustrations for this book were prepared by the Graphic Arts Division of The American Museum of Natural History. The photographs were supplied by The American Museum of Natural History unless otherwise acknowledged.

INDIANS OF THE PLAINS was originally published by the McGraw-Hill Book Company, Inc., in 1954. The American Museum Science Books edition is published by arrangement with The American Museum of Natural History.

American Museum Science Books edition: 1963

Copyright, 1954,
by The American Museum of Natural History

FOREWORD

When little boys play Indian, they often don feather headdresses and, if Santa Claus has been bountiful, costumes suggesting deerskin jackets and leggings decorated with fringe. When our European friends come to our shores, they sometimes expect to see, shouting war whoops, I suppose, along Broadway, Indians not unlike the ones that used to roam our Plains. Most of us, when we think of Indians, envision such items as tipis, war bonnets with trailing feathers, Sitting Bull, ponies, and buffaloes. In other words, we have all come to think of the Plains Indians as the genuine Indian, the ideal Indian—the very quintessence of Indian-ness. In many ways, however, the Plains Indians were a highly distinctive group and lived in a rather specialized way or at least in a manner quite different from other kinds of Indians. They were no more typical of the American Indian than the Navajo, the Hopi, or the Iroquois. Yet through the accidents of history, perhaps also by their own role, often heroic, in the epic of the West or indeed as the result of the insistent stereotype of the movies, they have come to usurp in the public mind all other Indians and to represent *the* Indian way of life.

But if in our symbolic use of the Indian we have rubbed out the fascinating local differences, the

product of ages of development, and created an
image not quite reflecting the Indian of the Plains,
we have shown equally little understanding of these
very Plainsmen, the variety in their tribal lives and
the significance of their customs.

Since the Sioux, the Crow, the Blackfoot, and
other tribes of the Plains have achieved a predominant position in the national symbolism—the
justice of which I shall not deal with here—let us,
at least, see the Plains Indians as they were and
understand what it was that made them the product
of their environment and their history. For it is these
Indians that many of us want to know more about.

There was, in my opinion, no one as qualified
to help us do this as Robert H. Lowie, the author
of this book. During his curatorial association with
The American Museum of Natural History, he carried on a series of brilliant and painstaking studies
of the Plains Indians; subsequently as Professor of
Anthropology at the University of California he
lectured about them; and throughout his long and
outstanding career he constantly thought about
them. I feel very fortunate that he consented to do
this book for the Museum. He was *the* authority.

Harry L. Shapiro
Chairman and Curator
of Physical Anthropology

The American Museum of Natural History
New York, New York

CONTENTS

Photographs

INDIANS OF THE PLAINS

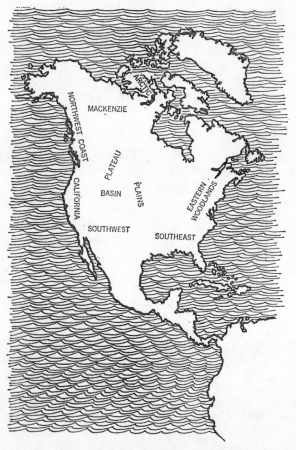

Fig. 1. *North American Indian culture areas.*

1 INTRODUCTION

The theme of this book is the culture of the Plains Indians from the time of their discovery until their virtually complete assimilation of the White man's ways. "Plains" is a geographical term that may be construed loosely to include the area between the Mississippi and the Rocky Mountains, along with adjacent parts of Canada. Or it may be limited so as to exclude the "Prairie" belt. However, it is not possible to apply the narrower definition at all strictly. The Plains proper are supposed to be marked off by their short-grass vegetation, a result of aridity; and the Prairie soil is allegedly distinguishable by its dark color. However, neither of these criteria is absolute. The shift in the character of the soil is gradual as one travels eastward, so that any line of demarcation drawn on this basis would be arbitrary. The true Plains are arid, with an average rainfall of less than 20 inches a year against 30 inches or more in other farming regions of our country. Hence the lack of trees and the dominant part of drought-resisting grama and buffalo grass in the vegetation. However, in this respect also no rigid definition will hold. In 1894 the town of Hays, Kansas, had a precipitation of only 11.80 inches, whereas in another year it rose to 35.40 inches. In some years the whole area will suffer from exceptional drought or share unusual humidity, but more frequently there will be no such uniformity in the several sections of the Plains. In consequence of such fluctuation the difference in vegetation from the Prairies may disappear, wet years bringing taller species of grass. Great variation also occurs with reference to temperature; in the same year subareas differ noticeably, so that in Texas the mercury may rise to 100° Fahrenheit for 30 consecutive days, whereas in North Dakota there may be only two such days during the same month; in the following year the figures may be reversed.

Even within a restricted section of the territory, appreciable differences are found. In South Dakota the southeastern valleys have an elevation of 1,100 feet against that of 5,000 feet in the Black Hills; and while the annual precipitation in the former district averages 30 inches, it drops to only 14 in the northwestern part of the state.

It is thus impossible to give a strict definition of the Plains Area in geographical terms. Culturally it would be even more arbitrary to set up absolute boundaries, for it is a matter of historical record or trustworthy tradition that many tribes of the Plains emigrated into them from the Prairies and Woodlands of the east. Hence we cannot confine ourselves to the short-grass regions, but shall include in our survey the natives of southern Alberta, Saskatchewan, and Manitoba; of Montana, Wyoming, Colorado, the Dakotas, Nebraska, Kansas, Oklahoma, and northern Texas; and of Minnesota, Iowa, Missouri, and Arkansas. As a matter of fact, it will not be possible to avoid mention of adjoining dis-

Fig. 2. Indian tribes in the Plains and surrounding areas.
The dotted line outlines the Plains culture area.

tricts in any direction, their natives being conveniently referred to as "marginal."

The Plains Tribes

Primitive peoples are most conveniently classified according to their linguistic affiliations. Groups whose speech is so similar that they are able to communicate with each other, notwithstanding minor differences, are said to be speaking *dialects* of the same language; if the differences are too great for mutual intelligibility, we speak of distinct *languages*. However, in many instances of the latter kind, the languages show many resemblances that can be explained only on the assumption that they have diverged from a common parental tongue, perhaps centuries or even millenniums ago. This holds true for English, Dutch, and Swedish, but even Russian proves to be connected with these languages when their vocabularies and grammars are closely examined. Such ultimately related languages jointly form a *family* (*stock*). In a large family it may happen that two or more of the languages are closer to each other than to the rest, in which case the family is for convenience divided into *branches*. Thus, most European languages plus certain Asiatic ones form the Indo-European family, which comprises the Germanic, Romance, Slavic, and other branches, most of them composed of several distinct languages, which in turn may split up into various dialects.

This mode of grouping, when applied to the Plains Indians leads to the recognition of six families. If we hyphenate the names of political groups speaking identical or virtually identical languages, we arrive at the following tabulation:

ALGONKIAN FAMILY	Blackfoot (Piegan–Blood–Northern Blackfoot) Cheyenne Arapaho–Gros Ventre	Plains Cree Plains Ojibwa (Plains Chippewa)
ATHABASKAN FAMILY	Sarsi	Kiowa Apache
CADDOAN FAMILY	Pawnee–Arikara	Wichita
KIOWAN FAMILY	Kiowa	
SIOUAN FAMILY	Mandan Hidatsa Crow	Dakota–Assiniboin Iowa–Oto–Missouri Omaha–Ponca–Osage–Kansa
UTO-AZTECAN FAMILY*	Wind River Shoshone–Comanche	Ute

* Although modern linguists recognize the relationship of these languages with Aztec and other Mexican languages, those spoken north of the Rio Grande are still sometimes conveniently referred to as "Shoshonean."

Though the several Plains tribes spoke so many different languages, they were not without a common medium of communication, *viz.*, a sign language not identical with that of deaf-mutes, but comparable to it. The gestures employed to designate various ideas were generally understood throughout the Plains. To illustrate the system, "cold" was indicated by clenching both hands and crossing the forearms in front of the chest with a trembling motion. "Chief" was represented by raising the forefinger, pointing it vertically upward, then reversing the finger and bringing it down. For "rain" or "snow" the gesture was to hold the hands at the level of the shoulders, the fingers hanging down, the palm down, and then to push downward. Though it might seem that this was an inferior system of communication, its possibilities were far greater than might be supposed. A Cheyenne could thereby recount his war deeds to a group of Crow Indians incapable of understanding one word of his speech. A Shoshone once explained to the author how the folk tale of a giant bird that snatched and ate people could be told wholly by signs; and the Kiowa correspondingly gave General Hugh Lenox Scott an account of their complex Sun Dance ceremonial.

Plains Culture

These tribes share a sufficiently large number of cultural traits to be classed together as representing a distinctive mode of life. Inasmuch as they inhabit a continuous territory, it is proper to speak of a "Plains" culture area, using the geographical term in its wider sense. In characterizing such an area we must keep in mind neighboring areas, for only by comparison can a type of culture stand out clearly. This means that lacks as well as positive occurrences must be noted. The Plains peoples, then, were typically large-game hunters, dependent for a considerable part of their diet on buffalo and using buffalo hides and deerskins for clothing and receptacles. Unlike the Basin and Plateau tribes to the west, they made little or no use of fish and of such small game as rabbits. Houses of stone or adobe, such as are still inhabited by the Pueblos of New Mexico and Arizona, were wholly absent. During at least part of the year the Plains Indians lived in conical skin-covered tents (tipis); these were larger than the similarly shaped tents of the Mackenzie River region to the north and further differed from them and from the occasionally skin-covered Eastern Woodland tents in having a special arrangement for a smoke vent. Characteristic was the seasonal grouping of tipis in a large circle.

The only aboriginal domestic animal was the dog, eaten by a few of the tribes, more generally used for packing and traction. The Spaniards introduced horses, which vitally altered hunting and transport methods, secondarily also affecting other aspects of life. The Plains Indians, favored by their environment, turned into equestrian nomads, sharply contrasting with Pueblo, Woodland, and Basin peoples. However, this transformation does not antedate the eighteenth century. The Spanish settlements in present New Mexico were the source of supply, and the new feature spread slowly toward the north (see page 42). Equestrian culture and its derivatives are therefore typical of the whole area only from well into the eighteenth century. Travel before and after the introduction of the horse was by land, the Woodland bark or dugout canoe being conspicuously absent among all but the easternmost tribes of the area.

As regards crafts, Plains Indians were good skin dressers and extensively used hides and dressed skins. In glaring contrast to their western and southwestern neighbors they displayed next to no aptitude for weaving and basketry. Woodwork likewise was not developed. However, the women made a good deal of fine porcupine-quill embroidery, and some skill was displayed in the attachment of feathers for decoration.

Several nonmaterial traits require mention at this point. Like the Eastern Indians, the Plains tribes were very warlike, thus again differing sharply from

the natives of the Basin and the Plateau. A periodically functioning police force is another characteristic of the area, and clublike organizations pro-
moting the military spirit as part of their functions
were widespread. The number and complexity of
ceremonials again distinguishes the Plains from the
Basin and Plateau, the climax being attained in
the usually annual festival of the Sun Dance. Decorative art in painting, quillwork, and beadwork emphasized straight-lined geometrical designs, the
style of painted figures on rawhide containers being
highly distinctive. Except near the eastern border
of the area, the absence of floral patterns until
recent times separated Plains from Woodland art.

The foregoing diagnostic traits suffice to set off
the Plains from other areas. However, some supplementary statements are required. In the first
place, a few of the outlying tribes, such as the Ute
and Shoshone, share the external features rather
than the religious and social traits, which tend to
be at best attenuated among them. Secondly, the
Southern Siouans together with the Pawnee, Mandan, Hidatsa, and Arikara unquestionably represent
a distinct subculture. That is, while displaying most
or all of the Plains criteria, they show additional
traits, notably agriculture and a semisedentary existence with pottery-making and part-time residence in fixed villages of earthlodges.

Finally, any classification on cultural and geographical lines has an element of arbitrariness
in borderline cases. Whether to include certain
peripheral groups is optional. Thus, the Upper
Kutenai, recently living in the extreme north of
Idaho and Montana as well as in British Columbia,
but once living east of the Rockies, were buffalo

hunters and adopted a few traits, such as the Sun Dance, from the Blackfoot or Cree. They have been regarded both as a stock by themselves and as another Algonkian group. Several other Plateau groups—Flathead, Nez Percé, Yakima, Spokane—also periodically invaded the Plains to hunt, but apart from dress and certain decorative art designs, they took over very little from the Plains tribes.

Two additional Uto-Aztecan tribes, the Bannock and the Northern Shoshone of Idaho, likewise exhibited a few Plains features. Finally, the Jicarilla Apache (Athabaskan) of northern New Mexico and southern Colorado similarly shared some Plains Indian traits. In all these instances, however, the similarities are of comparatively recent date and relate to superficial features. Thus, though the Jicarilla hunted buffalo in the Plains, they never felt comfortable there and promptly hurried out of the unfamiliar territory. According to Professor Morris Opler, who has made a comparative study of most Apache groups, "psychologically they are anything but a Plains people." Corresponding remarks hold for the other dubious cases. For example, the Northern Shoshone (Idaho) discovered by Lewis and Clark in 1805 largely depended on a fish diet and sometimes resorted to their ancient grass lodges for dwellings; their social and ceremonial life was always extremely meager, and their myths conformed to the Basin rather than the Plains pattern. Other borderline cases include members of the inadequately known Caddoan stock, encountered by the Spaniards as early as 1541 and 1542, and the Quapaw or Arkansas Indians. However, both are properly put into the Southeastern culture area, though linguistically the Quapaw are one with the Omaha subdivision of the Siouan family.

Political, Linguistic, Cultural Units

The term "tribe" may be used in a political sense, corresponding to the "nation" of civilized peoples. This is unobjectionable *provided* we remember that linguistic and political groups need not coincide. As the use of the same language did not prevent the American colonists from founding a new nation, so Omaha and Ponca Indians separated and at times even fought each other. In other words, linguistically they remained one, politically they became two tribes. The Piegan, Blood, and Northern Blackfoot differ only in minutiae of speech, but politically they were independent. The Dakota, popularly known as "Sioux," fall into three dialectic groups, roughly distinguishable by the use of *d, n,* or *l:* the Eastern dialect has "Dakota" for the tribal name of the speaker, the Central dialect (of which Assiniboin is a subvariety) substitutes "Nakota," the Western dialect "Lakota." So close are these variants that when missionaries reduced the language to writing in the Santee (Eastern) form the Teton (Western) groups read it without trouble, merely pronouncing the words after their own fashion— precisely as an American reads "clerk" in a British book though the author pronounced it "clark." Politically, however, there were many distinct Dakota groups.

In short, it is necessary to be clear whether the term "tribe" is to be understood politically or linguistically.

If two groups are identical, or nearly so, in speech, it seems a fair assumption that their separation took place a relatively short time ago, that accordingly both have preserved essentially the same mode of life. However, there is no regularity about this; a change of environment may bring with it new adaptations or the loss of adaptations to an earlier habitat. The Teton could not have split off from other Dakota many centuries ago, but by 1700 they were neither gathering wild rice nor paddling canoes after the Santee fashion. Of great importance in this connection are the alien contacts experienced, which may profoundly alter a people's culture. The Sarsi language differs very slightly from that of the Beaver Indians but moving southward, possibly about 1700, they soon attached themselves to the Blackfoot and assimilated the essentials of their culture, so that they are in historic times incomparably closer to the natives of the northern Plains than to their linguistic congeners. Naturally a complete transformation is rarely achieved within a short space of time; the Cree clung to snowshoes even in the Far West, and the Uto-Aztecan buffalo hunters preserved the Basin type of mythology.

Population

It is interesting to consider the size of the several units in aboriginal times. For the earlier contact period no censuses are available; hence, we must be content with the estimates of travelers and traders. At times the conjectures of different observers varied even for approximately the same date; in fact, in later days there were sometimes discrepancies between the figures of the United States Census Bureau and those furnished by Indian agents. Sometimes the reasons for such disagreement can be guessed; *e.g.*, in a matrilineal group a person whose maternal grandmother was Mandan would be reckoned as Mandan by the Indians even if his patrilineal kin and his mother's father belonged to other tribes. Apart from the influence of rules of descent, intertribal marriage would obscure the picture. A son of the Shoshone chief Washakie would naturally be classed as Shoshone, but he himself was half Flathead and had married one Crow and one Ute woman.

POPULATION OF PLAINS INDIANS

Northern		Kiowa	
Blackfoot	2,400 (1855)	Apache	300 (1805)
Blood	2,000 (1855)		184 (1930)
Piegan	3,200 (1855)		
All Blackfoot	7,600 (1855)	Pawnee	10,000 (1780)
	15,000 (1780)		4,686 (1856)
	9,000 (1801)		1,440 (1879)
	4,600 (1932)		959 (1937)
Cheyenne	3,500 (1780)	Arikara	3,800 (1780)
	3,055 (1910)		2,600 (1804)
	2,695 (1930)		616 (1937)
Arapaho	3,000 (1780)	Wichita	3,200 (1780)
	1,419 (1910)		385 (1937)
	1,241 (1930)		
		Kiowa	2,000 (1780)
Gros Ventre	3,000 (1780)		1,126 (1910)
	510 (1910)		1,050 (1930)
	809 (1937)		
		Mandan	3,600 (1780)
Plains Cree	4,000 (1835)		1,600 (1837)
	1,000 (1858)		271 (1930)
Sarsi	700 (1670)	Hidatsa	2,500 (1780)
	160 (1924)		2,100 (1804)
			528 (1930)
Crow	4,000 (1780)		
	1,674 (1930)	Ponca	800 (1780)
	2,173 (1937)		939 (1930)

Theoretically, we ought to compare the data for all groups at the same point of time, but our earliest information for the several tribes does not synchronize. The late James Mooney of the Bureau of American Ethnology made reasonable guesses for the year 1780, *i.e.*, before White influence had profoundly affected most of the western tribes; and his work forms the basis of A. L. Kroeber's estimate in his *Cultural Areas of Native North America* and J. R. Swanton's later studies for the Bureau. The table summarizes findings for a relatively early date and one or more recent dates.

POPULATION OF PLAINS INDIANS

Eastern and Central Dakota	15,000 (1780)	Osage	6,200 (1780)
			3,649 (1937)
Western Dakota	10,000 (1780)	Kansa	3,300 (1780)
			1,850 (1822)
			515 (1937)
All Dakota	25,000 (1780)		
	27,175 (1904)	Wind River	
	25,934 (1930)	Shoshone	1,500 (1820)
			1,250 (1878)
Assiniboin	10,000 (1780)		
	8,000 (1829)	Comanche	7,000 (1690)
	2,800 (1920)		1,423 (1930)
			2,213 (1937)
Iowa	1,100 (1760)		
	800 (1804)	Ute (incl. non-	
	112 (1937)	Plains Ute)	4,500 (1845)
Oto	900 (1780)	Jicarilla	
	500 (1805)	Apache	800 (1845)
			714 (1937)
Oto-Missouri	931 (1843)		
	332 (1910)	Kutenai	1,200 (1780)
	627 (1930)		1,087 (1905)
Omaha	2,800 (1780)	Nez Percé	4,000 (1780)
	300 (1802)		3,000 (1849)
	1,103 (1930)		1,415 (1937)

Compared with African Negro tribes, which commonly numbered tens of thousands of individuals and occasionally over a million, the Plains Indian tribes were numerically weak. In addition, we must remember that, where the figures in the table rise to 10,000 and above, they refer merely to linguistic, not to the much smaller political units. The Pawnee, for example, politically comprised at least four independent groups.

The apparently always inconsiderable size of the Sarsi and the Kiowa Apache explains their attaching themselves to larger tribes. In other instances, there has been a marked decrease since the earlier notices in consequence of devastating diseases. In 1837 the Mandan were so greatly reduced by smallpox that, instead of the 1,600 estimated just before an epidemic, only 150 remained in 1850. Since then they have increased only slightly. In other cases, too, spectacular decline due to sickness and warfare was followed by partial restoration. Because of the hazards of fighting and hunting, adult females preponderated over males in prereservation times, at least in the Northern Plains, but since then there has been a tendency toward sex equality. The birth rate has been high, while the death rate, as a result of the elimination of warfare and improved hygienic conditions, has decreased.

2 MATERIAL CULTURE

Food and Stimulants

HUNTING

Large game—elk, deer, antelope, and especially buffalo (bison)—formed the greatest part of the nomads' diet and contributed significantly to the villagers' food supply. An individual hunter would skillfully sneak up to his quarry, often disguised in a wolfskin covering his head and back, until close enough to shoot. In the winter Arapaho or Assiniboin hunters pursued buffalo and antelope on snowshoes, killing the game with ease as they became embedded in the snow. Sometimes a pair or a few men would combine in the chase.

Far more important, however, was the collective hunt in which the entire tribe participated. Even villagers like the Omaha abandoned the settlements after planting their crops and went on their big summer hunt, pitching tipis in a circle on the open prairie, which the cold prevented them from doing in the late fall or winter. Four methods of collective hunting may be distinguished—the "surround," driving game down a cliff, impounding, and encircling the victims with fire. The first of these became increasingly popular with the use of horses: the mounted hunters surrounded the herd, got the animals to mill around, and shot them down, usually with bows and arrows. The remaining methods, though not excluding horsemanship, did not require it. Grass firing by itself implied hemming in the herd by setting fire on all sides except for the hunters' ambush, thus driving the buffalo to the only opening, where they were promptly killed. This was a Prairie technique reported for the Santee, Miami, and other tribes of the Upper Mississippi country.

The more distinctive aboriginal Plains methods, then, were impounding and driving down a cliff; they could be combined with each other, *i.e.*, a corral could be built below the cutbank down which the beasts were stampeded, but if the height was considerable the enclosure below was unnecessary since the buffalo would be crippled or killed by the fall. Both methods could also be combined with either the use of horses or the firing of grass to force the animals into the required path. In either case, artifice was needed to start the herd in the proper direction, and great care had to be taken lest the beasts scent their enemies. Since the survival of the people might hinge on success in the chase, the directors of the undertaking issued orders that had to be implicitly obeyed, on pain of severe punishment by the police. Also rituals were performed to promote success.

The drive down a cliff requires no explanation, but impounding does. It involved the construction of a corral with an opening approached between two converging lines. These were formed by a solid fence in the vicinity of the entrance, but farther away there would be merely rock piles or bundles of brush at intervals; indeed, men and women sentries would string out for miles, screaming and waving robes (or in later times blankets) to frighten any animals that might try to escape outside the lines. First of all, scouts had to locate the herds,

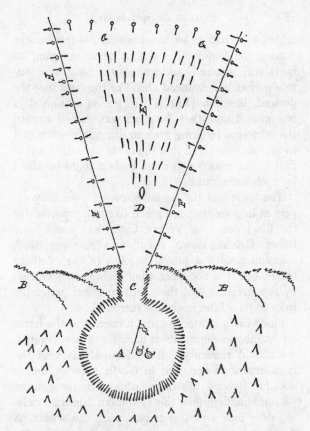

Fig. 3. An Assiniboin buffalo pound. Key: A) The park
below the cliffs; B) High range of hills; C) Gap or opening
through the hills and descent to the park; D) A person on
horseback leading in the buffalo; E) Buffalo on the level
prairie behind the bluffs and enclosed within the lines; F)
Dirt and stones thrown up about 3 feet high (straight
lines) and men (straight lines with small circles) lying
down concealed behind them; G) The buffalo having
passed the stations of these, they close in behind them. The
upside-down V's are Indian camps in the valley below the
cliffs. Courtesy of Bureau of American Ethnology, The
Smithsonian Institution.

which then had to be lured within the fatal angle. Among the Assiniboin a skillful mimic covering his body with a robe would imitate the bleat of a buffalo calf as he advanced ahead of the herd into the desired direction (Fig. 3). In pre-equestrian days we may assume that the herd was started toward the enclosure by firing grass or dung, a practice that in fact survived well into the horse period. It is said that as many as 600 or more buffalo could be killed by such techniques.

The Cree and the Assiniboin were especially expert at impounding, a method likewise reported for the Blackfoot, Gros Ventre, Crow, and some other tribes. Driving down a cliff was also practiced, sometimes with a pound below, by the northern tribes, but it is not clear what technique was used by the Arapaho and the southern tribes generally, prior to their later use of the surround.

Since the admittedly great influence of the horse on Plains developments is sometimes exaggerated, we should remember that effective drives of the type described occurred in North America before and far beyond the boundaries of horse culture. Champlain describes the Iroquoian Neutrals driving deer into a pen, thus capturing 120 within 38 days; and grass firing netted 200 buffalo a day for the Miami. In California the unmounted Maidu drove deer down cliffs, the Yokuts surrounded antelope in collective drives, the Washo charmed antelope into corrals. According to Tornaeus, a Swedish missionary of the period, horseless seventeenth-century Lapps drove reindeer between converging lines down an artificial "five-stepped slope, at the foot of which there is a lofty and strong enclosure, well protected like a stockade or blind alley, so that

no creature could escape from it." Collective drives
of the two aboriginal Plains types are thus widespread among the preliterate peoples, and there is
no reason to assume that the horse was prerequisite
to make them economically possible or effective.
Its advent did, of course, make the hunt considerably less arduous and more profitable.

FISHING

Nowhere in the area were fish the staple, but sundry tribes caught fish at least when other food was
scarce. Thus, if short of meat, the Cree caught river
fish with the aid of weirs (Plates 1, 2), scooped
them up, and clubbed them; in the winter, they
speared fish at open places in the ice. The Blackfoot, in times of need, trapped fish in crude basketry
traps (Fig. 4). The Omaha speared fish with sharpened wooden sticks or shot them with special head-
less arrows. Mandan and Hidatsa village sites
contain considerable numbers of catfish bones, suggesting that these villagers attached rather more
value to such fare than most people in the area.
This is likewise indicated by the ritualistic aspect of
catfish capture, the right to make a trap being regarded as a purchasable ceremonial privilege. The

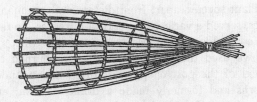

*Fig. 4. A crudely woven willow fish trap used by the
Blackfoot.*

fisherman set up a weir of 6-foot poles in deep quiet water and used a basketry trap. Modern Iowa deny that their ancestors took fish in any other way than by spearing. The Eastern Dakota, who are of course not geographically Plains people, consumed quantities of turtle and fish, but did not like to have them to the exclusion of meat. They hooked, speared, and shot fish with arrows. Whether the hooks were of native make remains questionable. The absence of reference to nets and the denial of the use of narcotics for drugging fish are noteworthy.

WILD PLANTS

Both farming and pure hunting tribes of the Plains made use of berries, chokecherries, wild turnips, and the like. The wild turnip (*Psoralea esculenta*) ranked as a prized subsidiary food, large quantities of the root being dug up in early summer to be peeled and dried for winter use. It grew in hard ground with the root extending some inches below the surface; consequently, women dug it up with some difficulty. The Eastern Dakota, like the Menomini and Ojibwa, harvested considerable quantities of wild "rice," one of two canoers paddling while his partner beat the seeds off into the canoe with a stick. To a lesser extent it was gathered in the Sand Hills of Nebraska.

Plant species, apart from dietary and ceremonial uses, served a variety of practical purposes. To take a few random instances from a single tribe, the Kiowa used the cottonwood for fuel; burned the wood of the post oak, ate its dried and pounded acorns and formerly made a drink of them; and manufactured points for bird arrows from the thorns of the prickly pear.

AGRICULTURE

The part of agriculture in Plains economy has often been underestimated, both by minimizing its place among the villagers and by ignoring that even the nomads obtained farm products from the semisedentary tribes in exchange for peltry, horses, and sometimes European trade goods. As early as 1541 the members of Coronado's expedition found Plains tribes bartering their "cloaks" against the corn (maize) of agricultural Indians. In 1736 a Jesuit missionary spoke of the Assiniboin visiting the Mandan in quest of corn as though this was part of the annual routine. Two years later La Vérendrye, the earliest explorer in these regions to record his experiences there, witnessed an exchange between these tribes, the nomads offering muskets, axes, kettles, powder, knives, and awls for grain, tobacco, etc. In Lewis and Clark's day the Cheyenne bartered buffalo meat and robes against Arikara corn and beans.

Although such exchange implies a surplus of maize among the Plains Indian farmers, we must not make the opposite mistake of exaggerating dependence on maize. Even among the Pawnee, who represent the acme of development within the area, the two staples—corn and buffalo meat—were very nearly equally stressed; there was not the intense agriculturalism of the Pueblos. Archaeologists find plenty of buffalo bones in Pawnee village sites; and "the dire straits into which the tribe was thrown by failure to find the herds shows very clearly how heavily the Pawnee leaned upon the bison economically, even with their fields of maize" (Wedel). What holds for the Pawnee holds still more strongly

for the farmers of the Upper Missouri. About 1800
the trader Tabeau records that the Arikara very
often lacked maize and were hard put to it when
buffalo likewise failed them. In 1834 the Mandan
suffered from the same cause. Probably the Eastern
Dakota were the least productive of the farming
groups; except near Lake Traverse (between Minnesota and South Dakota) most of their villagers
planted so little corn that according to the Rev.
Samuel William Pond, who spent many years
among these people, they "probably did not raise
enough annually . . . to feed the whole population
more than a week or two." Nevertheless, according
to George F. Will, who, with George E. Hyde, has
given special attention to the practical aspects of
the question, in 1878, a good year, the Santee are
credited with having raised 25$\frac{5}{7}$ bushels per acre,
and in a fair season the villagers of the Upper Missouri produced 20 bushels.

Maize, beans, squashes or pumpkins, and sun-
flowers were the principal crops, the first overshad-
owing the others in importance. As usual in North
America, except where agriculture was absolutely
predominant, women did most or all of the cultivating. They had to struggle with the same difficulties
that confronted subsequent White settlers—drought
and grasshoppers. They lacked plows, draft animals, and fertilizers, and did not know about rotat-
ing crops. But considering the crudeness of their
techniques and implements (Plate 3)—a hoe made
from the shoulder blade of a buffalo or elk, a digging
stick, and a rake—they obtained creditable results.
The plots varied in size from about one-half to three
acres. Since the tools were unsuitable for heavy
turf, the land sought for cultivation might be 5 to 8

miles from the village, in the soft Missouri or Platte bottom lands. Pawnee women cultivating at such a distance were exposed to the attacks of hostile raiders; so they sometimes had bodyguards of armed warriors. Enemies of a different sort were the birds threatening the maturing plants; women erected stages from which they and their children frightened away the intruders. According to an expert estimate, the Kansa and Osage probably cultivated one-third of an acre for each person in the tribe, while for the Mandan and other more intensive agriculturists the figure was one acre.

There were generally two harvests. The earlier one, lasting a week to ten days, occurred in the first half of August, when part of the green corn was gathered, boiled or roasted, shelled, dried, put into bags, and stored for future use. Though the corn thus processed is often referred to as "sweet," it was not the true sweet or sugar corn, but the common species of soft flour or starch corn. On the Upper Missouri, the real sugar corn was ripened and made into corn balls. During later historic times in Nebraska, the natives used sugar corn both in green and mature form, but had probably followed the northern practice previously.

The second and main harvest occurred in September or the beginning of October. The Hidatsa harvesters plucked the ripe ears and carried them home in distinctive baskets (Plate 4). Subsequently, amidst merrymaking and feasting, the maize was husked with the assistance of young men, braided, hung from a scaffold for drying (Plate 5), and threshed with flails of ash or cottonwood in a booth under the scaffold. After winnowing, the women deposited the corn, as well as other

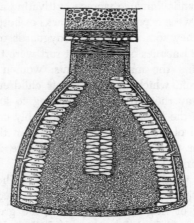

Fig. 5. *A diagram of a Hidatsa cache pit, based on a native sketch. Ears of corn are stored around the outside of the pit; in the center, shelled corn and squash. The pit is covered, from the top down, with ashes and refuse, then a layer of dirt, a layer of grass, and finally a circular skin cover. At the "throat," this pit is a little over 2 feet wide. After a drawing by F. N. Wilson.*

vegetables, in jug-shaped pits (Fig. 5), sometimes 8 feet deep, that were entered by a ladder. Since the mouths of these "caches" were 2 to 3 feet wide, people had to be careful in walking about at night. The Indians also stowed meat and various valuables in the pits when going off on a big hunt.

The Plains Indian farmers did not grow the dent corn preferred by White men, but had flour, flint, and sweet corns, which developed much variety of color within the area and differed in size according to latitude and soil. In the south, Pawnee corn grew up to 10 feet tall, but the stalks and ears diminished in size northward, so that in a poor year Mandan plants were dwarfed to 2 feet, with 4-inch ears. Yet the same plants attain a height of 5 to 6 feet under favorable conditions, the ears growing from 7 to 11 inches. The three native forms are very hardy, drought- and frost-resisting, requiring only 50 to 70 days to mature. In 1881, Oscar H. Will recognized the superior quality of aboriginal varieties under northwestern conditions and by experimentally improving the native types conferred a blessing on White farmers in the area, where a purely Mandan variety, Dakota White Flint, yields 40 bushels and more in eastern Montana and sections of North Dakota. In fact, on a model farm a yield of 70 bushels was achieved in 1914. Thus, as George F. Will and George E. Hyde have pointed out, the agricultural activities of Indian women have stimulated important development of Caucasian regional agriculture.

PREPARATION OF FOOD

The White man's flint-and-steel strike-a-light was adopted soon after contact, but the aboriginal fire-drill lingered in memory (Fig. 6). For tinder, the Crow used rotten bark or buffalo droppings, the latter serving very widely as a substitute for fuel in timberless country. The drill was revolved between the palms, the bow not being apparently employed for this purpose in the area.

Among the northern agricultural tribes, wooden mortars and pestles (Plate 6) served to reduce corn to flour; even Pawnee sites noticeably lack the familiar Southwestern stone metate or hand mill, which is however common in prehistoric sites of Kansas and southern Nebraska. The semisedentary

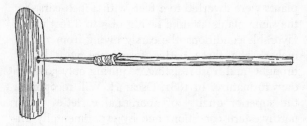

Fig. 6. Drawing of a model of a Crow firedrill, about 15 inches long.

tribes made crude earthenware pots for boiling, while some of the nomads practiced "stone boiling," *i.e.*, they lined a pit with a hide, filled it with water, and dropped red-hot rocks into it. The same effect was obtained by suspending a hide or paunch from four sticks driven into the ground. The Blackfoot and some other nomads, however, have traditions of ancient pottery vessels. Besides boiling, cookery techniques included roasting meat on a spit or broiling it on coals. The prairie turnip was often baked in hot ashes. For camas roots the Blackfoot dug a pit, placed very hot stones over the bottom, and covered them with wet willow foliage and branches, on which the roots were laid. Then they put willow brush on top, heaped earth over it, built a fire on the earth, and tended it for 36 hours at least, until the odor indicated that the camas was cooked. Raking away the fire, the women uncovered the food amidst a cloud of steam and took the roots out of the earth oven. Roots not eaten at the time were stored in bags. This technique is clearly borrowed from the Plateau, of which the camas is typical.

Pemmican, *i.e.*, preserved meat, merits special attention as probably all the tribes used it, since buffalo meat and venison were often not available fresh. Sun-dried slices of meat, pounded fine with a maul (Fig. 7), were mixed with melted fat, marrow, and the dry paste from wild cherries that had been crushed, pits and all.

TOBACCO

Though probably all tribes smoked tobacco, by no means all grew it. The Cree in the north obtained theirs from traders and mixed it with dried bearberry leaves; the Comanche were dependent for their supply on the Mexicans. In their agricultural state the Cheyenne raised the plant as late as 1802, but later they relied on the Arikara and White traders. About a hundred years ago Denig knew only the villagers of the Upper Missouri and the Crow to be cultivators of tobacco in the northern section of our area. Certainly neither the Arapaho nor the Gros Ventre have any tradition of raising the plant themselves. On the other hand, three nomadic tribes —the Blackfoot, the Sarsi, and the Crow—planted tobacco ceremonially as their only crop, first burning

Fig. 7. Blackfoot rawhide-encased stone mauls. The example at the top is about 12 inches long.

over the ground chosen as the site. Interestingly, the Crow smoked not the ceremonial tobacco they cultivated, but another species or variety obtained from the Hidatsa.

The species grown east of the Mississippi and to some extent west of it was *Nicotiana rustica*. The Blackfoot, judging from a somewhat defective specimen, planted *N. attenuata*, which was undoubtedly the species of the Thompson River Indians west of them and also of the Ute, Navaho, Zuñi, the Washo of westernmost Nevada, and some groups in southeastern California. The Hidatsa, Mandan, and Arikara cultivated *N. quadrivalvis*, the Crow *N. multivalvis*. Botanically, both these varieties are related to *N. bigelovii*, which appears wild as well as cultivated in California and Oregon; and they are conceived as having originated from this Pacific form by simple mutations. It is a suggestive fact that the word used by the Crow and Hidatsa for tobacco is *ōp*, *ōpe*, which is virtually identical with the terms applied to it by the Diegueño of southern California, the Shasta in the northern part of that state, and the Takelma of Oregon. Since the majority of Siouan tribes have other words for tobacco, it seems reasonable to suppose that *N. bigelovii* was diffused from the coast inland, along with the native designation, and mutated into *N. quadrivalvis* among the Hidatsa and *N. multivalvis* among the Crow.

Our data on the cultivation of tobacco are best for the Hidatsa. There, though women grew the other crops, only old men raised tobacco, women merely assisting in the harvest. The implements employed included a hoe and a rake, respectively, for softening and leveling the soil, and a buffalo rib for hilling up the earth around each plant. The seeds were inserted early in the spring, at the same time as sunflower seeds, but in separate fenced gardens averaging about 21 by 18 feet. About the middle of June the blossoms were picked and dried indoors; they were prized more highly than the stems and leaves, which were plucked just before the frosts, the stems furnishing the greater part of the tobacco smoked. Both crops were oiled with buffalo fat before being stowed away in a pouch for future use. Seeds were set aside, but without selection.

Tobacco was as a rule reserved for ceremonies and other solemn occasions, and its use was subjected to restrictions. Pipes (Figs. 8, 9), not cigars or cigarettes, were prevalent in the area. Mostly only the men smoked, though small pipes were used by Blackfoot and Cree women; among the Hidatsa only elderly men indulged to any extent, juniors being warned that smoking would make poor runners of them. The Pawnee prohibited all but a few old women from smoking, and these were doctors. Even of the men, only those relatively few who met special qualifications were allowed to smoke.

Fig. 8. A man's pipe, from the Comanche, with a carved red pipestone bowl and wooden stem, about 24 inches long.

Pipes were handled and passed according to definite tribal rules. A Blackfoot host handed a pipe to his vis-à-vis or to his left-hand neighbor, who puffed it several times, then passed it on to the left, and this continued till the end of the line was reached. Then the end man either returned the pipe to the host or, more generally, sent it back toward the right, no one who passed it taking a puff until the last man got it and returned it to the host, who smoked and sent it on a second round as before. Many tribes offered a pipe to the cardinal directions before smoking. In addition to such stereotyped tribal rules there was an infinitude of individual usages. Shoshone doctors removed their moccasins when smoking while treating a patient, and Lewis and Clark were requested to take off theirs among these people before accepting a pipe. Some Blackfoot would not smoke while an old pair of mocca-

Fig. 9. A Blackfoot medicine pipe, the principle ritual object in one of their sacred bundles. This particular example is a little over 3 feet long, trimmed with strips of white ermine and feathers.

sins was hanging up; others had to put the pipe on a slice of meat or a buffalo tongue. Presumably such taboos were those imposed by supernatural beings.

Spirituous liquor was completely lacking in aboriginal times.

Settlement and Dwellings

Whereas the nomads lived throughout the year in portable dwellings, *viz.*, the skin-covered tipis, the semisedentary tribes used tipis only when on the move, otherwise occupying fixed earthlodges in permanent villages. Seasonal migrations were typical of both groups. In the winter the Cree, for example, were able to subsist only if they divided into very small bodies, and the whole tribe would reunite in the spring, resume full social activity, and hold the Sun Dance. The Pawnee, after a second hoeing of the maize about mid-June, left their villages for the summer hunt and returned to harvest in September; after storing the crops, toward the end of October, they would set out for the winter hunt, returning to plant early in April. When the cold set in, the Omaha scattered to sheltered spots; similarly the Mandan and Hidatsa sought protection in forest land with access to fuel, erecting earthlodges similar to those of the permanent village but smaller and of cruder construction. When on the tribal hunt, these tribes also pitched skin tipis.

The permanent settlements were fortified, and advantage was taken of natural features, such as ravines, that would serve for protection. The Pawnee did not use palisades, but erected a 3- to 4-foot embankment, in front of which was a ditch 3 feet deep and 5 feet wide. On the Upper Missouri these features were supplemented by palisades.

Naturally sites were chosen with an eye to the water supply. In the disposal of the available space, differences developed. The Omaha did not arrange their lodges according to any regular plan, though on the hunt they put up their tipis in a circle and allotted definite areas to each clan. But the Mandan kept an open central plaza for ceremonial performances.

Among the purely hunting peoples a camp circle was formed for major gatherings, notably at Sun Dance time. Some tribes, among them the Cheyenne (Fig. 29) and Dakota, fitted their tribal subgroups into the circle according to a definite plan, while such a scheme was not clearly in evidence among the Blackfoot. Important gatherings of a political or ceremonial nature took place in a special lodge set up at or near the center.

THE TIPI

The tipi (Dakota word) was an approximately conical tent, originally covered with buffalo skins, later with canvas. Women put up and took care of the tipis and were generally considered their owners. The size and number of poles used varied a good deal. An Eastern Dakota tipi measured by Prof. Wilson D. Wallis of the University of Minnesota had sixteen supporting poles, was 14 feet high, and had a ground diameter of 14 feet; for the cover the tribe is said to have used only seven or eight buffalo skins. This would be small, indeed, for Crow tipis, which averaged fourteen, the normal maximum being eighteen and for a medicine lodge twenty or twenty-two skins. The Blackfoot, Cheyenne, Arapaho, and Dakota all used more poles. Favored by the proximity of the Bighorn Mountains, the Crow have kept up the erection of substantial tipis of extra height, some of the poles being 30 feet or even 40 feet long and towering so far above the cover as to suggest the shape of an hourglass for the tipi.

Basic and correlated with other differences is the use of either three or four poles as a foundation for the rest. The Cheyenne, Arapaho, Teton, Assiniboin, Kiowa, Gros Ventre, Cree, Mandan, Arikara, Ponca, Oto, and Wichita use three poles, whereas the Crow, Hidatsa, Blackfoot, Sarsi, Ute, Shoshone, Omaha, and Comanche use four. From observation and experience, Prof. W. S. Campbell finds that the three-pole type is the stauncher, offering greater resistance to winds, the Cheyenne form being the most serviceable of all; the Crow variety is the most elegant in shape, though inferior in painted decoration to that of the Blackfoot, Dakota, Arapaho (Plate 9), and Kiowa.

All the Plains tipis are far more impressive than the similarly shaped tipis found among North Canadian tribes, Siberians, and Lapps. In pre-equestrian days the humbler form must have been prevalent since only shorter, lighter poles could have been readily transported. Quite probably this simpler variety, covered with bark or mats, was the original one and spread over a large area in North America and Eurasia.

Distinctive of the Plains tipi as compared with similar structures elsewhere was the regulation of the smoke vent. The fireplace was in the center; as an outlet for the smoke a hole was left at the top and the tent cover was provided with flaps ("ears") attached to two poles outside the general framework. By moving these extra poles it was possible to close the opening in bad weather.

The entrance, a narrow opening in the cover, generally faced east, and the place of honor was in the rear. A skin curtain with two parallel sticks above and below shielded the opening and was lifted by a person entering and allowed to drop back into position after he had gained admittance. The Blackfoot and Crow, though like all Plains Indians without chairs and stools, had backrests made of parallel willow sticks united with sinew threads and hung from a tripod. These tribes slept on robes placed on the ground, but the Arapaho had a veritable bed, combining a backrest at the head and at the foot with a platform a foot above the ground. Apart from ceremonial objects in the rear, the bedding, and the backrests, the tipi held mainly rawhide containers and such utensils as wooden dishes, horn spoons, weapons, and implements. Several tribes used a skin lining at the back wall to keep out the draft.

THE EARTHLODGE

The earthlodge of the semisedentary peoples was a circular, dome-shaped structure roofed with earth, entered by a covered passage, and accommodating up to forty inmates or more. The heavy posts had to be fitted into place by men, and altogether the erection of the house was a communal enterprise, the owners compensating their fellow villagers with a feast.

Variations occurred, sometimes even within one tribe. Whereas the Omaha tied the wooden elements of the structure with cords, the Hidatsa depended on skillfully fitting the posts, beams, and rafters by appropriate joinery; no nails or pegs were used. The Hidatsa roofs were either conical or had the extreme top flattened. The Omaha used from

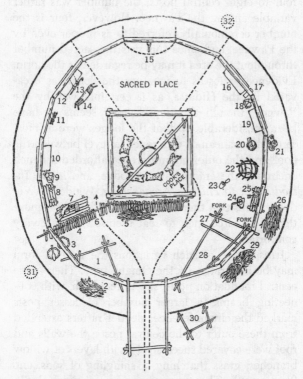

Fig. 10. *Diagram of the interior arrangement and equipment of Hairy-coat's father's Hidatsa earthlodge at Old Fort Berthold. Seats for the family are arranged around the central fireplace; 1, corral for stud horse; 2, 29, feed for the horse; 3, bull-boats; 4, partition; 5, 26, firewood; 6, door; 7, food platform; 8, 25, saddle platforms; 9, 18, clothing; 10, 12, 16, 19, beds; 11, arrowshafts and feathers; 13, lance; 14, backrest; 15, shrines; 17, arrow-making tools; 20, 31, 32, cache pits; 21, cooking utensils; 22, sweatlodge; 23, mortar; 24, stone hammers; 27, stall, for mean horse; 28, 30, corrals.*

four to eight central posts; the number was rather variable among the Pawnee. However, four is the number ceremonially referred to as proper even by the Pawnee, and since this was the sacred number throughout the area it may be regarded as the norm. Evidence varies as to whether the floor was excavated by the Hidatsa, as it certainly was by the Pawnee, though the depth never seems to have been considerable, so that the lodges were at most semisubterranean. A difference in level between the floor and the outer circumference afforded a bench encircling the entire Pawnee lodge, and in *An Introduction to Pawnee Archaeology,* Waldo R. Wedel remarks that there was "room sufficient for more than a hundred men to seat themselves on it very comfortably."

Irrespective of such variations the general form may be illustrated by the Omaha type. There were central foundation posts, say 10 feet high, with connecting beams; a larger number of lesser posts marked the circumference; slender rafters extended from these outer to the central posts; the walls and roof were covered successively with layers of willow branches, grass thatching, a shingling of sods, and finally earth. The entranceway was similarly built, 6 to 10 feet long, and had a skin curtain at either end. The fireplace was in the middle of the earth-lodge, and an opening was left for the smoke vent; on the Upper Missouri a bull-boat, a hemispherical wooden skin-covered frame, was inverted over this hole to shut out rain.

The Hidatsa estimate the duration of an earth-lodge at 7 to 10 years. By actual measurement some of their lodges extant in 1912 varied from nearly 11 to 13 feet in height and from 42 to 50 feet in outer

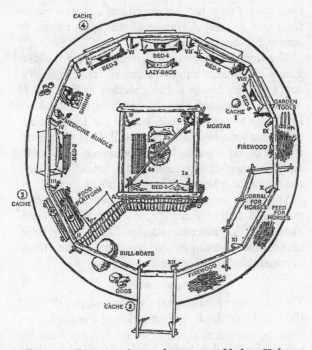

Fig. 11. *Diagram of a twelve-post earthlodge, Hidatsa.
The equipment and interior arrangement are shown in relation to the posts (I–XII). At the center of the earthlodge,
between the interior posts A and D and in front of the fire,
is a bed customarily occupied by the older people; across
the fire from this is a cowskin seat; 1a is the cook's place;
2a is a good seating place with no special distinction; 3a and
4a are places of honor for distinguished guests. Extended
diagonally across the fireplace is the pole from which the
cooking kettle was suspended. Pottery vessels, used as containers for water, were generally kept near the mortar and
pestle at interior post C.*

diameter. A Pawnee lodge excavated in 1930 measured 46 feet from north to south and 44 feet 6 inches
from east to west. Ceremonial structures might, of
course, be considerably larger.

The inside arrangements are clear from the dia-
grams of Hidatsa lodges (Figs. 10, 11). In Hairy-
coat's father's house a large section in the rear is
reserved for sacred objects, which in Small-ankle's
lodge are toward the rear, but on the left. In both
cases there are beds along the wall, food platforms,
a horse corral, a palisade as a fire screen, bull-boats,
and the essential implements of a household. Storage pits appear both inside and outside.

The beds were boxlike structures with corner
posts and a skin canopy, the opening being cur-
tained off for married couples. They were large
enough for several persons. Backrests of the villagers resembled those of the nomads.

GRASS LODGES

The permanent communal dwelling of the Wichita
differed from the foregoing in being a grass house.
That is, a conical skeleton of stout poles bent inward was overlaid with grass thatch, the whole
simulating the appearance of a haystack (Plate
8). The heavy thatching was tied with slender
rods, and decorative tufts of grass were fastened at
the junctures of the rods. Roof and walls were thus
continuous and carried to the ground. A relationship
to the earthlodge is indicated. The grass house is
characteristic of the Caddo and other Southeastern
tribes linguistically related to the Wichita and Pawnee, and archaeologists find remains of earthlodges
of Pawnee type in Caddo territory. In what probably
corresponds to present-day Kansas, Coronado dis-

covered a type of habitation differing alike from
the stone or adobe structures of the Pueblos and
from the skin-covered tipis of the nomads he had
encountered. "The houses which these Indians
have," wrote one of Coronado's Spanish captains,
"were of straw, and most of them round, and the
straw reached down to the ground like a wall." It
is generally assumed that he was writing of the
Wichita or a related group.

OSAGE HOUSE

The Osage (and possibly also the Missouri) houses
were oval or oblong in ground plan. Upright poles
were arched to overlap on top where they were
tied together, the lower poles being at the ends,
the higher near the center. These vertical poles
were interlaced with tiers of horizontal saplings.
The domelike structure, not unlike a sweatlodge,
was covered with mats or skins; it might be 30 and
even 100 feet in length, 15 to 20 feet wide, and 10
feet high. Bell-shaped pits indoors served for storage or refuse containers.

When hunting, the Osage used the skin-covered
tipi.

Domestic Animals and Transportation

The only domestic animal in precontact times was
the dog, which in this area existed in a larger wolf-
like and a smaller coyotelike variety. The Comanche are said to have kept dogs solely as pets. Several
tribes liked dog flesh—the Arapaho so much so that
neighboring groups called them "Dog-eaters." The
Dakota attached special importance to the eating of
dog flesh at various ceremonies and the custom
seems to have spread widely with a particular fes-

tival, the Grass Dance. Some tribes, however, never ate dogs, and the Blackfoot and Crow had a strong disinclination to do so. In any case, even among the dog eaters, there was no question of depending on the animal for subsistence. Nor were the dogs used in the chase by the typical tribes except for carrying the game; some of the marginal tribes of Plateau affiliation (Kutenai, some Shoshone) did find dogs a help in chasing deer and elk. Transport was, indeed, the general economic motive for keeping the animal in our area, particularly in the days before the Indians obtained the horse. Since the Indian dogs fiercely attacked strangers, they also had some value as sentries.

Dogs either carried loads on their backs or were trained to draw a crude vehicle, the "travois." Crow and Cree raiders packed extra moccasins on dogs' backs when setting out on an expedition. The true travois, prevalent north of the Platte and in later times adapted in larger form to horse transportation, consisted of two long poles whose front tips converged for attachment to the dogs' shoulders while the butt ends dragged along the ground; midway was attached a frame either in ladder form or made of a hoop with a netting of thongs (Fig. 12), and to this frame the load, sometimes 60 pounds and more, was tied. An important use for the dog travois was to relieve women in the transportation of firewood. A Hidatsa declared that women "with fifteen or twenty dogs could bring in enough wood to last the family a month"—presumably in the summer. The Indians similarly loaded meat secured in hunting, a quarter of a buffalo being considered a proper load among the Hidatsa. On the Missouri, bull-boats were sometimes lashed to

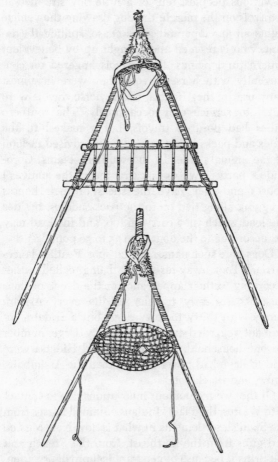

Fig. 12. *Blackfoot travois: at the top, for a horse; below, for a dog.*

the travois. A popular Plains Indian tale, known to various peoples, tells of a little boy strapped to a travois on the march; the dog drawing the vehicle sights an antelope and gives chase, spilling the infant, who is rescued and brought up by benevolent supernatural beings. Dog travois lingered on concurrently with horse travois; they were in almost daily use by the Hidatsa, whose horse travois were put into service only occasionally. The southern tribes had no true travois, but a makeshift, the poles and packs being carried in improvised fashion at the animal's side. In the southern Plains, Coronado's party saw "dogs carry their [the natives'] houses and they have the sticks of their houses dragging along tied on to the pack-saddles, besides the load which they carry on top, and the load may be, according to the dog, from 35 to 50 pounds."

Dogs bore such names as Red-spot, Feather-lance-carrier, Took-away-his-shield, being called either according to their appearance or the deeds of their masters. An early traveler credits every Arikara family with thirty to forty dogs, but a Hidatsa informant regarded twenty as a very large number for one household. The Mandan and Hidatsa were said to have had fewer in 1833 than the Assiniboin, Crow, and Blackfoot.

Of the two momentous innovations due to contact with Whites, the Plains Indians obtained horses from the Spanish settlements in what is now New Mexico and guns from the northeast, from the French and the British. Because of geographical proximity, then, the southern tribes had horses earlier than the northern tribes. We must assume that southern Indians impressed into Spanish service around Santa Fé learned to ride and to tend horses from their masters and that some herders abducted animals in their care and passed them on with the acquired knowledge to other tribes. This development presumably did not set in until after 1630, for in that year a group of nomadic Apache are known to have traveled exclusively with dog travois and to have hunted buffalo unmounted. Later the keeping of horses spread by barter and theft, but at first diffusion was slow. By 1690 the Hasinai (Caddoan) of Texas had four or five horses to a household, but along the Red River the Caddo had altogether only about thirty head. In 1719 two Pawnee villages on the Arkansas owned a total of 300—less than one horse to a man—while by 1800 probably every Pawnee village on the Platte and Loup rivers had several thousand. In 1724 a body of 1,100 Kansa traveled with dogs exclusively, and another group of the same tribe had only a few horses. Prior to 1735 there were no horses north and east of the Missouri; in 1766 the Dakota of central Minnesota were still traveling in canoes rather than on horseback, but by 1772 horses had become common, and by 1796 their canoes had been replaced by horses. Farther west the Shoshone, Flathead, and Nez Percé preceded the Blackfoot and Crow as equestrians and may be taken as the source of supply for them. The Blackfoot probably did not obtain horses before 1730. Paradoxical though it may seem, the essentially nonequestrian Indians of the Southwest and the region marginal to the Plains Area on the west had horses before the Plains tribes who became the chief representatives of equestrian culture in North America; and the typical horse Indians stole horses largely from tribes with an essentially nonequestrian pattern of culture.

Though the horse became integrated with daily life, it did not evoke much originality except in a minor way. Without creating new forms the Indians did make their own riding gear—saddles, bridles, stirrups, quirts, ropes, cruppers—and in this way they made their horse culture independent, whereas guns, axes, knives, cloth always had to be acquired from Whites.

The travois was adapted to the new animal, which could carry much heavier loads; even the Crow, who made sparse use of the horse travois, transported disabled tribesmen on it. As explained, dog and horse travois were used simultaneously: on a communal Hidatsa hunt in about 1870, one family made its two ponies drag only tipi poles, while two mules and three dogs each pulled a travois.

Concerning the saddles it is worth noting that in most parts of the area a high-pommeled and cantled form was mainly reserved for women; men generally used a pad saddle or a frame of elkhorn tree and cantle with wooden side bars. Stirrups were of wood, bound with rawhide.

Horses were pastured on the prairie grasses, often under the care of young boys and men, who watered and otherwise tended them. In the winter the animals fed on cottonwood bark and branches. Particularly valuable animals were tethered to the tipi pegs or, among the villagers, put inside the earthlodge. Gelding was practiced, but possibly it was merely copied from Whites.

The introduction of horses revolutionized the natives' economic conceptions. It created great differences in wealth and correlatively in prestige. Paupers in a settlement, and those who had no more than one or two head, would trudge afoot when a camp moved, while favored tribesmen owned herds of 70 or 100. In 1870 or thereabouts one Hidatsa family owned about a dozen, which included one stallion and two swift runners reserved for chasing buffalo and enemies.

In course of time a horse came to be the preferred standard of value. Men paid for a ceremonial privilege with a horse, and a suitor might offer ten horses for a virtuous girl. Social standing could be enhanced by giving away property; hence, a man who had horses to present or lend to those less favored enjoyed an opportunity to rise in prestige.

In order to see Plains Indian horse culture in proper world perspective, however, we must remember that it lacked significant features associated with Mongol and Turkic horse breeders. The Asiatic nomads gained subsistence directly from their herds —by eating the flesh of their animals and milking their mares. Few of the Plains Indian tribes ate horse flesh except in times of famine—even the Comanche used it as a distinctly subsidiary food— and no American natives ever dreamed of milking mares. The economic utility of horses in our area, then, lay in enabling riders to kill large numbers of big game animals more rapidly and efficiently than was otherwise possible and in facilitating transport.

It is hardly superfluous to explain that, as Prof. Julian H. Steward of the University of Illinois points out, the horse was not everywhere an unmixed blessing. In Nevada it could not be kept easily because of grass shortage. "It would in fact have eaten the very plants upon which people depended." Its utility for transport did not compensate for the cost of its keep where large game herds were lacking, so that horses acquired by the Western Shoshone were eaten. Dr. D. B. Shimkin (Federal Bureau of the Census) argues that even in Wyoming the economic improvement due to the horse can be questioned. The density of population in the Wind River area was no greater in horse days than in the nonequestrian Great Basin. The Shoshone of that region were tempted to slaughter buffalo merely for skins and tongues, and the need of providing fodder for their mounts proved a liability, making long stops in one locality impossible. More horses did mean more buffalo killed, greater transport facility, and improved military position, but also less fodder for each animal, frequent migrations, and the attraction of alien raiders.

As pedestrians, the Plains Indians had several auxiliary devices apart from the dog travois. Among these was the cradleboard, for, unlike its Pima equivalent, the Plains Indian cradle was not primarily a sleeping place for the infant but a means of transportation. While a Pueblo woman carried her child's cradle in her arms, a Plains Indian mother transported it on her back by means of a buckskin band across her chest and upper arms. On the march the baby in its cradle might be put into a willow basket attached to a travois; a horsewoman slung the cradle from her saddle. The Kiowa, Comanche, and Dakota put the baby into a skin pocket elaborately beaded and attached to a "lattice" frame of two tapering flat sticks converging toward the bottom. The Arapaho placed a U-shaped framework inside the buckskin cover for the child, the U being made by bending a willow branch and fixing the position by means of a transverse stick. The Blackfoot, Kutenai, Crow, Nez Percé, Shoshone, and

Ute substitute for this type of frame was a board
U-shaped at the top and tapering toward the bottom. The Southern Siouan form of frame is exemplified by a board 34½ inches long and uniformly
11¾ inches wide with a plain bow and two decorative zones at the head end, each carved and painted
with an X-shaped figure enclosing triangles after
the fashion of parfleche decoration (Fig. 13). In
many cases the cradle was profusely ornamented.

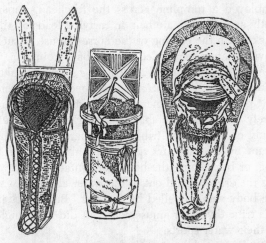

*Fig. 13. The three types of cradles used by the Indians
of the Plains area. On the left, the most typical, a bead-
covered case attached to two pieces of wood which form a
modified V, from the Kiowa. Center, a decorated flat wooden
board from the Pawnee; the baby was wrapped in fur or
fleece and tied onto the board with buckskin lacing. This
type of cradle was used mostly by the eastern tribes. Right,
decorated skin covering a wooden or basketry board; these
cradles were used primarily in the western area, this example
being from the Ute. The largest cradle, that from the Kiowa,
is about 45 inches high.*

The Cree and Assiniboin seem to have made little or no use of cradleboards in early days.

Dog sleds, though reported from the Mandan in 1833, are quite probably of alien derivation. On the other hand, the Cree used the snowshoe constantly in the wintertime, finding it very serviceable in the hunt and in fighting the Blackfoot, who lacked the device. Farther south, the Arapaho when in the Rockies pursued buffalo on oval snowshoes.

A carrying strap across the chest is recorded for the Hidatsa and Cree. The former simultaneously employed a tumpline across the forehead, apparently as a subordinate help in carrying loads on the back. With the coming of the horse the use of such devices naturally receded into the background.

At least a number of the tribes, *e.g.*, the Omaha, Hidatsa, and Arikara, are described as excellent and passionate swimmers, but the strokes used are rarely described. Fletcher and La Flesche in their study of the Omaha tribe report that "The Omaha swam by treading, moving hands and legs like a dog, or by keeping the body horizontal and throwing the arms up and out of the water alternately as the body was propelled by the legs." Both sexes in this tribe dived for amusement, but did not mingle in their water sports.

As for travel by water, the Cree of the seventeenth century are known to have made canoe trips and continued to do so in the following century. But as they turned more and more into buffalo hunters they, like their Blackfoot neighbors, knew only crude temporary hide rafts for ferrying across a deep stream. Blackfoot rafts, says Wissler in his paper on the material culture of this tribe, "were towed by the able-bodied men and women, usually the latter, swimming out and holding the lines with their teeth."

On the Missouri River, ferrying was done in a "bull-boat"; in later years cowskins replaced the buffalo hides originally employed (Plate 10). This tub was paddled; it was so light that a woman could easily carry it by means of a chest strap. Quite similar boats were used by the ancient Britons and are known from modern Wales, Ireland, Tibet, and elsewhere. The invention is so simple and distributed so spottily that it must have been achieved independently a number of times.

Dress and Personal Decoration

CLOTHING

Essential clothing was made of dressed skins. Because of the ease of obtaining cloth from the traders, it is difficult to give a comparative picture of tribal dress before White contact, for early travelers' accounts are much less ample for certain groups than for others. To indicate the kind of change brought about, we note that Omaha women came to wear skirts and to shorten their tunics, and quite commonly calico displaced skin shirts. Breechcloths were general in recent times, but there is doubt whether they are aboriginal; since ceremonial dress tends to preserve traditional forms, the ancient equivalent possibly was a deerskin apron or pair of aprons similar to those of Arapaho dancers.

The Crow costume (Plate 11) probably was typical of the northern Plains. It included a shirt, leggings reaching to the hip instead of trousers, moccasins, and a buffalo robe. Women wore a long dress of deer or mountain-sheep skin extending from the chin to the feet, knee-high leggings, and moccasins. The gala dress of Crow women was remarkable for its decoration—300 elk teeth—since no single hunter was likely to kill many elk and only two of the teeth of any one animal were acceptable for the purpose, rarity made such garments very pre-

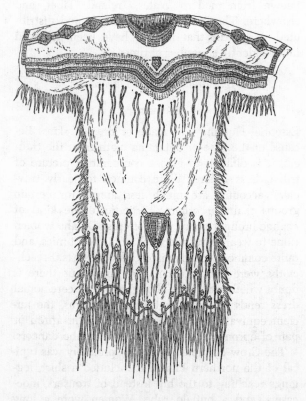

Fig. 14. A Blackfoot woman's dress, dating to the first half of the nineteenth century.

cious. A hundred years ago, a hundred elk teeth
were rated of equal value with ten ermine skins
(another decorative feature) or with one horse.
Crow women wore similar dresses with bone imitations of elk teeth. The Crow were also conspicuous
for the beauty of their buffalo robes.

Shirts are reported as originally lacking among
the villagers and several southern hunting tribes.
Indeed irrespective of the Canadian winter climate
the Cree never covered the upper part of the body
with anything but a robe, except ceremonially. The
widespread use of the ornamental shirt seems to be
a modern development in the Plains. The most
usual feminine dress (Fig. 14) was in one piece and
lacked sleeves; a two-piece garment is described
for the Cheyenne, Osage, and Pawnee, who are
said to have worn a skirt and a cape after the Eastern fashion. The ancient Omaha tunic was fringed
at the sides, with the arms free.

Heelless skin shoes, in other words moccasins,
were the general footgear (Fig. 15). Hard rawhide

Fig. 15. Patterns for Plains Indian moccasins. In the
two-piece pattern (A), the soles are of rawhide, the uppers
in one piece, the tongue may or may not be separate, the
ankle flap is separate. On the right is a one-piece pattern
(B) for the upper (a), the sole (b), and the tongue (c).

soles distinct from the soft uppers were common, but this may have been due to Southwestern influence, for one-piece soft-leather moccasins have been collected or seen among the Blackfoot, Sarsi, Crow, Cree, Assiniboin, Gros Ventre, Shoshone, Omaha, Pawnee, and Dakota. For winter wear, buffalo skin was used with the hair inside.

The essential clothing was made by women, who sewed with buffalo sinew for thread, punching holes with a bone awl. Very general were fringes, pendants, and ornamental strips, which served aesthetic purposes and often also symbolically indicated the wearer's military accomplishments.

HEADGEAR

In the sign language, a White man is indicated by drawing the right hand across the forehead to suggest a hat, a fact that implies the absence of native headgear in ordinary circumstances. The familiar war bonnet and buffalo-horn caps were reserved for festive occasions, and various headdresses in museum collections are ceremonial regalia (Plate 12). In the winter the northern tribes used fur caps; rawhide visors as a protection from the sun in the summertime are reported for the Cree, Blackfoot, and Crow.

HAIRDRESSING

Though combs were lacking, the Plains Indians brushed their hair—with the rough side of a buffalo tongue (Cree), or with a porcupine tail mounted on a stick, or with porcupine bristles tied to a stick with rawhide (Fig. 16) or, as among the Omaha, with stiff grass, one end being tightly wound about to provide a handle.

Coiffures were modified in the course of time by imitation of alien fashions and there were considerable individual preferences, at least among the men. A common feminine style was to part the hair in the middle, from the forehead to the nape of the neck, and to paint the parting line red. Omaha women arranged the hair in two braids, which were tied together at the ends and allowed to fall behind the ears. Blackfoot girls and young matrons used two braids or let the hair hang loose, tying it with a forehead band.

The Crow consider braids a departure from ancient usage for either sex. Their men in earlier times divided the hair roughly into two parts, they say, and let it flow loosely down the back and the sides of the face. Doubtless there were different fashions even then; one of Bodmer's subjects has his hair coiled in a bulky foretop. The Crow were conspicuous for artificial additions to their hair in the back.

Fig. 16. Blackfoot hairbrushes: left, porcupine bristles on a stick, bound with rawhide (about 4 inches high); right, horsehair, also bound with rawhide.

Horse hair . . . is arranged in 8 or 10 strands, each about as thick as a finger, and laid parallel with spaces between them of the width of a single strand. Fine gum is then mixed with red ocher, or vermilion . . . and by means of other hair, or fibers of any kind laid cross-wise, the strands are secured, and around each intersection of hair a ball of gum is plastered to hold it in place. About 4 inches further down, a similar row of gum balls and cross strings are placed, and so on down to the end. The top of the tail ornament is then secured to the hair on the back of the head. The Indians frequently incorporate the false hair with their own so as to lengthen the latter without any marked evidence of deception [Mallery].

A pompadour effect worn by Crow men was sufficiently common to be used as a tribal mark in Dakota pictographs (Plate 13).

Highly distinctive of the Pawnee and Southern Siouans was the practice of closely cropping the hair so as to have only a central ridge across the crown (Plate 14). The Osage, however, came to wear their hair long in imitation of the Ponca, who themselves adopted this style from the Dakota. On the other hand, various societies of other tribes adopted roaching of the hair as a ceremonial badge. The custom points to the western Woodlands, where the Sauk and Fox observed it.

A number of tribes, including the Omaha, separated a lock on the crown and kept it distinct and braided. Emblems of war honors were tied to it, and it was cut from the head of a slain warrior for use in triumphal processions.

ADORNMENT AND MUTILATION

There were innumerable minor decorative devices, some of them native, others obtained from alien tribes and, in historical times, from White traders. The Plains Indians wore bear-claw necklaces, earrings, shell earrings and drops, shell gorgets, and a variety of other articles, some indicative of status. Body and face paint were usual, red pigments being perhaps most frequent. Pigments were derived from animals and plants. Men plucked out their facial hair with the fingers or tweezers, and the Comanche removed their eyebrows even so recently as a generation ago.

Tattooing, though not so highly developed as in Polynesia or aboriginally in our Southeastern states, was far from rare. The Wichita indulged conspicuously in the practice, and so did the Southern Siouans. An eminent Omaha could get prestige for himself and a daughter recently come of age by having her tattooed in the center of the forehead with a black circle representing the sun and with a four-pointed star on her chest to symbolize the night.

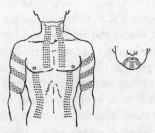

Fig. 17. Plains Cree tattoo designs: left, on a man's body; right, on a woman's face.

The Osage tattooed both sexes, a warrior gaining the privilege by deeds of valor both for himself, his wife or a daughter. However, the practice was not limited to the southern part of the area. The author has seen an old Hidatsa tattooed on one half of his chest; the Crow sometimes tattooed both sexes; and with the Cree, tattooing was common for men and women (Fig. 17), the former marking arms and chests, the women only as a rule the space between lips and chin. The custom evidently had ritualistic and social aspects apart from the aesthetic.

Tools and Artifacts

TOOLS

The obvious superiority of metal tools soon led the Indians to abandon their earlier equivalents of bone, stone, etc. It is accordingly difficult to reconstruct their aboriginal tool kit. Nevertheless some ancient implements have survived into the present or recent past, some have been described by early travelers, still others are revealed by archaeological excavation.

Even in recent years Indian women pounded chokecherries on a flat stone slab with a stone hammer grooved round the middle and hafted by wet rawhide shrunken to a wooden handle passed around the groove (Fig. 7). With such mauls a Crow or Blackfoot woman also mashed chokecherries for pemmican or broke up bones to extract the marrow. The stone heads of warclubs were mounted in similar fashion; some were spherical, others pointed at both ends (Fig. 18), still others ax-

Fig. 18. A Crow stone-headed war club, about 42 inches long.

shaped. Such clubs were sometimes used for killing a wounded buffalo in the corral.

Water-worn pebbles and slabs struck from their outer surfaces served as scrapers. Arrow shafts were smoothed between two grooved stones. Knives were of stone or bone (Fig. 19). Coronado saw buffalo-hunting nomads cut off mouthfuls of meat with

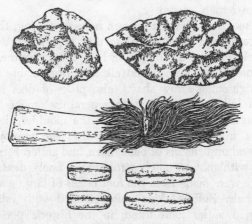

Fig. 19. At the top, chipped stone knives from the Blackfoot. Center, a model of a Blackfoot bone knife, decorated with fur, about a foot long. Bottom, Pawnee arrow-smoothers used for arrow shafts, 2 to 3 inches long.

flint knives. Blackfoot arrowheads are said to have
been more frequently of bone, deer, and buffalo
horn; the Omaha used flint or other stone points in
big-game hunting and warfare. In early historic
Pawnee sites the predominance of small, thin, triangular stone points is noteworthy, being suggestive
of Iroquoian connections. Pressure flaking with an
elk horn is reported as an Omaha technique in
stonework.

Pipes were commonly of stone, especially catlinite. The quarry for this red stone lies in southwestern Minnesota, which is in Eastern Dakota
tribal territory, but catlinite pipes were diffused
to distant tribes, such as the Arapaho and Crow.
However, other materials also were used; the Arapaho had black stone pipes as well, and the Blackfoot
shaped their pipe bowls from a dark greenish stone
found in their territory. Some pipes were venerated
as extremely sacred.

Bone awls served to punch holes in sewing; they
were noted by Coronado's men in 1541. Excavators
of old Pawnee dwelling sites have found fragments
of perforated buffalo and elk ribs, presumably for
straightening arrow shafts, also picks of deer and
buffalo bone for digging. In general use among the
villagers was a hoe made from the shoulder blade
of a buffalo (Plate 3). Skin dressers employed
several implements of bone, horn, and antler. Flesh-
ers with minute notches forming a finely dentate
edge were made from the foot bones of large game
animals. Buffalo skins were scraped with adze-
shaped antler tools fitted, in the historic period,
with iron blades, whose antecedents are unknown
since archaeological stone scraper blades do not
jibe with the handle. In dressing a deerskin the

hide was thrown over a log and cleared of hair with a rib or leg bone (Fig. 20).

CRAFTS

Throughout the area the textile crafts were poorly developed. Cotton was unknown. Thread for sewing was of sinew. The Blackfoot twisted the tough bark of some shrub into rope; the Omaha pounded the fibers of a nettle free from the woody part and braided it into rope, aboriginally probably weaving buffalo hair into lariats, scarfs, belts, and forehead bands. The women of this tribe doubled broad, short scarfs and sewed them together at the sides, using the resulting bags for practical purposes while men stowed away ceremonial articles in them. The

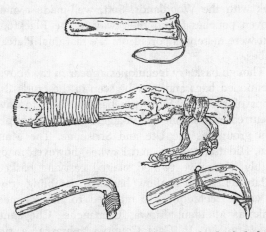

Fig. 20. At the top, two kinds of tooth-edged fleshing tools: above, shaft from tibia, Ute; center, shaft from tibia with part of femur attached and iron blade, Gros Ventre. This tool is about 15 inches long. At the bottom, adze-shaped tools used for scraping hides, with antler handles and iron blades. These are about 12 inches long.

Iowa wove floor mats of reeds over a bark-cord foundation, employing the same technique as the Winnebago and Central Algonkians. The same tribe made loosely twined rectangular storage bags, the fiber being basswood or nettle. Floor mats are definitely reported from the Pawnee, who also made them do service as bedding, bed curtains, and wrapping for corpses. The last-mentioned use is indicated likewise in a Pawnee burial site, where remnants of matting show a simple twining technique with narrow-leaved grass or rush fibers. The same excavation revealed bits of buffalo-hair cloth, the same piece being sometimes in different weaving techniques. Spindle whorls were lacking.

Soft twilled buffalo-hair wallets may be regarded as typical of the Southern Siouans and form another link with the Woodlands. Soft, well-made twined woven pouches found their way to the Blackfoot, but were merely imports from the marginal Plateau tribes.

Though basketry techniques appear in the above-mentioned bags and may be seen in the crude fish traps of the Blackfoot, true baskets seem to have occurred only among the villagers and such peripheral groups as the Ute and Shoshone. The Mandan, Hidatsa, Arikara, and Pawnee, however, made highly distinctive twilled plaited carrying baskets (Plate 4). Small shallow basketry gambling trays of coiled technique are credited to the Pawnee, Arikara, Mandan, Kiowa, Comanche, Cheyenne, and Arapaho. In Cass County, Nebraska, a site excavated by Prof. W. D. Strong of Columbia University harbored clay fragments with impressions of coiled basketry.

Pottery is not impossible for peoples without ag-

1. *A Plains Cree fish weir, located near the bend in the river.*

2. *A close-up, showing the construction of the entrance in the center of the weir.*

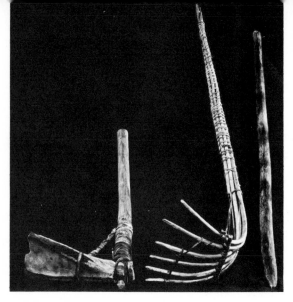

3. *Hidatsa agricultural implements: left to right, a bone hoe, a rake, and a digging stick.*

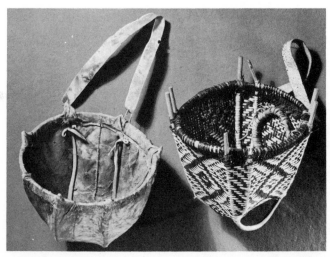

4. *Hidatsa burden baskets. At the left, a basket made of skin, used for carrying off debris when building an earthlodge; at the right, a willow bark harvest basket.*

5. *A scaffold with surrounding rack used by the Hidatsa for drying corn.* Photograph by F. N. Wilson.

6. *A Hidatsa woman pounding corn into meal with a wooden pestle and mortar.* Photograph by F. N. Wilson.

7. *Hidatsa agriculture: raking with a horn rake (left) and hoeing squashes with a bone hoe (right).* Photographs by F. N. Wilson.

8. *A grass-covered lodge and shade built by the Wichita.*

9. A painted tipi used by the keeper of the sacred pipe in 1900, from the Arapaho.

10. A Hidatsa woman paddles a bullboat on the Missouri River.

11. Crow couple in costume, about 1915.

12. *The Sun Dance headdress and hair-lock necklace of the Blackfoot.*

riculture, but if they are obliged to move constantly, as did the Plains Indian hunting tribes in search of buffalo, the maintenance of earthenware becomes extremely difficult. Accordingly, though the modern Blackfoot, Cree, Arapaho, and other nomads have occasionally referred to ceramics as a lost art practiced by their ancestors, the evidence on this point is contradictory; however, recent archaeological findings lend some support to such statements. The villagers of the Upper Missouri have been observed manufacturing pots (Plate 15), and the proof is perfect for demonstrably Pawnee sites. Accordingly, there is no reason to doubt relevant statements by the Omaha and other cultivators within the area who lost the art soon after access to metal substitutes.

Compared with the ceramic ware of other areas, Plains earthenware seems crude. However, this has been plausibly explained by assuming that the villagers lost interest in the craft when the trader's utensils became available and the Indians intensified their hunting. From unquestionably prehistoric Pawnee settlements, archaeologists have unearthed pottery of a much better quality than from later sites, and certainly much better than the earthenware observable in the recent period.

Technologically, Plains pottery, unlike that of most North American natives, was not coiled, *i.e.*, not built up spirally from little sausages of clay, but hand-molded. It largely comprised globular cooking vessels, but clay pipes as well as stone ones occurred among the Mandan. A noteworthy Pawnee feature is the collarlike rim of the pots with its incised ornamentation largely consisting of isosceles triangles enclosing chevrons or lines parallel to one of the sides. The importance of the phenomenon lies in the resemblance to the ware of the Iroquois of New York State.

Woodwork is another craft that is quite undistinguished among Plains Indians, though the skill shown in fitting the posts and beams of earthlodges commands respect. Such Arapaho carvings as the three-dimensional representation of a supernatural patron (Fig. 21) were rather unusual. The men did manufacture a number of utilitarian articles, of which mortars among the villagers and bowls more generally were important. The Omaha shaped a mortar from a section of a tree trunk about 1 foot in diameter and 3 feet long, chipping one end to a point for insertion into the ground and hollowing out the opposite end. They put coals on the surface, fanning them till they burned into the wood to an adequate extent, finally smoothing the mortar with sandstone and water. The pestle, 3 to 4 feet long, was much larger at the top than at the tapering end used for pounding; this held also for the Hidatsa equivalent (Plate 6).

The Omaha made their bowls from black walnut burrs, the excavating process being the same as for the mortars. Ladles were made so that the handle could be hooked over the rim of the bowl. Spoons were sometimes of wood instead of horn. Not all bowls were for food. The Crow had some for mixing tobacco seeds or paint or for throwing dice. Aboriginal ladders were notched logs; a Hidatsa woman reached her corn-drying stages by a notched cottonwood trunk pointed for security at the butt end.

If the Plains Indians achieved little as carvers, potters, and textile workers, their women were conspicuous for their craftsmanship as skin dressers,

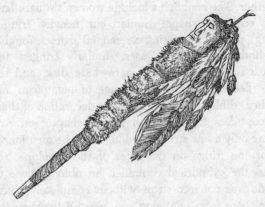

Fig. 21. An Arapaho wood carving (about 24 inches high), decorated with fur and feathers, representing a supernatural patron.

making not only clothes but also most of their containers from the hides of buffalo and other large game animals. Skin objects were either of rawhide or of leather. For both, the hide was first staked out on the ground, with the hairy side down, then the worker hacked away fat, muscle, and connective tissue with the toothed flesher. After several days' bleaching in the sun, the woman scraped the skin down to an even thickness with the antler adze; if she desired to remove the hair, the hide was turned over and treated with the adze. With this dehairing the rawhide process ended.

Rawhide served for binding or for the manufacture of receptacles. The handle of a stone cherry pounder or maul (Fig. 7) was attached to the head by a covering of green or wet rawhide, which

dried and shrank, thus firmly holding the parts together. The containers include women's square bags
of envelope shape; similar but heavily fringed
bags, usually for storing ceremonial articles; roughly
cylindrical medicine cases, similarly fringed and
closed at either end by a rawhide disk; and the
"parfleches," mainly for storage of pemmican and
other edibles (Figs. 22, 23). The decoration of these
receptacles is dealt with in the chapter on Art;
here only a few structural details will be mentioned.
For the fringe on the sides of the envelope bag
and the cylindrical container, an oblong piece of
hide was cut into strips without completely sever-
ing them from one edge and inserted between the
edges of the bag and sewed to them. The parfleche,
as defined by Clark Wissler, is "a sheet of hide
folded up into a package after the usual manner
of the powders prepared by a physician." In order

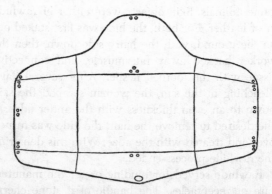

Fig. 22.   A pattern for a parfleche. To close, first the long
flaps and then the short ends are folded over and laced with
thong (see top illustration in Figure 23).

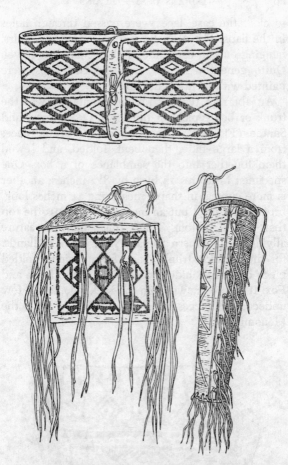

Fig. 23. Above, a painted rawhide parfleche (26 inches long, 13 inches high) from the Blackfoot. Lower left, a painted rawhide bag decorated with buckskin fringe. Lower right, a rawhide container for ritual objects (about 14 inches high). All these are from the Blackfoot.

to close the case, laces were passed through holes in the flaps. The Arapaho made parfleches in pairs, hanging one on each side of their mount in travel. Quite generally in the area the two flaps were painted with identical designs.

An aberrant type of rawhide container was the trunk or box typical of the Iowa, Oto, Ponca, and Santee (Fig. 24). The Iowa and Oto cut pieces from a large hide, then bent, folded, and sewed them together into the semblance of a box. One specimen measures 14 by 9 by 8½ inches; another is more cubical in shape, measuring 11 inches long, broad, and deep, but an inch shorter across the top than at the bottom. This is once more a feature allying the Southern Siouans with the Woodlands, for the rawhide trunk, made from a single folded piece of buffalo hide, was typical of the Sauk and Fox. It is also known from the Kickapoo, and a few undecorated pieces have been collected from the Menomini.

Fig. 24. A painted rawhide trunk from the Hidatsa, about 15 inches from side to side and 10 inches high.

Leather was required for clothing and soft pouches. In order to produce it the skin dresser had to subject the fleshed and scraped rawhide to a kind of tanning. She thoroughly rubbed into the surface an oily mixture of fat with buffalo or other brains, first with her hands, then with a smooth stone. Then the hide was dried in the sun and rolled up into a bundle. At this point it would shrink and had to be stretched back to its proper size. Next a rough-edged stone was rubbed over the surface, and the skin was run back and forth through a loop of sinew attached to a pole. This process dried and softened the skin, which thus became pliable. For some robes the hair was left on. Unlike buffalo skins, those of deer had the hairy surface rubbed down with a rib as a "beaming" tool before being rubbed over a cord. Some skins were browned by smoking: a smoldering fire was built in a small pit, and over it the skin was wrapped around a set of poles put up in the form of a cone. According to Catlin this operation made the skin capable of remaining soft and flexible irrespective of exposure to moisture. The Omaha made a practice of smoking skins to be cut up into moccasins.

Apart from articles of dress, which have been dealt with separately, leather was used in manufacturing a variety of soft pouches, including receptacles for smoking appurtenances, paint bags, women's workbags, knife cases, and toilet bags (Fig. 25).

Probably none of these articles, either of rawhide or of leather, was universal, but they were very widely diffused, partly through friendly visits associated with gifts and trading. For instance, the Cree did not make parfleches, but occasionally

Fig. 25. A bead-decorated soft skin pouch used for paint by the Arapaho. Note that the design differs slightly from the front to the back.

acquired them from other groups. However, parfleches are known from such borderline Plains peoples as the Nez Percé and Kutenai, while the peripheral Shoshoneans even developed a distinctive style of decoration for these containers.

Skin dressing was deeply influenced by the introduction of iron blades and the fur trade. Also robes and other skin manufactures spread widely from their centers of origin through gifts and trading among the tribes. The fur trade deeply affected native life. Whereas formerly the Indians had killed game for their own needs, they now hunted for gain on a much larger scale than before. One consequence was the rapid killing off of buffalo, another the increased duties of women in supplying the White men's demand for abundant dressed skins. Since, in addition, buffalo became virtually extinct and deer and elk scarce, it has not been possible to reconstruct in complete detail the aboriginal way of dealing with hides. Nevertheless early accounts and observation of processes preserved even recently on reservations, though mostly with the substitution of cattle skins, give a fair idea of this important native industry.

One of the feminine crafts highly developed in the area was porcupine-quill embroidery. It was best among the Dakota, Cheyenne, and Arapaho but lacking in the south among the Kiowa, Comanche, Apache, and Wichita. This absence is not wholly explained by that of the porcupine since quills could have been traded in. In the practice of this industry, too, White contacts brought changes in the use of new dyes for the quills and in providing glass beads as a replacement of quill embroidery.

Though the Omaha did not equal the skill of more northern tribes in this craft, relatively full information is available concerning their operations and will accordingly be drawn upon. The men killed the animals, from which the quills had to be promptly plucked to prevent breakage; these were sorted as to size and put into bladder bags. The largest quills, from the tail, served to decorate workbags and comb cases, while the hair of the animal was used for extra-fine ornamentation. The Omaha used fine quills for moccasin designs but were less given than other tribes to ornament other articles of clothing. The quills were not split, but put into the mouth to render them more pliable and flattened with the fingernails. With an awl the embroiderer punched holes for the sinew and quills.

A stitch was taken but not through the skin and the sinew was passed through and pulled tight. Then another stitch was taken in the same way but the sinew was not pulled tight. A little loop was left and through this loop the blunt ends of the quills were put. If, for exam-

ple, four quills were to be used, they were
placed one on the other through the loop,
which was then tightened. A quarter of an inch
from the first stitch of sinew a similar stitch was
taken and in the loop four quills were fastened
in the same way. Then the first quill was bent
toward the second loop and the first quill of the
second loop was bent toward the first loop, and
the braiding went on, back and forth, until all
four quills were in place, the last quill being
doubled under and the sinew used in a stitch
to hold it in place. In this way little by little the
pattern progressed.

The Omaha prepared a black dye by roasting
yellow earth and tallow, constantly stirring them,
and adding the blackened result to a boiling mixture of maple bast and leaves. In the very black
liquid thus procured the quills were steeped over-
night. For red dye the root of an unidentified plant
was boiled, the quills being added for a short time.
Yellow was obtained by boiling either early cottonwood buds or the roots of a vine. In other districts
of the area, corresponding results were attained
from other sources. Northern Plains tribes boiled a
moss growing near pine or balsam fir trees for a
yellow dye; and Denig credits the Crow with using
"several coloring herbs and mineral substances unknown to other tribes, which produce much better
colors." Interestingly enough, Crow, Omaha, and
Dakota deny the aboriginal use of blue, though
this figured in considerable measure after the introduction of aniline colors.

The embroiderer's outfit included only awls,

sinew, a bone marker for tracing designs, and the container for these articles. The Dakota and Arapaho also had quill flatteners made of bone or antler (Fig. 26).

Fig. 26. An Arapaho bone tool used for flattening quills and painting skins (about 9 inches long).

The Plains Indians generally employed the "two-thread" sewing technique in which the threads ran parallel, say one-quarter inch apart, and were caught under the skin at intervals; one or more quills were folded around the threads, passing back and forth between them. The resulting bands are usually straight and stiff. More rarely, as a rule only for rosettes, the Plains embroiderer caught a single thread under the surface of the skin and wrapped quills round it, singly, as she proceeded with the stitching. This produced a finer line, capable of curving in any direction, as explained by Frederic Douglas of the Denver Art Museum in the occasional publications of his institution.

In beadwork either the "lazy" or the "overlay" stitch was used. In the former, beads were strung on threads, which were fastened to the surface at the ends of short parallel rows. The result resembles some types of quillwork and suggests adaptation of the earlier technique to the new material. In the overlay stitch "strings of beads are tightly attached to the surface, in close-set rows, with other threads, thus producing a smooth finish." Whereas the lazy

stitch tends to restrict the craftswoman to angular
designs, curvilinear figures are easily made by the
alternative method (Douglas).

Bows and arrows, clubs, spears, and shields were
the weapons used in warfare and on the hunt.

Bows were either of wood or of horn and
were comparatively short, though according to the
Omaha they were longer before the horse was introduced, the greater length proving inconvenient
for a mounted warrior (Fig. 27). A Blackfoot specimen collected in 1870 is 3 feet 5 inches, and
Catlin, whose observations date back to the early
1830s, gives 3 feet as the standard length among
Crow and Blackfoot. Ash and ironwood were preferred by the Omaha, the Osage orange (*bois d'arc*)
by the Comanche, chokecherry wood by the Cree.
The material would vary according to geographical
conditions and even in the same tribe according to
facilities of access at any given time. Thus the Crow
tales refer to cedar as the material, and the Chicago
Natural History Museum has several Crow hickory
bows and one of ash.

Wooden bows were either simple (self-bows) or
strengthened with sinews glued on the back. Simple bows were typical of the United States Indians
east of the Missouri and occurred to the west as
toys, whereas sinew-backed bows characterized the
Far West. Accordingly, sinew backing was found
among the Ute, Crow, Blackfoot, Plains Cree, Cheyenne, and Hidatsa, but not among the Omaha. It
is highly probable that sinew backing was brought
into the western part of the Plains through contact
with Plateau and Basin tribes. The Blackfoot speci-

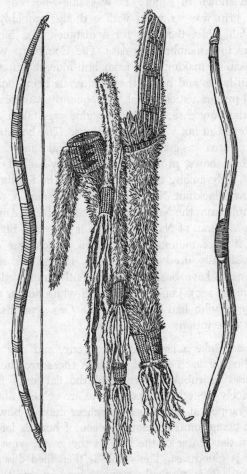

men shown in Figure 27 was sinew-backed, and the grip was wrapped with a thong, probably of buffalo hide; the ends for a distance of 4 inches were in a membranous case. The Comanche were typical in making glue from bull-hide shavings or from horns and hoofs, these materials being boiled and put on a stick, which subsequently was carried in the bow case, whence the glue was taken and softened in hot water for ready use. The bowstring of the area was generally made of buffalo sinew.

Horn bows, probably always sinew-backed, figured only among the western tribes, the Shoshone, Crow, Blackfoot, Nez Percé, and Cheyenne. A good sample from the Nez Percé collection of The American Museum of Natural History is shown in Figure 27; it is of mountain-sheep horn, which was also occasionally used by the Crow, though elk horn seems to have been more frequently employed by them. In 1875 James S. Belden, a white hunter and trapper who had lived with the Crow, published this description:

> They take a large horn or prong, and saw a slice off each side of it; these slices are then filed or rubbed down until the flat sides fit nicely together, when they are glued and wrapped at the ends. Four slices make a bow, it being jointed. Another piece of horn is laid on the center of the bow at the grasp, where it is glued fast. The whole is then filed down until it is perfectly proportioned, when the white bone is ornamented, carved, and painted. Nothing can exceed the beauty of these bows, and it takes an Indian about three months to make one.

Compound bows existed in ancient Babylonia at least as early as 2500 B.C. They appear among various Asiatic civilizations, composed of picked wood, sinews, and horn. Their origin is sought in steppe regions where long staves of wood could not be obtained. Scholars assume that the invention, in simplified form, was brought to North America, where the composite type consists either of wood and sinew or of horn and sinew, but not of all three materials joined. This view is supported by the complete lack of anything but simple bows either in the higher civilizations of the New World or in the eastern half of the United States. The Crow, Blackfoot, and Gros Ventre were likely to cover their horn bows with the skin of a rattlesnake.

Arrow shafts were proportionate in length to the bows. Blackfoot arrows in The American Museum of Natural History average 25½ inches, approximately the same as Sarsi, Dakota, and Cheyenne shafts. A shoot of the favored wood was straightened and rounded by passing it through a hole drilled in a piece of horn and by rubbing it between two grooved stones (Fig. 19). To increase the accuracy and carriage of the projectile, three feathers were generally attached to the butt end of the common shaft which was usually notched. Arrows for shooting birds, small game, or at a target did not require heads. For more serious purposes the Indians used sinew to fasten the stone, bone, horn or, in later times, metal points.

The bow was retained long after the introduction of firearms, not from sheer conservatism, but because old-fashioned muskets were difficult to load on horseback and could not be fired with equal rapidity.

As a protection against the rebound of the bowstring, Crow and Cree archers wore a wrist guard of hide, the Omaha and Iowa a leather band. A Blackfoot quiver with bow case attached, both of otterskin, is shown in Figure 27. The combination is widespread, being found among the Omaha and Iowa, but not in the Woodland Area.

Most Plains Indians released the arrow by holding the nock between the ends of the index and middle fingers, while the first three fingers are hooked on the string. The Plains Cree, however, are said to have shared the Eskimo technique of drawing the string with the first, second, and third fingers, the nock being lightly held between the first and second fingers.

Clubs were of several forms. The Cree favored a stone in a hide bag attached to the end of a 2-foot stick, the hide not fitting tightly round the stone. In the Assiniboin equivalent the stone weighed about two pounds, was sewed in leather, and was whirled round the handle, to which a wrist loop was attached. A Crow warclub with double-pointed stone head is shown in Figure 18.

Spears (lances), invariably thrust, not hurled, served in the chase as well as in fighting. Mounted Comanche often charged buffalo with this weapon; in warfare only brave members of this tribe were privileged to carry spears. Straight, hooked, or at the end of a bow (Plate 16), the spear played a considerable part in the military societies of many tribes.

Shields were circular and made of buffalo hide. The Blackfoot generally decorated the shield itself, whereas the Dakota and Crow tended to put designs revealed in visions and other ornamental features on the buckskin cover that normally enclosed the shield proper (Fig. 28). Sometimes the painted cover was itself put into another case.

Fig. 28. *Two painted and feather-decorated shields used by the Crow (about 20 inches in diameter).*

3 SOCIAL ORGANIZATION

Marriage and the Family

Though some Plains Indian customs connected with sex depart widely from our norms, they adhered as a rule strictly to their own. As in many civilized societies, there was a double standard: elders carefully watched over the behavior of young women, while a young man was rather expected to philander. Feminine chastity was highly prized; it was only a virtuous girl for whom a suitor was likely to offer many horses, and certain honorific tasks at sacred ceremonies could be executed only by a woman of irreproachable purity.

Romance was by no means lacking in the sex life of these Indians. Lovers would court a girl when she was fetching firewood or water, or they tried to attract attention at night by playing a flageolet. There is an affecting tradition of a young Hidatsa woman who heard that her sweetheart had been crippled and at his own request abandoned by his companions on a raid. She at once set forth, braving all dangers, traversed hostile territory, reached him, and with her brother-in-law, who had stayed with the deserted man, managed to rescue him.

All the Indians had definite rules barring marriage with the closest relatives and in some tribes even with distant relatives and with unrelated clansfolk (see page 95). On the other hand, there were also some positive prescriptions. An extremely widespread primitive view treats siblings (a sibling is either a brother or a sister) of the same sex as socially equivalent and looks upon marriage as a bond primarily between families rather than between individuals. In consequence, by way of maintaining the family tie, a widower would marry his dead wife's sister and a widow her husband's brother. The former custom is known as the "sororate," the latter as the "levirate." Although not always binding, these unions were regarded as desirable, so that an Omaha has been known to marry his brother's widow though she was many years his senior. Among the same people a man might also marry the daughter of his wife's brother or his wife's father's sister.

Although elopements were far from rare and might be accepted by society if the union proved stable, the most generally approved form of marriage was by purchase. There was nothing at all derogatory to a girl in being paid for, quite the contrary. It must be emphasized that she did not thereby become a chattel. In fact, in certain cases, as among the Mandan, there was actually no purchase, but rather an exchange of gifts between the two families, each furnishing precisely the same number to the other. In other instances there was clearly the conception of a payment by the groom's side, or its equivalent in the form of services rendered by the groom, who acted somewhat like a hired man during a year or two. This was of course most easily done by his taking up residence with the bride's family (matrilocal residence). On the Plains there was no universal rule concerning the place where the newlyweds were to live; Cheyenne and Arapaho marriages were generally matrilocal, while the Blackfoot had the reverse custom (patrilocal), and the Crow seem to have been indifferent on the subject.

Temporarily a Pawnee youth was allowed access to his maternal uncle's wife and an elder brother might share conjugal rights with a junior brother, but these practices were not characteristic of the area. Full-fledged polyandry (marriage of one woman with two or more husbands) was not a Plains institution, though polygyny (marriage with two or more wives) was commonly allowed. Among these warlike Indians many men would fall in fighting, a situation which created a surplus of marriageable women. However, polygyny never reached the excessive degree found in some African kingdoms, where the ruler would appropriate several hundred women for his service. A prominent Plains Indian might have several wives, but rarely more than four or five, and most marriages were monogamous. It was by no means degrading for a woman to be one of several wives. As a matter of fact, a man of distinction who married the eldest daughter in a family established a preemptive claim to her younger sisters as they reached maturity. Small-ankle, an eminent Hidatsa, married Yellow-head and subsequently three of her junior blood-sisters and a fourth girl classed as a sister because she was adopted by the wife's mother. Polygyny was not restricted to the "sororal" form, but this was the most common; with astonishing unanimity the tribes declare that sisters in a polygynous household were less likely to quarrel than unrelated co-wives. One reason for taking two or more wives was that a man of distinction owed it to his status to entertain, which in the

absence of domestics involved considerable work
for a single mate. "I must take another wife," said
an Omaha; "my old wife is not strong enough now
to do all her work alone." Not infrequently an additional wife was captured from a hostile tribe.

In the absence of religious sanctions for marriage,
it could be dissolved without much ado and often
was. But a faithful, industrious woman was not
likely to be deserted.

The division of labor between the sexes followed
a general primitive pattern in so far as the husband
hunted while the wife supplied the vegetable fare.
This meant that among the semisedentary tribes she
did the cultivating and among the nomads dug up
wild roots and collected berries. In all cases she
prepared the meals, brought fuel and water, put
up and took down the tipi, dressed skins, and made
all the clothing. Men butchered game, cleared the
plots for planting, and also cut and transported
the large posts for an earthlodge among the villagers. The manufacture of weapons, stone implements, and all woodwork everywhere devolved on
men. In art, the men painted realistic designs on
robes, shields, and tipis, the women painted geometrical figures on hide and were responsible for
all beadwork and quilling.

The position of women was decidedly higher than
is often assumed. An adulterous wife was liable to
severe punishment and, as in all societies, instances
of wanton abuse are on record, but these were
definitely disapproved by public opinion. In cases
of matrilocal residence the wife's relatives would
protect her from arbitrary cruelty. A good woman
enjoyed the esteem of her husband and of the community at large. As there was at times romantic

devotion in youth, so there was probably more frequently a deep attachment between old partners in matrimony. Institutional recognition of the wife's status is shown by the fact that among the Crow she took part jointly with her husband in sacred rituals. Altogether there was nothing like the Melanesian or Australian native's social segregation and exclusion of women from ceremonial life.

Indians had a generic love for children, touchingly illustrated in a Blackfoot story. A scout sent out to detect the enemy discovers a lonely tipi inhabited by a couple from the hostile tribe. Their baby, just able to walk, was dipping up soup from a kettle and detected the stranger peeping in by a hole. Toddling over, it fed the man again and again, unnoticed by the parents. The scout left and was assailed by qualms. It was his duty to announce the discovery, but he could not bring himself to bring death to the infant and its parents. Sentiment overcomes his sense of duty, he returns and warns the couple so that they and the baby are able to escape.

As might be expected, then, parents deeply loved their own offspring and were inconsolable over their loss. In such cases they generally adopted some youngster who seemed to resemble their deceased child. Informally a parent would give instruction to the children of his or her own sex, who were thus initiated into the skills necessary in life. Discipline was not lacking but was mild compared to what was, until recently, customary in Western civilization. Often it was applied not by either parent but by, say, an elder brother. Very rarely was a child beaten; an unruly youngster of two or three might have water dashed on him or be frightened by

a bogy, the owl or coyote especially being often
chosen for the role. For praiseworthy conduct an
Arapaho youngster might be rewarded by words
of commendation or some delicious tidbit. When a
Crow lad had shot his first deer or done well on his
first raid, a father's kinsman would advertise the
fact by singing a song of praise.

It was a foregone conclusion that siblings should
aid one another in every way possible. An elder
brother loomed as his junior's natural protector;
horses offered by a girl's suitor were rightfully ap-
propriated by her brothers; sisters made moccasins
and finery for brothers. This genuine affection and
mutual helpfulness did not prevent a rigid taboo:
as soon as a boy and his sister attained maturity,
they no longer played or chatted together but had
to avoid each other. Only a few years ago a ninety-
year old Arapaho woman declared that she had
never spoken to her brother. In case of absolute
necessity a message might be delivered curtly, with
averted eyes. The mutual avoidance of adult brothers and sisters falls under the head of what are
known as "respect relationships." Siblings being regarded as socially equivalent, the Indians generally
extended relationship terms far beyond what seems
reasonable to us (see page 103).

Contrary to our own notions, primitive tribes attached very specific duties or privileges to relatives
outside the immediate family circle. For example,
the paternal aunt of an Arapaho girl would take it
upon herself to instruct her niece, and a maternal
uncle did the same for his nephews. This uncle, like
a young woman's brother, might receive horses from
a suitor and have the right to marry her off. An
Omaha uncle of this category had more power to

dispose of his nieces than their own father. Among the Crow a father's brothers and sisters were entitled not only to great respect but also to gifts, especially whenever a nephew returned with loot from a raid.

Marriage created a series of new bonds with one's relatives-in-law, and most Plains tribes prescribed definite rules of conduct between a person and his (her) mate's kin, though the details varied in the different tribes. Extremely widespread was the mutual avoidance of a person and his (her) parents-in-law, especially if not of the husband's (wife's) sex. In accordance with the principle that brothers (sisters) are equivalent, the siblings of the persons involved were included in the prohibition. A Crow never spoke to his wife's mother; if he had to convey a message to her, it was relayed through his wife. He even refrained in conversation with anyone from uttering a Crow word that happened to be part of her name, being obliged to paraphrase his meaning. The underlying sentiment was not one of hostility, but of supreme reverence. An Arapaho wife might not speak to or look at her husband's father; even quite recently an interpreter could not question her father-in-law's brothers and an informant refused to answer questions with her son-in-law sitting 15 feet away from her. An attempt at conversation by either of two individuals subject to the taboo was viewed by the other as a lack of respect.

Considering the intensity of feeling on this point, it seems strange that a few tribes in the area, such as the Pawnee and Arikara, completely lacked the taboo. It is also odd that where it did hold it could be overcome by a man's presenting his parents-in-law with a scalp or a substantial gift. Again, the Crow and the Blackfoot, who insisted on the taboo between a man and his mother-in-law, had no parallel to the Arapaho rule for the wife and her father-in-law.

A particularly friendly relationship obtained between Crow or Hidatsa brothers-in-law. However, the Crow did not permit a man to indulge in obscene talk in his brother-in-law's presence. Considering this circumspect behavior between two connections of the same sex, it is remarkable that the Crow permitted the utmost license between a man and his sister-in-law; they romped together, might expose each other's nakedness, and addressed each other in vile language. In "The Social Life among the Blackfoot Indians," Wissler reports that among the Blackfoot "this is often carried to a degree beyond belief. . . . There is not only the same freedom here as between man and wife, but the conventional necessity for license." The Arapaho also favored mutual obscenity and teasing, such as pouring water on the in-law. In this context, we must recall that the marriage customs of the Plains would make of these connections possible spouses.

The Life Cycle

Because of the numerous folkways associated with marriage and family life, these have received treatment separately from other stages in individual existence. These phases did not receive uniform emphasis throughout the area. It will be best to treat the consecutive periods for a single tribe, the Plains Cree, and then supplement with an account of noteworthy deviations elsewhere.

During childbirth a Cree woman knelt, attended

by midwives, one of whom cut the navel cord. The afterbirth, wrapped in a piece of hide, was hung on a tree in the woods. The cord was subsequently put in a decorated skin bag worn by the child round its neck. The infant was not bathed but dried with dry wood or moss and after several days was placed in a hide bag stuffed with moss. Cradleboards were not typical of these people until relatively recent times.

Soon after birth a child received a name, formally bestowed at a feast by a person of the same sex and credited with supernatural power, who prayed to a spirit on behalf of his godchild, took the infant into his arms, and pronounced a name derived from an episode or character in the name-giver's vision. More rarely great warriors named a child after one of their exploits, *e.g.*, one chief called a baby Dragging-him, because he had once dragged an enemy out of a trench. Informally a person might gain a name in commemoration of a war experience of his own. If a child got sick, another medicineman would be asked to give him a new name. Sometimes a nickname given to an individual would stick to him for life. It was reckoned impolite to ask anyone for his name if it referred to a supernatural experience; and the names of the dead, unless they had been outstanding braves, were not mentioned. Fine-day, Bear, Fringe, Many-birds, Red-dog, Star-blanket, Upturned-nose, Rattlesnake, Wolf are some typical Cree names.

The nursing period often lasted much longer than with Whites; sometimes a child of four would seek the breast. Much time was spent with grandparents, who displayed a great deal of affection for their descendants. Two unrelated boys often be-

came comrades in the preadolescent period, lived
in each other's households, and subsequently went
on the warpath together, joining in the same risks
so that both might be killed at the same time.

At puberty a girl was secluded for four nights
in a small tipi under the guardianship of an old
woman. A married woman also had to withdraw
while menstruating, as did the unmarried daughters
of the owner of sacred objects, which otherwise
were supposed to become polluted. To return to
the pubescent, she had to chop wood, sew, dress
hides in her retreat, and listen at night to tales related by her mentor. She got little food to eat, cried
a good deal, and when necessary scratched her
head with a pointed stick. This four-day period
was the most likely for a female to acquire a vision,
which otherwise might be experienced at any time.
On the fourth night the women of the camp went
to the shelter; four of them controlling spirit power
prayed for the girl, piled up the wood she had
chopped, and pushed it over, whereupon each
woman carried off some of it. The girl was led to
her home ceremonially and was once more prayed
for. A feast followed, and then the parents distributed presents among the guests. No comparable
ritual was celebrated for boys, but they were usually told by their elders to fast and try to gain a
vision (see page 170).

At death the corpse was disposed of in any one
of several ways, interment at a depth of about 5
feet being commonest. In the winter, when the
ground was frozen too hard for excavation, the
body was either put into a log chamber with brush
heaped over it or wrapped up and placed on a
platform of poles laid across the forks of a big tree.

At the special request of a dying man he might be placed against a willow backrest inside a tipi set up on a hill, a low stone wall being built indoors round the corpse.

Before disposal the corpse was painted and dressed in the dead person's best garments; the legs were bound together for a while, with knees somewhat flexed and hands folded over the chest. In the grave were placed a filled pipe and a container of grease—according to one authority, all his personal possessions. The corpse was pulled out of the side, not the door, of the tipi by a famous brave and carried to the grave amidst general lamentation. A warrior cut off a braid from the hair of the deceased. Close relatives gashed their forearms and legs and wore their hair loose, remaining in mourning until a man of eminence declared the period terminated. On the fourth night after the death there was a feast with ceremonial pipe and food offerings to the spirits. The braid was put into a sacred bundle with braids of other dead members of the family. Such bundles were highly regarded and carried by the women when camp moved. Whenever subsequently the bereaved got near the grave, they would give a feast and tidy the site. The dead person's personal property was given away lest their sight arouse sad memories; his tipi was abandoned or, more frequently, exchanged for another; the horses were distributed among sons and daughters with one reserved for the widow.

Several of the usages described for the Cree were widely shared. Delayed weaning, for example, was a common primitive practice; Assiniboin children were never weaned under two or three years old, and among the Arapaho a child was conventionally nursed until it was four years old. Widespread, too, were the change of name of an ailing infant and the reluctance to inquire after a person's name or to mention that of a dead person. Probably quite general in the area was the notion of comradeship, especially between boys, that suggests the blood-brotherhood of other continents. Arapaho girls as well as boys formed these bonds in preadolescence and maintained them for life.

The dread of menstrual blood and of its contaminating sacred objects by contact or proximity extended far beyond the bounds of the Plains, sometimes attaining a morbid degree, considering the freedom with which natives often discussed sexual matters. Even ten years ago Arapaho women displayed the utmost disinclination to speak of the subject to a woman investigator, Sister M. I. Hilger. "Very few give instructions to their daughters about it. . . . You know if a menstruating woman enters a sickroom, it will kill the sick person." Yet though some restrictions were usually imposed on a girl when coming of age and at subsequent periods, neither the retreat to a special shelter nor the puberty ceremonial for a girl, as described for the Cree, was general in the Plains; the Blackfoot, for example, lacked both, as did the Arapaho—notwithstanding their intense feelings about menstruation. As for adolescent boys, the Plains Indians had nothing comparable to the *tribal* initiation of African or Australian indigenes, though initiation into ceremonial organizations was a familiar practice.

The rule that a corpse should not be taken out by the regular entrance occurs in various tribes, the Crow reason being that otherwise some other inmate of the lodge would die soon after. The practice has been reported from Woodland natives (Ojibwa, Menomini, Saulteaux) and even from the Greenland Eskimo and the Lapps. Disposal of the body never seems to have been by cremation in our area, but both interment and tree burial after the Cree fashion were typical of the Plains, where the body was also often put on a four-pole scaffold. After decomposition the bones might be deposited in rock crevices. Quite general in the area were demonstrative mourning with laceration of the body and mutilation of a finger, the distribution of the deceased person's property, the abandonment of the tipi. Economic conditions wrought some significant modifications. In the Basin the destruction of a man's property wrought no great loss, but when the Comanche as Plains people acquired large herds of horses there was a revulsion against sacrificing a large number, and Professor Ralph Linton tells us a compromise solution was found by killing only one favorite horse and distributing the remainder among the survivors. Again, it was much easier for nomads to abandon a tipi than for semisedentary folk to leave their earthlodge after a death, which the Hidatsa do not seem to have ever done, presumably because of the material sacrifice involved.

Bands, Clans, Phratries, Moieties

In the very simplest societies the family or a union of a few families, often related to one another, coincided with the local group or "community." West of our area, the Shoshoneans of Nevada had so difficult a time existing at all in their habitat that during much of the year they had to live in minute nomadic bands rarely much larger than a single family. Only for brief periods, when provisions were ample, could several of these small groups unite into a larger body to hold a dance. The Plains tribes developed greater complexity of organization, but it should be noted that during the winter economic reasons caused them also to split up into very small units. D. G. Mandelbaum, who has studied the Plains Cree, has written that in January and February these people, sometimes on the verge of starvation, "scattered in small family units into the more densely wooded country." One year, about 1837, the Cheyenne departed from ancient custom by sticking together during the cold season, but they very nearly perished in consequence. Economic factors, then, normally enabled the Plains tribes to carry on their more complex social activities only from the beginning of spring until the beginning of winter. This applies perhaps particularly to the nomads, but even a semisedentary people like the Mandan took up special and less pretentious dwellings in the cold season.

LOCAL UNITS

A "band" is a local group of people jointly wandering in search of sustenance. Its size varied considerably in our area, as did its make-up. The Kiowa, numbering altogether about 1,600, embraced ten to twenty bands, each formed by the inmates of twelve to fifty tipis. A new band came into being when a leader separated from the parent group with a following of brothers and sisters with their spouses and offspring. The Comanche at one time had thirteen bands, four of which were especially important. They bore such names as Burnt Meat, Making Bags While Moving, Those Who Move

Often—*i.e.*, nicknames. The Plains Cree bands each claimed a range of territory that, however, was ill defined. In the nineteenth century at least eight of these units were recognized, most of them bearing a geographical designation, such as Upstream, Calling River, Touchwood Hills People. The Crow comprised two politically independent major subdivisions, the Mountain and the River Crow, the former roaming mainly over southern Montana and northern Wyoming, the latter along the lower Yellowstone. Bands, called by such names as Ugly People and Red Willow Men, jointly formed the Arapaho and occupied distinct positions in the

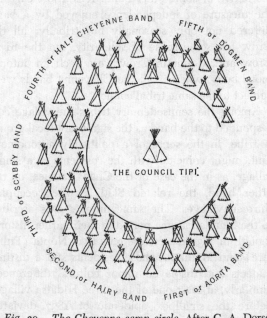

Fig. 29. The Cheyenne camp circle. After G. A. Dorsey.

camp circle when the entire tribe was united. Eleven comparable subdivisions have been noted for the Cheyenne (Fig. 29); characteristic sobriquets were Small Windpipes, Hair Men, Shy People, Eaters.

It should be noted that, though bands were consistent with another and more rigid type of grouping (as among the Crow), the band itself was a unit of shifting constitution. A Plains Cree could freely pass from one to another; among the Arapaho a husband usually lived with his wife's family so that the children came to be identified with her band rather than with the father's, but there was nothing to prevent his taking wife and offspring to his native or some other band. It is also clear that the measure of independence enjoyed by a band differed not only seasonally but tribally: all the Crow felt some sense of solidarity, but the River Crow and Mountain Crow were each an autonomous body, whereas all the Cheyenne bands were subject to the same tribal council.

Among the semisedentary tribes the village corresponded to the band as the significant local group. A tribe, in the sense of a politically autonomous unit, might coincide with the residents of a single village, as in the case of the Chaui Pawnee; on the other hand, the related Skidi Pawnee occupied thirteen villages. The same number was ascribed to the Mandan at one period in their earlier history, though in 1833 there were only two, Núpta (Puhptare) and Mi'tutak, whose residents spoke distinct dialects and displayed minor cultural differences. Similarly, at least one of the three Hidatsa villages before the smallpox epidemic of 1837 deviated

somewhat in speech from the others and had some
ceremonial peculiarities.

KINSHIP UNITS

In contrast to local groups, where membership
rested on the accident of residence, were the units
in which membership was fixed by heredity. This
might be done by consistently ignoring one side of
the family and stressing the other. If children were
all reckoned as of the father's unit, the principle of
"patriliny" held; if they belonged to the mother's
unit, we are dealing with "matriliny." All persons
of either sex descended from the same ancestor,
through males only, form a "patrilineage," all those
descended from one ancestress, through females
only, form a "matrilineage." Actually it often happens that primitive folk regard themselves as sharing the same ancestor or ancestress without being
able to trace the genealogical blood relationship,
either because they have lost track of the links or
because the connection was once established by
legal fiction. In this case we speak of patrilineal or
matrilineal clans.

The clan, then, differed from a band in absolutely fixing membership. Whereas an Arapaho
child shifted its affiliation when taken out of the
Ugly band to settle in the Red Willow band, the
situation would be different for a Crow youngster.
If his Mountain Crow parents decided to join the
River band and he remained there, he would indeed belong to the River Crow, but he could never
change his clan affiliation; once a Sore-lip, always a
Sore-lip.

Further, the clan differed from the family in being a unilateral group; whereas the family takes

cognizance of both parents, a clan system one-sidedly ignored either in favor of the other. It must be remembered, however, that though the *clan* neglected either patrilineal or matrilineal kindred, this does not mean that the people as a whole did so. For since family ties are universal, both parents had a definite place with reference to the child. What is meant, then, is simply that for *certain* specific purposes only one half of one's relatives counted, while in respect to other matters the half excluded from one's clan might be quite as important. For instance, the Omaha had patrilineal clans, so that a mother's brother was never in his sister's daughter's clan; yet he had to be consulted when his niece was to be married (page 84). On the other hand, while the Crow clans were matrilineal, the father's relatives were nevertheless entitled to respect and to gifts from their brother's children.

Even the most remotely related, or only fictitiously related, fellow clansfolk were morally obligated to help and shield one another, and in case of intratribal murder the bereaved clan might try to punish the offender or, on the principle of collective responsibility, even a clansman of his. Such a situation might precipitate a feud between the two clans involved. Another general function of clans was the regulation of marriage: because fellow members of a clan were related by blood or were considered relatives, they were not permitted to marry one another, *i.e.*, the clans are "exogamous" (Greek *exo*, outside; *gam*, marriage).

Of the Plains Indians, the Crow, Hidatsa, and Mandan are known to have had matrilineal clan systems. The same is reported of the Oto and Missouri by Lewis H. Morgan in his *Ancient Society,* but our information on these tribes is fragmentary, hence not quite satisfactory. One authority believes that the Cheyenne once had matrilineal clans that degenerated into the recent band system, but other observers reject his conclusion. The Pawnee were unquestionably matrilineal in the sense that an individual permanently belonged to his mother's village, and since a woman never left the settlement she was born into, she with her mother, mother's sisters, daughters, and daughters' daughters formed what elsewhere would be the permanent core of a matrilineal clan. A Pawnee village, however, was not a clan; by permission a man might marry into another village, but this was very rarely granted, so that the settlement was not exogamous, but the reverse—"endogamous."

The Omaha, Ponca, Iowa, Kansa, and Osage all had patrilineal clans. As to the Blackfoot and Gros Ventre, there is a disagreement on the part of authorities. The decision hinges on the fixity of the tie between an individual and his tribal subdivision. Wissler's evidence, published in papers of The American Museum of Natural History, indicates that a Blackfoot was free to select his subdivision and that marriages within it were frowned upon simply because of "the suspicion that some close blood relationship may have been overlooked"; hence, he prefers to speak of Blackfoot bands. It must be conceded, however, that they represent a borderline case, for on Wissler's evidence the general feeling assigned a child to his father's group and migrants were often reminded of their original membership. "Thus, it seems that the bands are in part, at least, gentes [clans]." There is also doubt concerning the Dakota and the Assiniboin. In 1767 a visitor to the Eastern Dakota recorded names of tribal subdivisions that certainly resemble the clan names of other Woodland tribes. It is therefore probable, though not certain, that the subdivisions mentioned were clans.

The Southern Siouan clans were generally subdivided into what may be called "subclans." Frequently the name of the smaller unit was a variation of the clan's: the Iowa Elk clan embraced a Big Elk, a White Elk, a Bull Elk subclan.

Sometimes two or more clans within a tribe regarded themselves as related to one another more closely than to other clans. Such a union was called a "phratry." The Kansa had seven larger units, which they called "those who sing together"; three comprised two clans, three were made up of three each. The sixteenth clan was reckoned co-ordinate with the phratries, possibly because it had formerly been linked with another clan that died out. Often the phratries had no important function beyond assembling friendly clans. They might be nameless (Crow) or bear such names as Fire and Earth (Ponca).

More significant was the "dual organization" by which a whole tribe was split into two complementary units or "moieties" (French *moitié*, half). These tribal halves, if exogamous, may be considered the equivalent of major clans; but it is possible that their origin is historically different from that of a multiple-clan system. Among North American Indians we find both undivided moieties and moieties subdivided into clans. In the latter case the moiety might still regulate marriage, which inevitably made the clans exogamous; or it might have nothing to do with marriage; or there may have been a disinclination to marrying inside the moiety without a strict rule to that effect. In the last of these possibilities, realized among the Omaha, we may reasonably suspect that the moieties were formerly exogamous. The Pawnee, though devoid of clans and exogamy, nevertheless had a strong sense for a dual division. Whenever they played important games or seated themselves for ceremonial performances, the Winter people sat in the north half of the circle, the Summer people in the south half. Membership was hereditary, every individual permanently belonging to his mother's moiety. The Southern Siouans similarly expressed the complementary nature of the moieties in spatial terms when camping on the march or on a hunting expedition. Among the Omaha one moiety was associated with the sky, the other with the earth; the Osage halves represented, respectively, peace and war. Such linkage of moieties with opposite concepts occurs in various parts of the world, including Brazil and Australia. It is also a widespread feature for moieties to render each other services. When an Osage child was sick, the parents asked members of the other moiety for food.

Apparently the Mandan and Hidatsa moieties were less striking phenomena than those of the Southern Siouans. Designated as Three-Clans and Four-Clans, respectively, each comprised the corresponding number of clans. They did not regulate marriage and functioned as distinct units mainly when political issues, such as treaties, were at stake. In the old days each had its own territory for eagle hunting.

Clans, phratries, and moieties were variously combined. The Pawnee had moieties without clans;

the Crow lacked moieties but grouped their thirteen
clans in six phratries, five pairs of clans and one
trio; among the Omaha each moiety embraced five
clans, divided into subclans; the Ponca moieties
were divided into four clans each, paired into
phratries; the phratry grouping of the Kansa partly
crisscrossed the moiety division, so that the Earth
and the Elk clan, though of opposite halves, formed
one phratry.

The designations of the clans present variations
of historical significance. The Crow clans bore fairly
uniformly such names as Treacherous, Filth-eaters,
Sore-lip, Greasy-inside-their-mouths. This type of
nomenclature was shared by the problematic tribal
subdivisions of the Blackfoot and Gros Ventre, who
had such groups as Ugly-ones, Those-who-do-not-
give-away, Fighting-alone, Fish-eaters, Liars, Bad-
guns. Obviously the same type held for the band
names of the Arapaho and Cheyenne quoted above.
The Dakota equivalents were as a rule similarly
labeled, witness Wears-a-dogskin-round-the-neck,
Breakers-of-the-law, Not-encumbered-with-much-
baggage. In short, over a wide region in the western
Plains nicknames were common.

In sharp contrast to this system was that of the
Southern Siouans. Here the nomenclature is preponderantly derived from the animal kingdom or some
cosmic phenomenon, the particular species or natural feature being, in technical language, the "totem" of the tribal subdivision. Among the Omaha,
even when the clan is not actually named after an
animal, it is in some way conceived to be associated
with the species or natural phenomenon. The
Omaha have an Elk, Black [Buffalo] Shoulder,
Wind, Deer clan; and even when a name is of a

13. *Costume and hairdress from the Crow.* Courtesy of Bureau of American Ethnology, Smithsonian Institution.

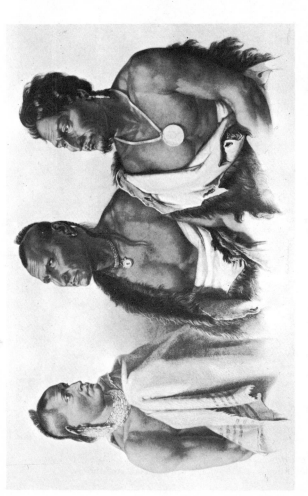

14. *The hair roach, as worn by the Missouri and Oto Indians (left and center), and a Ponca chief. Carl Bodmer engraving in Maximilian.*

15. *Mandan pottery vessels.*

16. *An Assiniboin warrior with shield and bow spear.* After Carl Bodmer in Maximilian.

17. *A Hidatsa Dog dancer.* Carl Bodmer engraving in Maxi-
    milian.

18. *Mandan Half-shaved Head Dance.* Carl Bodmer engraving in Maximilian.

19. Mandan Bull Society Dance. Carl Bodmer engraving in Maximilian.

20. *Two young warriors returning with their first scalps; their faces are blackened as a symbol of the attainment of a "coup."* Courtesy of Bureau of American Ethnology, Smithsonian Institution.

21. *An Assiniboin scalp dance. The legend reads "Scalp Dance. Drawn by an Assiniboine warrier. Fort Union. Nov. 10, 1853."* Courtesy of Bureau of American Ethnology, Smithsonian Institution.

22. *The Cree double-ball shinny game.*

23. *The Hidatsa hoop-and-pole game as played in a winter earthlodge village.* Carl Bodmer engraving in Maximilian.

different character, its bearers are connected with a totem. Thus, the Earthlodge-makers are also expressly referred to as Wolf and Coyote people, the Gray-eyes as Thunder and Reptile people. The names of subclans may refer to taboos imposed on the members, *e.g.*, Do-not-touch-buffalo-heads or Do-not-eat-buffalo-tongues. Among the Crow there is no suggestion of such a clan nomenclature; and though a Prairie-chicken clan is common to the Mandan and Hidatsa and the former also have an Eagle clan, there is no evidence of any deeper meaning to these designations.

Further, the clans of the best-known Southern Siouans each owned a set of ordinal birth names. An Omaha Elk man's eldest son was called Soft-horn; the second, Yellow-horn; the third, Branching-horns; the fourth, Four-horns. No trace of such a custom has been reported from the three matrilineal Siouan tribes.

Apart from names, the Southern Siouan system had another feature not encountered in the north—the holding of distinctive ceremonial and political functions by particular clans. Among the Omaha the Black [Buffalo] Shoulder people kept the peace pipes, one of the Buffalo clans was in charge of two sacred tents, and only the Pipe subclan of the Deer-head clan had the privilege of wearing down in their hair. Osage policemen were always recruited from particular clans.

A remarkable point about all this is that, while the Southern Siouans of the Plains differed so markedly in their clan system from their northern fellow Siouans in the area, they closely resembled the pattern of patrilineal Woodland peoples, including the Algonkian Menomini and the Siouan Winnebago, both residents of Wisconsin. The Menomini clans all bore animal names, a fair number coinciding with those of the Southern Siouan divisions, *e.g.*, Bear, Wolf, Eagle, Beaver, Elk. The clans also owned distinctive personal names, bestowed on children according to the order of their birth; and governmental functions belonged to the Bear clan. Furthermore, though less explicitly than the Omaha and their closest tribal relatives, the Menomini recognized a dual division suggestive of moieties: in playing lacrosse the clans with bird totems were regularly pitted against those with animal totems. As might be expected, the correspondence was still closer with the Siouan Winnebago: here there were not only totemic nomenclature, ordinal birth names peculiar to each clan, and specific functions, political and ceremonial, of particular clans, but also explicit moieties, associated with sky and earth, and in the old villages the dwellings of men of these halves are said to have been divided by an imaginary northwest-southeast line.

In short, if we mapped culture areas exclusively on the basis of social structure, the traditional Plains Area would have to be split up so as to unite the Southern Siouans with the more westerly Woodland tribes. Knowing that the Southern Siouans came from the East, what happened is simply that they brought an Eastern clan pattern with them into their new habitat. Altogether the historic Plains Area presents an extraordinary diversity in this respect: matrilineal and patrilineal descent, nontotemic and totemic clan systems, tribal subdivisions approximating but not quite attaining clan status, and completely loose band organizations are all found between the Rocky Mountains and the Mississippi.

Kinship Terms

In this connection another fact is significant. Most primitive tribes have a way of designating relatives by blood and marriage that differs markedly from ours. They draw distinctions we ignore and on the other hand fail to distinguish where we consider differences of the utmost importance. Thus, most of the Plains tribes have separate words for an older and a younger brother and also for an older and a younger sister. But nearly all of them call the father and the father's brother by a single word, while carefully separating the uncles on the father's from those on the mother's side. Correspondingly, they generally called a mother's sister "mother," but distinguished both the real mother and the maternal aunt from the paternal aunt. Since the natives were usually very logical in applying these terms, they also recognized a vast number of brothers and sisters; for persons who call the same individuals "father" or "mother" naturally regard one another as siblings.

Now this phenomenon is doubly interesting, both in its sociological and in its historical aspects. Sociologically it appears that the rule of descent has a good deal to do with the relationship system. Where the individual family and the local group are the only essential social divisions, people are as likely to distinguish uncles from the father and aunts from the mother as we do. But where a one-sided rule of descent prevails, it tends to go with the classification described above. That is, relatives are then considered with reference to whether they stem from the father's or the mother's side; accordingly, the paternal and the maternal uncle cannot be called by the same name, but father and paternal uncle can be, because interest centers on the lines of descent, not on the physiological relations of individuals. So we find that among the Dakota, whose eastern branches probably had patrilineal reckoning, a person had many fathers and mothers, for in addition to the uncles on the father's side all his cousins would be reckoned as "fathers" provided they were in the same clan as the father, and correspondingly for the mother's sisters and female cousins.

Certain Plains tribes emphasized the matrilineal or patrilineal side even more strongly, so as to ignore even differences of generation. Thus, in the Crow and Hidatsa languages the word we translate as "father" meant not only "begetter," "begetter's brother," and "clansman of begetter's generation," but also "father's sister's son." This is quite logical, for if a Crow was of the Sore-lip clan, his sister was likewise, and by matrilineal descent her children must have been the same. Hence, one cousin, the mother's brother's son, addressed the other, his father's sister's son, as "father" and logically was called "son" in return.

The same notion in reverse appears among the patrilineal Omaha and other Southern Siouans. Here a boy called his mother's brother's son by the same word he applied to his maternal uncle, while the mother's brother's daughter was a "mother," for patriliny united these relatives in one social subdivision.

Evidently the Dakota, Crow, and Omaha schemes are distinguished from one another by their treatment of cousins. A fourth possibility in this respect was realized by the Arapaho, Gros Ventre, and Sarsi, who drew no distinctions between any cousins and siblings. Interestingly enough, none of the three had a clan organization.

Historically, the noteworthy fact is that once more the Southern Siouans fall in line with western Woodland peoples. Their system shows virtual identity with the systems of the Winnebago, the Sauk and Fox, Menomini, and Kickapoo. In other words, the resemblance cuts across linguistic family lines. Some Siouans are much nearer certain Algonkians than to some other Siouans. The social structure and a kinship nomenclature in harmony with it has undoubtedly been diffused over a considerable number of tribes in the central states, irrespective of linguistic affinity. Whether the Algonkians or the Siouans were the originators, it is impossible to tell, for the features in question are not general in either stock.

Clubs and Societies

Apart from a person's social ties with his family, band, and clan, he was in most Plains tribes connected with organizations in which membership did not rest on kinship. These associations served a great variety of purposes, and those essentially religious in character are best considered under another head (page 191). However, since religion and magic penetrated every phase of life, even predominantly secular societies rarely lacked at least a tinge of supernaturalism. Also, in a set of organizations within the same tribe and obviously related to one another, it happened that particular societies had much more of a religious flavor than others. Because of the breakup of tribes into small fragments with the coming of the cold season, associational activity was largely suspended until early spring, when a formal reorganization occurred.

Societies were far more frequently masculine than feminine, but neither from this nor from other phases of life were women so sharply excluded as in Australia or Melanesia. As a matter of fact, women auxiliaries figured even in the military societies. Further, the village tribes of the Upper Missouri had exceedingly important women's organizations (page 113), and the Pawnee had a curious association of single women and widows who displayed obtrusively shabby regalia and tortured prisoners of war. Among the Kiowa a man starting out on a raid was likely to appeal to a body of possibly forty Old Women whom he feasted on his return in gratitude for their prayers. Guilds of skillful tipi cover makers and of expert quill workers are known from the Oglala Dakota.

However, on the whole, men's clubs doubtless loomed larger, and among them the category popularly known as Dog Soldiers, or otherwise as military, police, or age-societies, stands out. None of these designations is adequate, for only a few tribes graded their organizations by age and everywhere the functions tended to be manifold. Since The American Museum of Natural History specialized in a comparative study of these societies, their insignia are well represented in the exhibits, especially those of the Arapaho, Hidatsa, Mandan, Blackfoot, and Crow.

Although Indians originally never reckoned their age by years, five tribes—Mandan, Hidatsa, Blackfoot, Arapaho, Gros Ventre—are known to have had a system of age-societies. This resulted probably from two causes: youngsters, inevitably more or less of the same age, would imitate the activities of their seniors; and among these it was customary to buy the right to a certain set of regalia, dances, and songs, usually linked with privileges of other kinds. The buyers did not join the sellers as members, but displaced them. The sellers, however, remained a fixed group that jointly bought the corresponding emblems and privileges of an older group; and this process was repeated at intervals until the original group of boys had reached the highest existing grade. When they had sold that, they retired from the associational scheme altogether. Virtually if not literally all males of the five tribes entered the system and remained with it until old age. Because the initial gang of youngsters who mimicked their seniors could not vary greatly in age and since they always bought new memberships in a body, fellow members throughout the series continued to be roughly age-mates.

The procedure in these purchases had some quaint features. At least among the Hidatsa and Mandan the younger group was eager to advance and the next older, who were called their "fathers," made the most of their advantage, professing great reluctance to give up their beloved dances, badges, and correlated behavior patterns. Hence the prospective buyers came to the sellers' lodge with a heap of gifts and offered them a pipe, which would be accepted only as a token of agreement to sell. The seniors were likely to declare that this first installment was insufficient; so the buyers scurried around to cadge more property from their relatives. The older men still acted as if doing their juniors

a great favor, but finally smoked the pipe, ordering
the buyers to bring food to feast their "fathers" for
four or more successive evenings. Kinsfolk again
helped the purchasers to collect enough food to sat-
isfy the higher group; then, on the evenings stipu-
lated, the sellers enjoyed their feast and began
teaching the buyers the songs and dances distinctive of the society in question. To some extent the
buyers would participate in the songs and dances
on these occasions. The owner of the lodge would
exhort the "sons" to pay generously for the emblems
they were to receive and to emulate the example of
some distinguished "fathers" as warriors. After the
final evening of instructions, the insignia were
turned over to the new members, and there was a
public procession and dance by them, advertising
the fact that they were henceforth the representatives of the grade just entered.

A smallpox epidemic in 1837 and other disturb-
ances prevented the system from being maintained
in the traditional way, but the collapse revealed its
true basis. In 1910 a Hidatsa ninety years old declared that he was still a member of the societies he
had joined at twenty, twenty-seven, and forty-five
years of age *because he had never had the chance
to sell his memberships.* In other words, for the natives membership in any organization meant merely
ownership gained by purchase—not as in some aboriginal associations elsewhere, where it meant some
particular age or marriage status. Other facts support this conclusion. The associations called, respectively, Kit-foxes or Dogs in any one of the five tribes
with supposed age-societies resemble namesakes in
the other tribes so much that there must have been

a single Kit-fox or Dog prototype for all of them (Plate 17). However, the status of both differed notably in different tribes. The Mandan Kit-foxes comprised only unmarried youths, forming the second of the eight to ten grades; in 1833 the Hidatsa counterpart stood fourth in a series of ten; the Arapaho affixed the name to a preliminary order of boys not as yet properly within the series; but its long extinct Piegan namesake ranked high and was credited with sacred functions. In all Blackfoot lists the Kit-foxes take precedence of the Dogs; yet elsewhere the Dogs definitely rank higher. Among the Arapaho their average age has been estimated at fifty as against eighteen or even twelve for the Kit-foxes; in one Mandan list the Dogs are the seventh, the Kit-foxes only the second society in order of purchase; the corresponding figures among the Hidatsa were six and four in 1833, subsequently, seven and four or even nine and two according to later informants. In short, the same society was not essentially connected with a particular age or matrimonial status, but varied in rank in different tribes, indeed, even in the same tribe at different periods. If a new society, *i.e.*, a new combination of privileges, was created or imported from without, it was naturally assimilated to the existing scheme by the innovating tribe. This automatically altered the sequence it had followed there, but need not have affected the position of the societies anywhere else.

The shifts that occurred during the nineteenth century in a single tribe are brought out by comparing Maximilian's Hidatsa list (1833) with that supplied as correct for the period of his youth by an old informant in 1910:

MAXIMILIAN	BUTTERFLY
1. Stone Hammers	1. Stone Hammers
2. Lumpwoods	2. Kit-foxes
3. Hērerōka (Crow Indians)	3. Lumpwoods
4. Kit-foxes	4. Little Dogs
5. Little Dogs	5. Half-shaved Heads
6. Dogs	6. Enemies (Black Mouths)
7. Half-shaved Heads	7. Crazy Dogs
8. Enemies (Black Mouths)	8. Ravens
9. Bulls	9. Dogs
10. Ravens	10. Bulls

In the course of, say, 30 or 40 years several notable transpositions had evidently taken place, proving that the grading of the societies could vary. This was bound to happen if one society sold its rights to a foreign group, as we know happened within the area.

Societies of similar type, but not graded, loomed large among the Dakota, Assiniboin, Cheyenne, Crow, Pawnee, and Arikara. In much attenuated form they were found among the Southern Siouans, where they were eclipsed by fraternities of a strictly sacred order, and among some marginal tribes such as the Sarsi and the Wind River Shoshone. The Plains Cree had distinctive features, each band having only a single Warrior society into which worthy young men were invited, but which might buy new dances from another band or an alien people. If they had sold their old dance to younger band fellows, the Warriors might have started something like the Mandan scheme, but this did not happen. The one society merely held two sets of insignia and ceremonial privileges.

Typical of the ungraded societies are the Crow and Cheyenne schemes. Membership was voluntary and not dependent on age but, though theoretically coordinate, particular societies might eclipse others at particular periods. Among the Crow the Lumpwoods and the Foxes and among the Cheyenne the Dogs were conspicuously important in historic times. An age-system rather precluded rivalry between societies, but where these ranked as equals competition could and did set in. Thus, the Lumpwoods and the Foxes both tried to outdo each other annually in striking the first blow against an enemy, and the same kind of rivalry obtained between some Dakota societies.

As regards the functions of the military societies of both the graded and the ungraded type, we may distinguish private and public functions. For the individual his society was a club, and at its lodge he would lounge, sleep, eat, dance, sing, and generally have a good time with his fellows. But there were also serious public duties that devolved on either a special society in the series, or on all of the societies, or on one after another. Foremost among such obligations was the policing of the people at crucial times, such as the collective hunt, the march, or the Sun Dance. Each spring the Crow chief would appoint one of the societies to act as police until the tribal breakup in the fall, whereas this task always belonged to the Black Mouths among the Mandan. Further, as the epithet "military" implies, the majority of these organizations fostered the warlike spirit so typical of the area. Songs, always an important feature, constantly stressed the

ideal. Thus, a Kit-fox of the Oglala Dakota would
sing:

> I am a Fox.
> I am supposed to die.
> If there is anything difficult,
> If there is anything dangerous,
> That is mine to do.

But while every man was expected to be brave,
most of the societies chose a few especially valorous
members as officers, distinguished by their regalia,
who were deliberately to flout danger. Thus, the
rank and file of the above-mentioned Oglala organization wore kit-fox skin necklaces, a forehead band
decorated with kit-fox jawbones, and at the back
of the head a bunch of crow tail feathers and two
erect eagle feathers. But in a dance the officers
painted their bodies yellow, and four of them,
carrying lances, were under obligation to lead in
battle and not to retreat. Such lances, straight or
bent at the top, were very common regalia in Plains
organizations, as in the Half-shaved Head society of
the Mandan and in an Arapaho organization (Plate
18).

At an annual reorganization of the military societies in the spring, as well as on some other occasions, they offered public entertainment by march-
ing in procession or performing a dance outdoors.
Maximilian's artist, Carl Bodmer, has caught such
a spectacle presented by the Mandan Bull society
(Plate 19). The rank and file are seen wearing a
piece of a buffalo head with horns, but the officers, pledged never to retreat from an enemy, are
masked by a complete buffalo skull, provided with
eye slits. Spectators, some brandishing or discharg-

ing guns, as do two dancers, are perched on the roof of an earthlodge.

Some of these organizations had virtually or literally no religious features; others were highly charged with them, the Pawnee and the Arapaho societies perhaps most of all. Pawnee social life was largely dominated by their scheme of sacred bundles, and to this they assimilated ten associations exercising the military, social, and recreational activities elsewhere largely or wholly secular. A number of other societies, unconnected with the bundles, nevertheless had a religious basis in that the founder derived his sanction for starting a new club from a supernatural inspiration.

A remarkable trait found as an essential part of behavior in some societies, military or otherwise, is the obligation to say the opposite of what is meant, do the opposite of what is demanded, and generally to act contrary to common sense. Typical is the Heyōka association of the Oglala. As an example Wissler says, "One of their most spectacular feats is that of plunging the arms into boiling water and splashing it about over each other complaining that it is cold."

The village tribes of the Upper Missouri had several women's societies, which followed the pattern of the age-societies as regards collective purchase, but naturally lacked military and constabulary features. The two highest of them were the Goose and the White Buffalo Cow society. The Goose women performed ceremonies in order to make the corn crop prosper and to attract buffalo herds. The White Buffalo Cow women were also called upon to lure buffalo. They wore a feathered headdress of albino buffalo skin in hussar fashion and danced in position, raising each foot alternately higher than the other and waddling from side to side.

Warfare

Plains Indian warfare, compared with the practice of civilized peoples, had many distinctive features. Prolonged wars, standing armies, and officers holding permanent rank were lacking. The objective was never to acquire new lands. Revenge, horse lifting, and the lust for glory were the chief motives and readily blended since a fleeing horse thief might come to kill his pursuer, a raid for revenge might incidentally result in the capture of horses, and honor could be gained in either type of expedition. Though it did happen that major tribal forces were pitted against each other, this rarely happened, the usual military adventure involving only a few warriors. It was considered of the utmost importance that a party return without the loss of a man; deliberately to incur losses for strategic ends was wholly repulsive to Indian ideas.

Strange from our point of view was the mingling of supernaturalism with warfare. Dakota shields were invested with protective power mainly because of the symbolic designs and trimmings on them. A bad omen sufficed to make men give up an intended raid. Only if inspired by a supernatural being did a Crow venture to go on the warpath: the spirit appearing in a dream or vision would specify where the party was to go; how many horses would be driven off; that the prize animal had a docked tail, was painted with zigzag lines, and would serve as mount for a thumbless Cheyenne. Because of his supernatural sanction the leader enjoyed absolute control and theoretically claimed all the loot. In practice he shared it with his companions in accordance with tribal ethics; otherwise he would find himself without a following on his next venture. A man who scored repeated successes as a leader came to be renowned for his war medicine, so that novices would beseech him to give them a replica, entitling them to a share in its blessings, and would pay him large fees for the favor.

The Indians distinguished between a party organized for killing enemies and one for capturing horses, the latter type being the more usual enterprise in historic times. Generally the would-be raiders started on foot, equipped with plenty of moccasins, which might be packed on dogs; and they hoped to return on the backs of stolen horses. Valuable beasts were likely to be tethered to their owners' tent pegs, and it was obviously dangerous to slink into a hostile camp in order to cut loose such an animal; accordingly some tribes attached special merit to the accomplishment of this task.

Chiefs did not always favor such expeditions and might order the police to prevent them on grounds of safety. Hence the organizer and his chum would steal away at night, to be subsequently joined by volunteers. Various details of procedure were widespread in the area. The leader carried his medicine, which supposedly would benumb the enemy at the time of the surprise attack or cause weather that frustrated the pursuit of the raiders. Scouts, carrying wolfskins and howling as they approached their party to report, kicked over a pile of buffalo droppings to symbolize the truth of their statements. When the whole party returned to their tribe, they signaled from a distance, waving blankets according to a code to indicate how they had fared. In case of success they dressed up and paraded round the camp with blackened faces (Plate 20), showing off their scalps and their booty. Scalps were attached to sticks and carried by women dancers to the accompaniment of drumbeats and songs (Plate 21).

Prisoners might be adopted into a tribe, but were often jeered, abused, and even tortured. It was not uncommon, however, to marry a captured woman.

Fortifications were used both for the protection of settlements and to ward off pursuers of horse thieves. The villagers of the Upper Missouri built palisades too high to be easily scaled, put loopholes into the fence, and dug a ditch inside the village. About a century ago a Ponca fort harboring many earthlodges had an embankment over 6 feet in height. Situated on a bluff with a ravine at the rear, it could be entered only from one side and by passing for over 200 yards along the ravine. Approximately contemporary with this fort was a structure 4 feet high which the Omaha erected round their camp on learning of an attack contemplated by the Dakota and Ponca. The embankment was topped with interlaced tipi poles covered as far as possible with tipi covers, through which loopholes were cut; trenches were dug for the women and children.

From infancy a Plains Indian boy had it dinned into his ears that bravery was the path to distinction, that old age was an evil, while it was a fine thing to die young in battle. He would hear famous warriors reciting and perhaps enacting their ex-

ploits on public occasions; he would see such men
honored and likewise drawing material rewards, as
when a great brave outfitted a would-be captain
with part of his medicine or when he named a
newborn child and was paid for his offices. Thus,
every lad was conditioned to emulate the example
of eminent warriors.

In accordance with what was said above, a captain who had never lost a follower rated higher than
one who, however successful otherwise, had failed
in this respect. The emphasis on this point explains
why a small body, even a single resolute brave,
could hold off a force at ridiculous odds, why the
Cree gave up revenge parties after the spread of
firearms.

Scalping was general, but with a marked tribal
difference in attitude. Whereas in the Southeastern
culture area, the capture of a scalp was a primary
aim so that a Creek was a nobody unless he had at
least taken seven scalps, such one-sided emphasis
was lacking in the Plains, where only a few tribes,
such as the Teton and the Cree, set a high value on
scalping. "You will never hear a Crow boast of his
scalps," it is said; a Blackfoot dwelt rather on the
number of horses and guns he had captured; and
elsewhere, with few exceptions, the "coup" proper
greatly overshadowed scalping as a deed of merit.

Often loosely applied to all recognized war
deeds, the term coup (French *coup*, a blow) cor-
rectly designates the touching of an enemy's body
with the hand or with a special stick, striped like
a barber's pole among the Cheyenne. On the same
enemy the Cheyenne permitted three men to
"count coup," the first toucher taking precedence;
the Crow, the Assiniboin, and the Arapaho allowed

four men to score in descending order of merit. Nearly everywhere the coup definitely outranked the killing of a man. "Killing an enemy counts nothing unless his person is touched or struck" (Assiniboin). A man who had killed an enemy from a distance and raced to count coup but was outrun and forestalled by a tribesman had to content himself with the second honor.

As indicated, tribes differed about the exploits worthy of public recital and also as to their relative merit. The Crow systematized their notions, recognizing four categories of exploit: carrying the pipe, *i.e.*, leading a successful party; the genuine coup; the theft of a picketed horse; and the snatching of a bow (or gun) in a hand-to-hand encounter. In order to rank as a "chief," *i.e.*, a distinguished warrior, a man had to have at least one deed of each type to his credit. However, there were some rare exploits, such as rescuing another Crow from imminent death, that rated especially high; and a series of lesser deeds might also be recited as evidence of valor, though not counted toward the chiefly status. Thus, a man did cite his capture of loose horses or his having been wounded in battle. The Iowa recognized three grades, the highest being that of victorious captaincy; next came the killing of a foeman; and the lowest type included as of equal value the coup, the cutting off of a head, scalping, and cutting off a lock of hair.

Some tribes specifically emphasized the element of danger in an exploit: a Cree who had shot an enemy while himself exposed outranked a killer from ambush; to use a club in slaying a man was worthier than to lay him low with firearms. However, many tribes regarded the killing of a woman or a child as a feat entitling to war honors. Altogether the actual sentiments of Plains Indians were a result of the tribal ideologies that impelled a man to defy death and the universal human urge to survive. In consequence, all sorts of contradictions occurred: a man normally tried to get as much glory as possible without risking his neck. There were, of course, sporadic daredevils and likewise men laboring under great grief or disillusionment who deliberately sought death.

Given the exaltation of a splendid war record, men naturally tried to exhibit their brave acts for general admiration. They achieved this end by reciting their deeds at any major gathering, by pictorial representations of them on a tipi cover or robe, and by details of personal decoration. The pictures were predominantly realistic (Figs. 30, 31), showing such episodes as the untethering of picketed horses, the capture of a gun, the seizure of an enemy's shield or bonnet. Sometimes, however, the representations merged into symbolism, as when a horseshoe stood for a horse. In the symbolic ornamentation of costume, styles varied. An Assiniboin who had killed enemies wore an eagle feather for each deed; feather heraldry was highly developed by the Dakota while barely known to the Blackfoot, who made corresponding use of white weasel skins. A Crow coup striker wore wolf tails at the heels of his moccasins, a gun snatcher put ermine skins on his shirt, a captain trimmed his shirt and moccasins with hair.

The introduction of the horse gave a great impetus to raiding, thus multiplying martial enterprises. This means that an economic motive was added that had not previously existed. However,

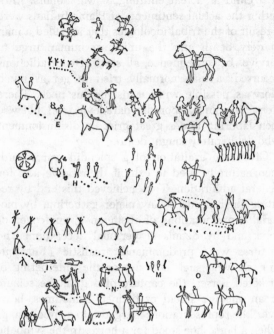

Fig. 30. War episodes as depicted on a tipi cover, Black-foot. A, Bear-chief, afoot, escapes from Assiniboin Indians; B, Double-runner cuts loose from horses; C, he captures a Gros Ventre boy; D, he and a companion kill two Gros Ventre, counting as a coup; F, he takes a gun from a Crow; G, he kills five Flathead; H, a Cree takes shelter in some brush, but Big-nose goes in for him; I, a Cree killed while running off Blackfoot horses; J, Double-runner with medicine-pipe takes a bow from a Gros Ventre and kills him; K, he takes a shield and horse from a Crow and is pursued; M, he kills two Gros Ventre and takes two guns; N, he captures a Gros Ventre woman and a boy; O, he takes four mules.

the strictly economic aspect of this phenomenon should not be exaggerated. The Plains Indians did not require herds of, say, 100 horses in order to supply their material wants. A few pack animals and a few for riding and hunting would have been quite adequate for that purpose. Since, unlike Mongols and Kirghiz, they neither milked mares nor as a rule ate horse flesh, anything beyond that limited number served purely social purposes of ostentation, like the several hundred wives of an African king. A Cree raider derived few direct benefits from his booty, for if he captured ten horses the tribal code would make him give away all but one or two to relatives and friends.

Certainly it is an error to assume that the desire for horses was responsible for the warlike spirit characteristic of the Plains. Apart from the overwhelming evidence for the craving of glory, it is clear that precisely the same eagerness for distinction prompted the tribes of the Southeast and of the western Woodlands, from which the majority of the historic Plains Indians emigrated into their subsequent habitat. In his report on the Indians

Fig. 31. The capture of horses as recorded on a Blackfoot tipi cover.

of the Creek Confederacy, J. R. Swanton says that
Southeastern warfare "was a social institution and
warlike exploits necessary means of social advancement"; its motive was not plunder, but scalping.
Still more to the purpose is what we know about
the tribes of Wisconsin and Illinois in the earlier
days of Caucasian contact. According to W. Vernon
Kinietz' study of the area from 1615 to 1760 "Indian [Miami] warfare was waged primarily for the
glory of the participants. Acquisition of territory
was not a motive, but the acquisition of scalps or
tokens of the bravery and skill of the warriors was
very important to them." And Paul Radin's research
discloses that the Winnebago, linguistically close
to the Omaha branch of the Siouan family, shared
some of the most essential features of Plains militarism: "A man may go on the warpath for two
reasons: either to revenge a slain relative or in a
general way because he thinks he has received
sufficient power and wishes to obtain glory." This
tribe prized the coup and set it above mere killing;
a headdress with a feather denoted a coup striker,
killer, and scalper, while other decorations indicated other deeds conventionally recognized; a captain required spiritual sanction and was held responsible for the death of a follower (also true of
the Illinois); a son was told that "it is good to die in
war"; a warrior was expected to accompany his
comrade on the warpath; oaths were sworn to at-
test the truth of one's military claims, perjury being
punished with death. From Kinietz too, who quotes
from the memoirs of Antoine Denis Raudot, we
learn that in the very beginning of the eighteenth
century the Illinois evidently counted coup with a

stick or rock, thereby gaining the coveted right to claim a captive.

In other words, the typical Plains Indian war complex existed in a nonequestrian culture; and there, as in the Plains, the dominant motives were noneconomic.

Rank, Law, and Government

Aboriginal North American society was in the main democratic, and by and large the Plains Indians conformed to the prevailing pattern. Distinctions of rank occurred, but no *hereditary* classes, and to speak of "castes," as has been done occasionally, is preposterous since there was social mobility, and marriage was not legally restricted to one's own class. All that can be said in this respect is that, as everywhere, the children of distinguished men enjoyed certain advantages. As the son of a Rockefeller or Morgan has a better chance to become a great businessman than has a guttersnipe, so a Cree chief's son was more readily acclaimed as a brave man than an orphan would be. The tendency to stress such hereditary advantages was not uniform, on the whole probably increasing southward. Most of the tribes attached great importance to "incorporeal property"—immaterial privileges corresponding to our patents and copyrights. Naturally the owner of such prerogatives tried to bequeath them to his descendants, an urge that would foster the germ of hereditary privilege. Where specific public functions belonged to a particular clan, it might be regarded as socially superior, but since even the chiefly office implied little power, the practical significance of this phenomenon was slight. The essential point is that in the Indian's view a person of lowly origin could by supernatural favor gain wealth and standing; inevitably a boy with rich or eminent parents and many kinsmen had a better chance than an orphan. Characteristically, the worst Crow insult was to tell a man that he had no relatives, for it meant that he was a social nobody subject to abuse. To a spirited lad this taunt, however, was a challenge: he could court spiritual blessings, distinguish himself in fighting, gain wealth, and ultimately shame his detractors. The situation was utterly different from that of the Hindu or Tahitian social scheme that condemned the majority to an obscure social role.

A most important difference between the Plains Indians and Tahitians concerns material property. Whereas in Tahiti a monarch could appropriate the possessions of a lesser man, on the Plains any comparable act was unthinkable. On the contrary, a great man could maintain his status best by lavish generosity to the poor. Such liberality, next to a fine war record, was the basis for high standing. The Oglala had a society of chiefs enjoying superior prestige, but when a novice was admitted, he was urged to look after the poor, especially the widows and orphans. Among the Blackfoot a man aspiring to become a leader tried to outshine his competitors by his feasts and presents even at the cost of impoverishment, but not without thereby gaining the coveted status of a headman. J. O. Dorsey, in his study of the sociology of the Omaha, writes that the Omaha recognized two classes of meritorious tribesmen—"such as had given to the poor on many occasions, and had invited guests to many feasts," and those who, in addition, "had killed several of the foe and had brought home many horses." Rank is in fact so largely dependent on the military code that it has to some extent been considered under the head of Warfare.

As hinted above, the Plains Indian "chief" was by no means an autocrat. Autocratic chiefs did indeed exist in the Atlantic and Gulf regions, but not in our area, where the title was honorific and implied little authority for the bearer, though an exceptionally powerful personality could exert great influence. As a rule, the chiefs were titular, and any power exercised within the tribe was exercised by the total body of responsible men who had qualified for social eminence by their war record and their generosity. Until 1880 the Omaha had two principal chiefs, but they never made vital decisions without consulting the lesser titular chiefs, i.e., without regard to public opinion. Coercive authority was exercised only indirectly through appointment of police for the hunt; when a quarrel occurred within the tribe, the chiefs did not quell the disturbance by force, but put sacred pipes between the combatants, "begging them to desist." This latter situation may be taken as typical of the area: in normal times the chief was not a supreme executive, but a peacemaker and an orator. So far as essentials go, it is therefore of no significance whether there was one chief, or a pair of chiefs or, as among the Cheyenne, a council of forty-four in a population of about 4,000, nor whether a man by virtue of his lineage could or could not ever qualify for the title of chief.

Nevertheless germs of governmental power existed in connection with special occasions. Especially during the collective hunt or a major festival a police force might exercise coercive authority.

Whereas normally the greatest chief would not dare lay hands on the meanest tribesman, the police appointed by him or, at some festivals, by the priest (page 179) did have the power to restrain a recalcitrant individual. The time of a great buffalo hunt, above all, required careful obedience to the leader's instructions lest the whole people suffer; hence the police would issue orders that no one must hunt by himself and thereby prematurely startle the herd. The Cheyenne police, more lenient than that of other tribes, nevertheless whipped even eminent offenders; among the Omaha, too, a highly esteemed man was once flogged so violently that he never fully recovered. Elsewhere the criminal's tipi might be destroyed and his goods confiscated; in extreme cases, if he resisted, he might be killed.

Such germs of strict government, however, never developed into a permanent oligarchy or monarchy because the spirit of Plains culture militated against it, as did also the splitting up of most tribes during a large part of the year.

Nevertheless, even apart from police activity, there were definite legal conceptions, though no courts in our sense. Sometimes religious ideas affected the attitude toward an undesirable action. Thus, the Cheyenne regarded murder of a tribesman as a sin and a crime; it polluted the Sacred Arrows, their holy of holies, and called for the penalty of possibly ten years' exile at the order of the forty-four councilors. But for the Crow a murder was a purely secular misdeed, though highly regrettable, since it might precipitate a feud between the clans involved. The camp chief and the police took cognizance, not as a punishing agency but as appeasers, trying to reconcile the parties by making the murderer's kin pay a substantial indemnity to the aggrieved family.

Crow and Cheyenne shared a form of oath or ordeal. If one Crow disputed another's claim to a meritorious war exploit, each contestant would take a knife, point it toward the Sun, and invoke the god to smite him with misfortune unless he spoke the truth. If one of the litigants soon after suffered death or misfortune, he was regarded as the perjurer.

A deterrent from reprehensible actions lay in the tremendous power of public opinion. The Indians were extremely sensitive to gossip that might affect their social standing. According to Clark Wissler, a Blackfoot who had made himself a nuisance would be "held up to general ridicule amid shrieks of laughter," and the mortification of the victim sometimes drove him into exile or upon the warpath. The Crow and Hidatsa recognized a definite relationship for exercising discipline of this order. It obtained between persons of either sex whose fathers were of the same clan. These "joking relatives" teased each other like certain true relatives by blood or marriage (page 86) but also had the serious duty of publicly upbraiding each other for deviations from proper conduct. A man thus exposed and jeered at for cowardice would feel like sinking into the ground with shame.

Trade; Economic Values

Within a particular local group there was little trading, for the necessities of life were freely shared and the crafts described elsewhere were not plied by professionals who devoted themselves exclusively to their practice. Nevertheless, some individuals excelled as bowyers, arrow makers, and skin dressers, and such persons were not as a rule inclined to exercise their skill gratuitously on behalf of unrelated tribesmen. If one of them did place his services at a stranger's disposal, the beneficiary understood that some compensation was expected. Good arrow makers were at least likely to be adequately feasted by prospective customers. With the development of equestrian life, the horse became a convenient unit of value; at an earlier period good arrows seem to have served the purpose, ten of them being subsequently reckoned the equivalent of a horse among the Crow.

Although reciprocal obligations were recognized, altruistic behavior was imposed in certain situations. A Blackfoot or Crow stumbling on a fellow tribesman butchering was sure to receive an ample portion of meat. Any self-respecting man gave presents to the poor, and no one could hope to rise to the position of a headman who failed to live up to his people's ideal of generosity.

The economic ideas attached to ceremonial privileges belong to a distinct category. Anything falling under this head commanded, from our point of view, exorbitant prices. Even the right to paint a simple design on one's face during a religious ritual might be worth a horse; and for so much as looking at the contents of a medicine bundle a man might have to pay the equivalent of $100. One Crow bought the prerogative of preparing a blanket, the modern substitute for a skin robe, as described in the seller's vision for a horse valued at $62; in addition the purchaser had to hire a draftsman to do the painting and to buy the proper feather trim-

mings. Another Crow paid ten horses to his sponsor
in the Tobacco organization, and the novice's kin
supplemented the fee with twenty-three more. Further, often even the closest kinship did not absolve
the buyer of a privilege from making the usual
payment. Thus, Hidatsa children inherited from a
father who owned a medicine bundle merely the
prerogative of buying it from him.

Why were people willing to give up valuable
property in return for ceremonial privileges that
seem to us quite worthless? To illustrate by Blackfoot data, the ownership of a bundle was supposed
to ensure long life, success, happiness; in consequence, it also brought social prestige. To buy a
bundle was a safe investment, for it was readily
negotiable and the new buyer was under pressure
of public opinion to offer at least the price exacted
at one time from the seller. Apart from this, a one-
time owner received perquisites in the form of fees
whenever those conducting the pertinent ritual
called upon him to participate because of his familiarity with the procedure. "While with us young
men are exhorted to open a savings account, among
the Blackfoot they are advised to become owners
of medicine bundles" (Wissler).

Intertribal trade cannot be sharply separated
from that between Indians and Whites. There was
doubtless a fair amount of exchange of native commodities, as when visiting Crow Indians bartered
fine robes against the corn grown on the Upper
Missouri. Farther south, the corresponding phenomenon was observed by Coronado in 1541. But
during the historic period the goods passed from
one local group to another were largely those obtained from Whites. Broadly speaking, horses came

from the Spanish settlements (page 42), hence first reached the southern Plains, while guns (as well as other wares) came mainly from the British and French in the northeast. This explains why, when the Cheyenne and the Kiowa-Comanche met amicably in 1840, the latter deprecated gifts of horses, of which they had plenty, but readily exchanged their surplus for guns, blankets, beads, calico, and metal kettles. Considerable relaying developed: in about 1820 the Arapaho are reported as holding "a kind of fair" on a tributary of the Platte, obtaining British goods from the Cheyenne, who in turn had got them from the Mandan.

The effects of White trade were far-reaching, as has already been pointed out in several connections. The acquisition of guns enabled the Cree to crowd out their western neighbors and helped to turn them from a Woodland into a rather typical Plains people. Quite generally, the Indians were for the first time tempted by fur traders to kill game for gain. They adopted totally new foods and stimulants—bread, sugar, coffee, spirituous liquor. Metal utensils superseded earthenware and wooden ones, strike-a-lights proved easier means of getting fire than the drill, cloth was made into clothing with less labor than skins, steel knives cut better than flint. Thus a large portion of aboriginal culture became obsolescent, fragments being retained only for ceremonial occasions.

4 RECREATION

The Plains Indians had a relatively wide range of amusements, including games, dances, attendance at major festivals, and storytelling.

Games

Children often played in imitation of their elders. Little girls would put up miniature tipis, and young boys would bring them rabbits or other food as though they were adult men returning from the hunt. Boys also imitated the performances of the military clubs and indulged in all sorts of pranks, including the snatching of meat from the racks set up in camp and then dashing off to a safe distance for a leisurely feast. In the winter, Dakota and Crow boys spun conical tops by whipping them on the ice. Adolescents and mature young people were allowed to go with their sweethearts berrypicking or bringing in the requisites for a major ceremony.

Adults were addicted to games of chance, at which a man might gamble away all his property —if legends are to be believed, even his wife and his own body. Conspicuous among most tribes were dice and the equivalent of our "Button, button, who's got the button?" Both extended far beyond the Plains area; in his report published by the Bureau of American Ethnology in 1907 Stewart

Culin found dice among 130 and the "button" game among 81 North American peoples.

The dice used were not cubical in shape, but sticks with different faces, plum stones, little pieces of bone, or similar objects (Fig. 32). One form of Pawnee dice sets consisted of cane slips. One cane was painted red on the concave side and had an incised line painted red on the convex side; the second was blue on the concave side and had featherlike marks on the reverse; and so forth. But instead of throwing sticks, Pawnee women might toss three large and three small plum stones from a flat twined basket. The smaller stones were burnt black on one side; the large ones, plain on one side, were marked with a curved band and seven dots on the other. The player held her basket near the ground, tossed the stones into the air, and moved the basket smartly against the ground, catching the stones in it. Tallies rested between opposing parties, and each woman laid bets against her vis-à-vis. Crow women also used either sticks or plum stones (or bone equivalents). Every combination of throws scored according to a definite system that seems arbitrary to the outsider. For example, the Blackfoot called one bone with thirteen pits the "chief," and this piece turning up with three blanks counted six points. A player continued so long as she scored; and in order to win, one side had to get all the tallies.

The "button" or hand game was played with pairs of small objects, one of them marked, say, by a string round the middle, the other plain; usually the guesser had to guess the hand holding the un-marked object. In case of more than two players, each bet against his vis-à-vis. The Blackfoot reck-

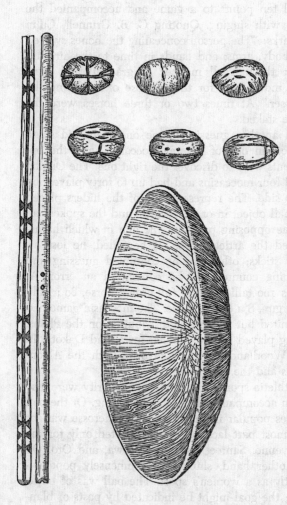

Fig. 32. Stick dice, decorated plum-stone dice, and a wooden bowl, all used in Crow games of chance. The stick dice is about 9 inches long, decorated on both sides with designs that were burned in; one side is flat, the other rounded.

oned ten points to a game and accompanied the play with singing. Quoting G. B. Grinnell, Culin remarks: "The person concealing the bones swayed his body, arms, and hands in time to the air, and went through all manner of graceful and intricate movements for the purpose of confusing the guesser." At times two or three horses were the prize staked.

In another guessing game one team hid small objects in one of several moccasins, and the opponents were to discover the right one. The Omaha used four moccasins and had up to forty players on each side. The representative of the hiders placed a small object in one moccasin, and the spokesman of the opposing party hit the one in which he assumed the article to be. If he failed, he lost his tally sticks; otherwise he continued guessing and winning counters till he committed an error. At times 100 tallies won a full-grown horse, 60 a colt, 10 a gun, 8 a buffalo robe. The moccasin game had a limited but suggestive distribution on the Plains, being played by the Omaha, Iowa, and Dakota. In the Woodlands it was a favorite with the Algonkians and the Winnebago.

Athletic sports and games of dexterity were also often accompanied by heavy gambling. Of the ball games popular in the Woodlands, lacrosse was for the most part lacking, being reported only for the Cheyenne, Santee, Assiniboin, Iowa, and Oto. On the other hand, shinny was immensely popular— mostly as a women's sport. The ball was of buckskin; the goal might be indicated by posts or blankets or terminal lines. The Omaha field was about three hundred yards in extent, and the moieties might be pitted against each other, while the Crow sometimes had men play against women. A game with two balls joined was played by Cheyenne, Cree (Plate 22), Arikara, Pawnee, Santee, and Omaha women. The hoop-and-pole game, an exclusively masculine sport, was widely distributed. The players, generally two in number, rolled a hoop, either netted or plain, on a level course and threw darts at it, the precise way of striking the hoop or a portion of the net determining the count. The Pawnee used either a plain rawhide ring 4 to

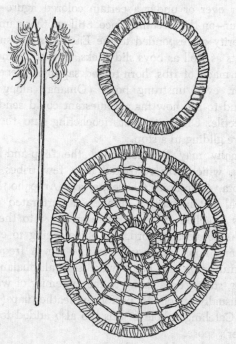

Fig. 33. Ring, hoop, and dart for the Crow hoop-and-pole game (see also Plate 23).

6 inches in diameter, to be pierced by a hooked dart, or a netted hoop up to 25 inches in diameter; they sometimes played the game as a magical performance for calling buffalo. As well as using a hoop the Hidatsa rolled small stone disks; the Comanche hoop, except for its smaller size, exactly resembles the Crow form (Fig. 33). Variations occurred tribally in the darts, which might be arrows, forked saplings, hooked sticks, or long poles. The Arapaho sticks were tied and thrown in pairs, the aim being to hit the hoop so that both sticks were either over or under a certain colored figure—one of four—on the circumference. Still another game of dexterity corresponded to the Eastern snow snake. Adults as well as boys slid sticks, arrows, feathered darts made of ribs, horn-tipped saplings, pieces of antler, even unstrung bows (Omaha) along the ground to see how far a contestant could send his projectile. Often it went ricocheting into the air before gliding to a stop.

Finally may be mentioned the "cup-and-ball" game, which was restricted to a few tribes, the Dakota, Assiniboin, Cheyenne, and Arapaho. In a typical Teton outfit a number of perforated deer hoofs attached to a pin were swung into the air by the connecting cord, the object being to catch as many hoofs as possible on the pin. A frequent substitute for the hoofs were several phalangeal bones, strung on a thong to the extremity of which was usually attached a perforated leather flap (Fig. 34). Catching a hole in this tab also added to the player's score.

Archery contests and foot and horse races figured among other forms of diversion. The public part

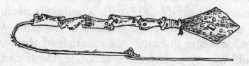

Fig. 34. Assiniboin cup-and-ball game.

of important ceremonials provided a great spectacle for the people at large and may be regarded as the equivalent of our theatrical shows. The "dances" during such religious festivals, however, generally were unimpressive and required a minimum of physical effort, such as alternately raising one's feet on tiptoes while standing still or alternately advancing the clenched fists while in position. An exception must be made on behalf of war dances and those associated with some military societies (Plate 18), which were executed with great vigor. Dances of men with women, though not unknown, did not represent an important or typical form of entertainment. Probably the commonest form was to have a group of men and women in alternation form a ring, each man putting his right arm around his partner's shoulders and both shuffling their feet slowly to the left, the entire group describing a circle.

Storytelling

Folk tales were told of a winter evening when the people had stretched out to rest for the night. A Crow narrator expected to get a periodic response from his auditors, failing which he assumed that they had fallen asleep and would stop talking.

Folk tales cannot always be distinguished from sacred myths; and we must remember that what seems obviously fraught with a religious meaning did not necessarily strike Indians in the same way. Thus, in many instances the creation of the world is told merely as any other folk tale. On the other hand, in certain tribes, such as the Blackfoot and the Hidatsa, the owners of medicine bundles often explained the origins of these sacred objects as the climax of a generally known story. There would thus be both an esoteric and a popular version, the former known only to the handful of bundle owners and differing mainly by its infinite dullness since the narrator was likely to graft on the plot a circumstantial statement of all the ceremonial details impressed on the original bundle owner by his spirit protector.

From a literary point of view the stories of the Plains show much greater affinity with the Woodlands than with the Basin Area. The Basin has a preponderance of tales revolving about the deeds and adventures of animals and a minimum of novelettes with distinctly human heroes, such as are very common in the Plains and the Woodlands. Of course, the animals of the Basin speak and act like human beings, and in view of the religious notions of the Plains tribes animal helpers automatically turn up in the novelettes, but they remain as a rule secondary characters.

A feature the Plains share with many other regions is the conception, though not so explicitly brought out by some tribes as by others, of a mythical era in which things were different from what they are now. The people at one time had to eat their food raw because fire was hoarded by some mean character, from whom some cunning Indian managed to steal it for the good of his fellows. Hunting was once unnecessary, for all the game animals were impounded in a corral where they could easily be shot at will. The ancestors of the race were not liable to death. The seasons were different from what they have been in recent times; the mole had good eyesight; the crow used to be white. The relevant myths explain what happenings led to the present state of the universe and man. Usually some one character of ancient times brings about many of the changes in question and may therefore be called a "transformer." Often the same person also teaches the ancestral Indians how to impound buffalo, chip arrowpoints, perform a victory dance, and so forth, in which case the transformer is at the same time his people's "culture hero." In Crow myth Old Man Coyote appears when the entire world is still covered with water and summons water birds to dive for mud from the depths. Three of the birds fail, the fourth fetches a little mud, from which Old Man Coyote molds the earth. Later he creates mankind, bids them multiply, and instructs them.

To us it seems paradoxical that the transformer and culture hero who is so definitely represented as a benefactor also frequently appears in the contradictory role of a "trickster." Thus, Old Man Coyote is forever greedily seeking food and resorts to all sorts of low wiles to gain his ends, *e.g.*, simulating friendship for a buffalo, whom he then lures to leap down a cutbank. He even covets his own daughter and in order to be able to marry her feigns death and returns in disguise to woo her, thus flouting the very strict Indian rules of incest. Even when he does not outrage custom, he is likely to play an undignified part, being outwitted by other characters or beaten in trials of strength. The inconsistency of these traits—creative power and impotence, philanthropy and unscrupulousness, establishment of social rules and deliberate flouting of them—does not seem to have disturbed the Indians.

Another frequent mythical conception is that of man-destroying monsters whom some conquering hero killed for the benefit of man. The Crow tell a long story about Old Woman's Grandchild, the offspring of the Sun and a Hidatsa woman. He tames a ferocious bear, allows himself to be sucked in by a huge buffalo that used to swallow Indians, in order to stab the beast, chops off the heads of snakes accustomed to crawl into human bodies, and so forth. Ultimately he ascends to the sky to turn into a star. Similar feats are often ascribed to twins.

Boy heroes are common in Plains stories of later times too. A favorite theme worked out in harmony with the ideology of the area is the rise to fame and fortune of a poor orphan who has been pitied by some supernatural being. Another popular subject is that of a proud beauty who spurns all suitors, only to fall prey to a Bluebeard from whose clutches she is rescued with difficulty. If the haughty maiden has insulted her admirer, he may seek a vision and obtain such power from an elk spirit that women become infatuated with him, so that he is now able to turn the tables on the girl who humiliated him.

Some highly specific motifs in these traditions have an amazing distribution far beyond our area. The conception of a primeval ocean and earth divers was found among Algonkian tribes on the Atlantic Coast in the early seventeenth century and was sometimes interpreted as a distorted fragment of the Biblical deluge story; it has been reported from California, Siberia, and even eastern Europe. Again, there is a frequent North American idea of a perennial conflict between the Thunderbird and a water dragon; in the Plains version the monster regularly rises from a lake to destroy his enemy's fledglings while the parents are gone. At last the distressed father seeks the aid of a skillful Indian hunter, who kills the dragon by throwing red-hot rocks into his mouth. The generic notion of conflicting air and water powers extends at least from Dakota to British Columbia. Several Plains episodes or conceptions have been reported from South America. A Cree story of an adulterous wife killed by her husband embodies the notion that her skull rolls after him and her children. This curious idea of a rolling skull occurs as far south as the Gran Chaco. The Assiniboin tell of a hunter who whittles one of his legs to a point and with it tries to impale his companion, and this odd conceit is likewise found in British Guiana. More amazing still, the trickster simulating death in order to attain an incestuous union with his daughters turns up in Tierra del Fuego, among the Ona and the Yahgan, the southernmost natives of the New World.

Where parallels are so specific and intrinsically strange, it is difficult to suppose that the motifs were independently invented. We may assume that early migrant tribes carried part of the ancient American lore with them as they traveled south. Theoretically, one might of course also guess that these details were diffused in comparatively late times, but this hypothesis suffers from the fact that the intervening territories have not so far yielded any evidence of the features in question.

A Plains Indian raconteur was not limited to the traditional body of fiction. He could also narrate ever-interesting tales of actual warfare or hunting adventures or, if he had a streak of the comedian, get up a topical story showing some well-known tribesman in a ridiculous light.

Clowns

Clownish behavior sometimes blended with serious and even sacred observances, as when those so instructed in a vision did the reverse of what they were asked by their tribesmen, pretended to freeze in the sweltering summer heat or to be overcome with the temperature on an icy winter day. But on some festive occasions buffoons might appear for the sheer purpose of amusing the crowds—dressed in the shabbiest of clothes, riding a miserable pony, and disporting themselves in the most absurd and at times most obscene fashion.

All in all, the natives evidently enjoyed a respectable number of entertainments and attached considerable importance to them.

5 ART

Among the Plains Indians, stone sculpture was absent and wood carving as a craft too little developed to foster artistry, as demonstrated by some ceremonial objects (Figs. 35, 36). On the other hand, there was a good deal of painting and of decorative art in quills and later in beadwork.

Painting on Skins

Painting was executed on buffalo robes, tipi covers, parfleches, and other hide or skin objects. The colors were derived largely from iron-containing clays, which yielded brown, red, and yellow, while a black earth or charcoal provided black. The aboriginal use of green and blue, though contested, seems established. Paints were pulverized in stone

Fig. 35. A ceremonial carving carried by an officer of the Crow Lumpwood Society (about 2 feet high).

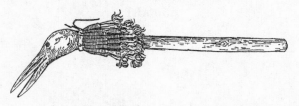

Fig. 36. A ceremonial carving surmounted by a crane head, used in the Crow Hot Dance (about 2 feet high).

mortars and mixed with a gluey material that made the colors stick. The artist, in action, held the paints in hollow stones, shells, or sherds. Brushes, one for each color, were of bone, horn, or wood; later a tuft of antelope hair was mounted on a stick. The Hidatsa first pressed the designs into the hide, then applied the paint over them, and finally set the paint with the glue. The glue outlined the patterns and could be used without colors on parts of a hide. The hide to be decorated was extended on the ground, the artist crouching over it, sometimes aided by a colleague, especially in pictographic work.

In general, geometric designs were done by the women, realistic forms by men; the two styles were very rarely combined on one "canvas."

The geometrical patterns on robes fall into a small number of categories, of which two are especially prominent among the Dakota. The women's robe typically shows a frame around an oblong field that encloses many minor figures and is in a characteristic position above the center (lower illustration on page 146). The characteristic men's robe bears the "black warbonnet" pattern, *i.e.*, concentric

circles with numerous small radiating figures each
composed of two isosceles triangles and designated
by the Indians as "feathers" (illustration this page).
Widely distributed, but common only among the
Comanche and their neighbors, seems to have been
a frame with a central hourglass pattern enclosing
minor designs (top illustration on page 146). Red is
the dominant color in the geometrically decorated
specimens, but yellow and blue are also very
popular.

Pictography might be regarded as a means of
communication rather than as an expression of the
artistic urge. It is certain that the realistic pictures
on robes or tipi covers drawn by the Indians served

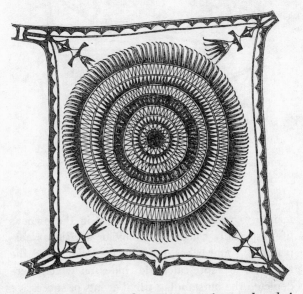

*Fig. 37.   Three examples of patterns often used on buf-
falo robes are shown on this and the following page.*

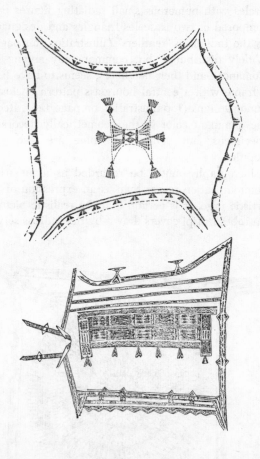

mainly to record significant events in the owner's
life, especially a martial exploit or a visionary experience; some tribes, notably the Dakota and the
Kiowa, also kept "calendric" hides on which were
depicted the outstanding tribal events of successive
years. Nevertheless all these representations can be

viewed likewise from an aesthetic point of view. As hides became scarce, materials introduced by Whites were used. Even sacred events were recorded on cloth, and historic occurrences were sometimes depicted in notebooks with crayons furnished by the trader.

As for theme, the robes preponderantly represent scenes of battle and raiding. As John C. Ewers notes, in his book *Plains Indian Painting*, human and equine figures are by far most common, jointly appearing in 90 per cent of the specimens examined; even the buffalo is rare, the dog completely lacking. Perspective was absent; figures, both human and animal, generally appeared in profile; and though there was composition in the portrayal of hand-to-hand encounters of the looting of an enemy's horses, there was hardly any attempt to coordinate all the scenes of a hide into a unified painting. Individual figures are variously represented: hoofs may be either realistically drawn or provided with a hook; human legs and arms may be lifelike or merely suggested by straight lines; the head is often merely outlined, in other cases only an eye and the nose are indicated; manes may be omitted or emphasized; figures are either in solid color or merely in contour. Notwithstanding technical deficiencies a fair number of pictographs display an estimable dynamic quality.

We do not know how far back into the past Plains pictography extends. The fact that horses are so frequent on Museum specimens does not prove the art modern, for shields and their buckskin covers show a variety of animals—buffalo, deer, eagles—which could well have been drawn in precontact days (Fig. 28). That skins were painted in the southern Plains in 1540 appears from a letter by

Coronado, though he is reporting on hearsay and
does not state whether the decoration was realistic.
The oldest known piece, now in the Peabody Museum at Harvard University, was collected by
Lewis and Clark among the Mandan in 1805 and
is supposed to represent a battle that took place
in 1797 (Plate 24). Though many horses appear
on this robe, the prevalent weapons shown are
bows, spears, and shields. An interesting early robe,
donated to the Historical Museum in Bern in 1838
as a Crow robe, may also be of Mandan origin.

Occasionally a scene normally painted was imitated in quillwork (Plate 25).

Rawhide Decoration

In the decoration of their parfleches the Plains Indians achieved a distinctive style. Though the simplest geometric forms—straight lines, triangles, rectangles, diamonds—predominate, they are arranged
in a variety of combinations, some of which charac-
terize subdivisions of the area. The overwhelming
number of specimens housed in museums are
painted, but according to Dakota informants the
patterns were originally incised, *i.e.*, an artist
would scrape away portions of the pigmented layer
of the buffalo skin, leaving sections of lighter or
darker shading. Whatever may be the relative antiquity of the two procedures, incising was certainly
practiced at one time, for two Crow samples are to
be seen in the Chicago Museum of Natural History
along with a few Eastern Dakota and Blackfoot
specimens.

The two main parfleche flaps are symmetrically
decorated; in addition, the northwestern tribes—
Sarsi, Blackfoot, Crow, Assiniboin, Dakota, and the

marginal Nez Percé and Kutenai—decorate the side flaps, though with less care. Straight lines preponderate, but curves crop up among several northwestern peoples, most of all among the Blackfoot. The Crow stand out for the precision of their lines, the Wind River Shoshone and Southern Ute coming next.

The decorative area is mostly oblong, but the northwestern tribes again show distinctiveness in substituting a trapezoid for the rectangle, this being always the case among the Sarsi and Kutenai, frequently among the Blackfoot and Assiniboin, occasionally elsewhere. Some tribes enclose the decorative field in a frame, which others completely lack.

A very common trait is a central stripe that extends through the middle of the flap and either forms the basis of a large central figure (Fig. 38) or divides the field into two symmetrical panels. Although there has doubtless been a great deal of trading back and forth in recent times, some patterns remain absent or rare in certain tribes and common in others. The Crow, for example, are fond of vertically unbisected large diamonds in the cen-

Fig. 38. Designs painted on parfleches: left, Crow; center, Cheyenne; right, Hidatsa.

ter, while favoring neither the clear-cut two-panel
system nor the slender figures that often seem to
divide the decorative field of the Arapaho or Cheyenne into five as against the three longitudinal
units of the Crow. A framed central rectangle and
a central hourglass figure are also common among
the Crow. Details are at times continuously distributed, proving historical connection. Thus, the
Crow and the Wind River Shoshone place solidly
colored rectangles in the four corners of the field;
less frequently this feature appears among the Nez
Percé, Gros Ventre, and Dakota.

Altogether the northwestern tribes show marked
similarities of treatment, and there is also a strong
resemblance between the Crow and Shoshone
styles. On the other hand, despite the affinity of

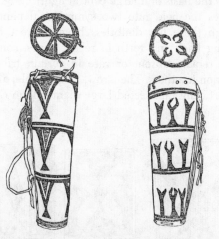

Fig. 39. *Two painted rawhide cases used for ritual objects by the Arapaho. The design on the cover of the case
is also shown.*

Crow and Hidatsa in other respects, their parfleches
reveal no specially close relationship.

Rawhide containers other than parfleches, such
as the envelopelike square cases with a flap (Fig.
23), resemble the parfleches in ornamentation. This
applies in part even to the cylindrical medicine
bags; but since the shape of these objects modifies
the visible decorative field, deviations may be expected to occur both on the main body and the
cover. This certainly holds for Arapaho specimens,
on which inverted tents and distinctive fishtail-like
and stemmed crescent designs figure prominently
(Fig. 39).

Embroidery

Since a draftsman enjoys far greater freedom than
an embroiderer, we should expect a much wider
range of decorative designs on rawhide containers
and on nonpictographically ornamented robes than
in quillwork and bead embroidery. Actually the reverse holds, the embroidered patterns being very
diverse and sometimes markedly complex; a craftswoman might even succeed in quilling bird forms,
horses, and mounted braves in full regalia (Plate
25). Elaboration, however, was a comparatively
late development.

A chronological study by Frederic H. Douglas,
based on early reports and drawings as well as on
authentically early museum specimens, affords the
following as the probable sequence of events. In
the quillwork that unquestionably preceded beadwork, angular geometric designs predominated;
floral patterns in the Plains were either intrusions
from the Woodlands or, later still, due to French
influence. This angular style, based on triangles,

rectangles, and their combinations, is to be correlated with the prevalent "two-thread" technique
(see page 71), but since "one-thread" sewing was
not wholly lacking, some curvilinear effects were
achieved, notably in the production of rosettes.

Bead embroidery hardly developed on the Plains
prior to 1835–1840, when White traders began to
introduce large china and glass beads on a considerable scale. The early beads, most commonly white
and sky blue, are about ⅛ inch in diameter, nearly
double the size of the beads brought in from about
1850 and thereafter. Again, the dominant technique
employed, "lazy-stitch" sewing, affected the style,
largely excluding curvilinear patterns. The figures
worked out in this period seem to have been shared
throughout most of the area; they include equi-
lateral and isosceles triangles, generally resting on
or hanging from a transverse stripe; chains of right-
angled triangles; bars and oblongs; and series of
concentric oblongs. The impression conveyed is one
of massiveness. Characteristic of this earlier period
is the general smallness of the beaded areas, even
6-inch bands being infrequent. In a study of the
influence exerted by quilled decoration on its successor, this earlier beadwork style would obviously
be of crucial importance.

The modern style set in with the availability of
much smaller beads, whose precise character indicates the age of the decorated pieces, and came to
fruition from 1880 to 1900. Tribal differences, both
technological and stylistical, asserted themselves in
this later period. The Dakota, Cheyenne, and Arapaho adhered to the lazy stitch; the Blackfoot, Sarsi,
Plains Cree, and Flathead made exclusive use of the
overlay; the Crow, Assiniboin, Gros Ventre, and

Plains Shoshoneans employed both techniques. In the south, where beadwork was used only for trimming, the lazy stitch was in vogue among the Pawnee, whereas the Omaha preferred the overlay.

In the ornamentation of long, narrow strips, say, on men's leggings, the style is rather uniform throughout the area. The forms that appear comprise almost exclusively solid triangles or hourglasses, characteristically stepped, circles, crosses, and rectangles. Though eclipsed by later elaborations, these elements, which are proved by photographs to have been the commonest everywhere in the area during the 1870s (Douglas), persisted into the most recent times.

Apart from the widespread features just listed, subareal differences evolved. We may distinguish a northwestern style typical of the Blackfoot, Sarsi, Plains Cree, and Flathead. Hundreds of little oblongs or squares are united to form large patterns, usually of a single color with borders of varicolored squares. The figures include stepped triangles, squares, diamonds, crosses, oblique wide bands with stepped long sides. The style is markedly simple and restricted as compared with that of other subareas and bears "the closest affinity of any of the Plains to that seen in porcupine quillwork" (Douglas). Highly characteristic of Blackfoot moccasins is the U-shaped figure on the instep, often associated with subsidiary designs. This decoration was the most fashionable on Crow moccasins in the second decade of the present century (Fig. 40); on the other hand, it is completely lacking in the large collections from the Arapaho and Gros Ventre to be found at The American Museum of Natural History.

The embroidery of the Crow and Shoshone sug-

gests definite affinity with parfleche decoration; nor
is the relationship confined to these two tribes.
There may be something in the Dakota theory that
painting preceded even quillwork and that before
manipulating quills the Indian women painted moccasins with conventional patterns. Taking the area
as a unit, we find in both embroidered and painted
compositions the same arrangement of hourglasses,
diamonds, and triangles. Thus, the Hidatsa parfleche (Fig. 38) shows essentially the same central
figure as some Dakota pipe pouches. Generally
speaking, the Crow-Shoshone style seems to be
more massive than that of most other tribes; large
triangles and their combinations, hourglasses and

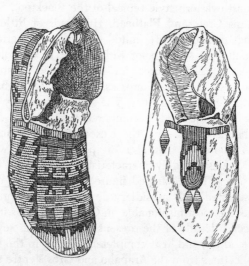

Fig. 40. The difference in moccasin designs is shown
here in examples from the Arapaho (left) and the Crow
(right).

lozenges, are characteristic; a vertical chain of them often has one triangle balanced on a transverse stripe resting on the apex of another.

As might be expected from their geographical position, the Crow share design features not only with the Blackfoot, but also with the Dakota, Arapaho, and Cheyenne. By and large, the efflorescence of bead embroidery can be best illustrated by Dakota and Arapaho specimens. To take only moccasin decoration, the poverty of the Blackfoot with their ever-recurring U motif contrasts with the profusion of designs among the two tribes mentioned (Fig. 40, Plate 26). The Dakota have names for the most popular of their design elements (Fig. 41), though not for the major compositions they build up from them. Typical of these latter are the patterns on pipe and tobacco bags, which have been called the culmination of Dakota decorative design (Plate 27). Dakota and Arapaho decorations generally impress one as comparatively light rather than massive. Both favor a small central diamond with symmetrical appendages, say, of "forked trees" (Fig. 41). The Dakota usually have these additions on all four corners of the diamond, while the Arapaho as a rule content themselves with a single pair; the former are also more inclined to insert crosses and stars by way of varying the background.

Scholars have shown that some of the simpler embroidered designs extend beyond our area; thus, the isosceles triangle enclosing the rectangle, often conceived on the Plains as a tipi with its door, crops up likewise in Pueblo territory. That there is a historical connection involved seems likely, but we

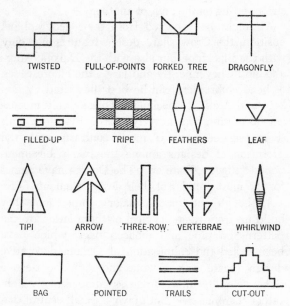

Fig. 41. Conventional design elements and their interpretation from the Dakota.

cannot be sure in what direction this motif and others spread.

Designs and Symbolism

Plains Indian art sheds light on an important problem. Among the design units of the Dakota there is one called "dragonfly" (Fig. 41), and the doubly crossed vertical line in question could easily suggest the shape of the insect. Since many primitive tribes interpret purely geometric forms as animals, plants, natural phenomena, or other parts of the real world, theorists once generally assumed that art began with an attempt to depict real objects. In later times, they suggested, the representations had become less and less like the originals until at last only the name remained as evidence of the original artist's intention. Everyone admits that this process, known as conventionalization, is possible and has at times actually taken place; the problem is whether *all* geometrical figures originated in this way. The question can be discussed from more than one point of view, and we shall confine ourselves to considerations pertinent to our area.

Turning first to our Dakota design names, we find that by no means all of them refer to any concrete object. There are such purely descriptive designations as "twisted," "full-of-points," "filled-up," "cut-out." The suspicion arises that they evolved for convenience of reference and that the whole of the nomenclature of which they form part is nothing but the craftswomen's technical vocabulary. That some shapes suggested either an animal like the dragonfly or an artifact like an arrow seems natural enough. In the case of the "whirlwind" sign, one simply cannot conceive of a native's first trying to give a lifelike picture of the phenomenon indicated, and it is equally inconceivable how such a picture would ultimately assume the semblance of a narrow diamond. The obvious inference is that native craftswomen were familiar with certain simple forms and, for convenience' sake, came to label them. In other words, the association between form and name is secondary.

There are even more cogent considerations. The attempt to link meaning with designs is by no means universal in our area. It seems to have been lacking among the Blackfoot and was very slightly developed among the Crow, though these latter do sometimes call a right-angled triangle a "spear-head," a couple of such figures with facing hypotenuses "two facing tipis," and a plain cross "a star." The only persistent association seems to be that of a diamond with an infant's navel cord. Incidentally, the Arapaho regularly symbolize the navel by the same figure, which however may bear a variety of other meanings. A strong urge to interpret typical geometrical forms is confined to relatively few tribes, such as the Arapaho and the Dakota; and even among them informants frequently declared that their decoration had no significance but served a purely aesthetic purpose.

It might be argued that the Indians had merely lost the memory of the original meanings, but here a vital point enters. Where meanings are offered for a particular design, they vary within the tribe. Among the Dakota, Wissler discovered that often the woman making a decorative pattern and the man wearing the garment bearing the design connected different meanings with the design. Obviously an interpretation was secondarily read into it, certainly by one sex. This is sufficient to prove that our Indians do tend to invest a given geometrical figure with meaning. In the present case we can even point out the underlying drives. Dakota males were obsessed with the objective of military glory, hence used any occasion to inject relevant ideas. So it came about that, while a woman beaded designs on moccasins merely for decoration, her husband wearing them would see in the designs a picture of warfare: a diamond became a man's body, triangles stood for the tipis around which a battle raged, straight lines represented arrows, pronged figures symbolized wounds. When women interpreted geometric figures, they naturally expressed interests of a different order. For instance, the Dakota believed that the turtle presided over female physiological functions; hence this reptile played a conspicuous role in feminine thought. Sometimes a woman might actually start with the idea of making a fairly lifelike representation of a turtle in shaping an amulet, and such efforts may be regarded as parallel to the men's paintings of their war records. But more commonly she would use the most diverse figures—the U on a dress, diamonds with pronged appendices on leggings, an arrangement of triangles on a rawhide case—to symbolize the turtle or its breast (Plate 28).

Another interesting symbol conceived by Dakota women is a series of parallel lines on cradles, saddle blankets, and moccasins to represent the childbearing stage in a woman's life. The identical arrangement on a moccasin is interpreted by the Arapaho as the poles of a sweatlodge. This decoration on footgear is so distinctive that it cannot have originated independently in two tribes of the same area; hence, we infer once more that the design existed before the interpretations, was diffused as a decoration, and used for different symbols by the Arapaho and the Dakota. Other designs shared by these tribes confirm the conclusion. A simple four-branched cross usually represents the morning star for an Arapaho but is rarely connected with an astral body by the Dakota, who more generally see in it the four quarters of the globe or corpses or the rescue of an imperiled fellow tribesman.

What is more, Arapaho explanations were highly variable within the tribe, depending on the individual informant and on the context. A triangle with a curved hypotenuse may be a horse's ear, a buffalo horn, a lake, or a fish. A solidly embroidered disk serving as a tent ornament stood for the sun or the whirlwind; near the top of a cradle it denoted the infant's head. The diamond was associated with no less than ten different meanings—the navel, a person, an eye, a lake, a star, life or abundance, a turtle, a buffalo wallow, a hill, a tent interior. Surely it is inconceivable that so many distinct attempts at realism should all converge by deterioration toward a diamond—apart from the fact that it is not easy to imagine how an artist could ever realistically represent "life or abundance." Further, the meanings cited also occurred with quite different figures: a square, a trapezoid, a triangle, a pentagon, a circle no less than the diamond symbolized a lake; the life symbol could be a small rectangle, a green square enclosing a white and red square, a diamond. Evidently both a set of forms and a set of symbolic concepts were conventional in the tribe and came to be variously combined.

The course of development may, then, be summarized as follows. The Plains Indian artist was familiar with a number of geometrical designs, some of which were named for obvious resemblances to natural phenomena or artifacts, others being associated for reasons no longer clear. But in any case the association was as a rule secondary, not due primarily to an urge toward realism, which found expression in pictography.

Plains Indian symbolism offers some points of interest apart from the problem of conventionaliza-

tion. The Arapaho only exceptionally professed to
represent plants, rather infrequently interpreted
designs as human beings, and rarely as the larger
mammals. Dogs and horses, deer and elk did not
appear at all in this context, whereas small members of the animal kingdom were fairly common.
Yet altogether animals loomed far less conspicuously than topographic features—mountains, rocks,
the earth, etc. Of celestial bodies, only stars turn
up very frequently, especially the morning star.

Information is too meager to permit tribal charac-
terization from this point of view; yet a few facts of
historical interest stand out. The marked paucity
of interpretations among the northwestern tribes
goes hand in hand with other resemblances, *e.g.*,
in their parfleche decoration, so that they consti-
tute a subarea. The Crow, however, show some kinship with the Dakota and the Arapaho. Like the
former, though on a lesser scale, they had what
looks like a technical nomenclature for design elements. On the other hand, the occasional identification of the cross with a star and the regular association of a lozenge with the navel point toward
the Arapaho.

It remains to speak of the use of color. A white
background is frequent in the beadwork of all
tribes, being used almost exclusively by the Arapaho, while the Cheyenne showed an additional
preference for yellow, the Shoshone for a light gray-
ish blue. The Blackfoot were far less given to white
than other tribes, employing rather light red, yellow, and blue backgrounds. As previously stated,
the Omaha assert that blue was unknown to them
in pre-Caucasian times. The same belief held
among Crow informants.

Colors often had symbolic meanings, in art as well as in warfare (page 116) and in religion. With the Dakota, red suggested the sunset or thunder; yellow, the dawn, clouds, or earth; blue, the sky, clouds, night, or day; black, the night; green, the summer. Black betokened victory for the Crow, Arapaho, and probably other tribes. The Arapaho employed red to signify blood, man, paint, earth, sunset, or rocks; yellow, for sunlight or the earth; green, for vegetation; blue, for the sky, haze, smoke, far-away mountains, rocks, and night. White formed the normal background, but occasionally denoted snow, sand, earth, or water. The Crow used red paint to represent longevity and the ownership of property; it figured prominently in the Tobacco organization. White clay stood for ablutions intended to induce a vision and a knowledge of the future.

Music

Compared with African Negroes, the American Indians had only a few types of musical instruments, and those of the Plains are no exception.

Probably universal in the area was the flageolet (often referred to as a flute) used mainly by a lover when courting his sweetheart. By a code previously agreed upon, a young Assiniboin from a distance of a hundred yards could convey messages to his girl while she was inside her tipi without her family's catching on. He was able to express such ideas as, "I am here waiting for you," "I am watched," "Remain," "I'll come again," "Meet me tomorrow." An old Dakota specimen was 25 inches long and $\frac{5}{8}$ inch in diameter. It consisted of a straight stick carved at one end into a crane's head with open beak; it has been described by Frances Densmore in Bulletin 61 of the Bureau of American Ethnology as "an open pipe with the usual whistle or flageolet mouthpiece." The Hidatsa speak of a "singing whistle," a flageolet of box elder wood with the pith removed; it had seven holes. Several forms of whistle made of the wing bones of birds or of wood were noted by Maximilian as distinctive of the several Mandan military societies.

Rattles were made of gourds mounted on a handle and enclosing pebbles or of rawhide shaped in the form of a pear, globe, or open ring (Fig. 42). The rawhide was stretched over a frame of woodwork while wet and dried, pebbles being inserted at holes in the top or handle. Rattles were shaken by doctors when treating their patients and also served as emblems of organizations or of officials in them. Often they were decorated with feathers. The "deer-hoof" or dewclaw rattle consisted of a stick to which deer or antelope hoofs were attached; among the Hidatsa it was one of the badges of Dog society membership (Plate 17).

What may be called a rasp was distributed over

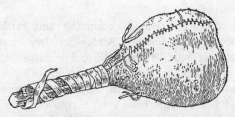

Fig. 42. A Blackfoot skin rattle (about 9 inches long); the handle is wood covered with leather and bound with thongs.

a large portion of the area and beyond. The Assiniboin type consisted of a 3-foot piece of wood that had notches cut along its edge. "The performer drew a stick backward and forward, along the notches, keeping time" (Henry). The instrument was the emblem of a Hidatsa organization (Fig. 43), being "played" at its dances, where the "female" stick was smoked with incense and propped up on two forked sticks; it represented a horned snake. The rasp was regarded as "male." The Ute employed the simple rasp to make music for their Bear dance, and the Paviotso used it for charming antelope.

Two main kinds of drums appear. The type more closely approaching ours was hollowed out from a section of a tree, with strips of hide serving as heads. A Wind River Shoshone sample, with decorated drumheads, is shown in Figure 43; the willow drumstick had its end wrapped with buckskin. This type could be suspended from forked sticks. Unequivocally aboriginal is the tambourine-like "hand drum" with a single skin head, the other side having a grip of cordage. This form figured in many situations, such as the military clubs, the Crow Tobacco organization, the Goose Women society of the Hidatsa.

Songs accompanied drumming and rattling at dances and ceremonies. Altogether they formed an important part of native life. For instance, some tribes at least regarded them as an indispensable, if not the most important, element of supernatural revelations. Apart from such sacred contexts, there were lullabies, secular songs distinctive of organizations, snatches composed in derision of a rival club or a personal enemy or a joking relative (page 127).

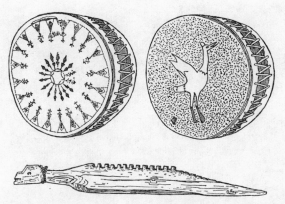

Fig. 43.   Above, a Shoshone double-headed drum (about 22 inches in diameter and 14 inches deep). The bird representation appears on the reverse side of the drum. Below, a wooden rasp (a little over 4 feet long and 5 inches wide), the musical instrument of the Notched Stick Society, Hidatsa.

Investigations of this vocal music have been pursued for many years by Frances Densmore, but the highly technical results do not lend themselves to a brief popular summary. It seems noteworthy, however, that she finds the Dakota, Mandan, Hidatsa as presenting more similarities among themselves and with the Ojibwa than with the Ute.

6 SUPERNATURALISM

Beliefs

THE SUPERNATURAL

Magic, the use of supernatural techniques for gaining one's ends, is often contrasted with "religion," the appeal to supernatural beings. In the practice and theory of primitive peoples it is hardly possible to maintain a rigid distinction between the two concepts: for example, a magical cure may be taught by a benevolent spirit, and a magical rite may be held quite as holy by the performers as a ceremony dedicated to the worship of a god. Accordingly, it is useful to have a single term for the whole system of beliefs and practices involving power beyond that of mortal beings, and this combination of beliefs and actions may be called "supernaturalism."

Of course, the native cannot conceive of nature as the modern scientist does, and accordingly he cannot oppose to such a concept another that transcends what are called natural laws. But he can and does react vehemently to perceptions that are wholly out of the normal range of his experience. American Indians have a variety of words to describe what strikes them as mysterious, weird, or miraculous, thrilling or awe-inspiring. The Crow word is *maxpé,* corresponding to Hidatsa *xupá,* Dakota *wakan,* Algonkian *manitō.*

To the abstract notion so designated, a particular experience is or is not assimilated. The word and its derivatives may be applied to persons or things and may even be used as adjectives or adverbs. The Dakota said of a child who speaks surprisingly well for his age, *ie wakandagi*. A Crow who magically lured deer into a corral was described as a *maxpé* man; in the myths the same epithet is applied to heroes and witches; and a word from the same root, *xapāria*, designated tangible objects viewed with special veneration, such as feathers seen in a vision. It is quite possible for an Indian to assume different attitudes at different times toward the same object that is called "wonderful" by any of the preceding terms. Sometimes an inanimate object, because of its oddity, was treated as a "supernatural" person. A Crow who found a peculiarly shaped rock (Plate 29) suggestive of an animal would treasure it, grease it, wrap it up with beads and other offerings, and believe it capable of reproduction. Periodically the owner would pray to the rock to grant him long life and wealth.

The first thing that strikes an observer of most primitive peoples is the way in which supernaturalism pervades every sphere of social life. In the communal antelope hunt a Comanche magician tried to block the escape of the game by crossing certain sticks decorated with antelope hoofs. When the herd had been surrounded, he could supposedly kill a particular antelope by simply pointing one of his hoofs at it. Other tribes employed corresponding devices to lure and destroy buffalo. In a time of scarcity, the Mandan believed, the dance of the White Buffalo Cow women enticed the herds near the village. Elsewhere a hoop game was played in order to call buffalo. Much of the magic rested on the principle that mimicry of a desired event could produce it. Such "imitative magic" may appear unobtrusively in many different ways as part of a complex ceremonial. At one stage of the Tobacco Dance the Crow Indians raised their drumsticks aloft to symbolize and to promote the growth of the plant; and the semisedentary tribes of the area, skillful farmers as they were, did not rely solely on their knowledge of farming, but also on the efficacy of their agricultural rites.

As supernaturalism intruded into economic life, so it also asserted itself in warfare. A Crow brave did not venture on a raid without the prompting of a supernatural protector in a dream or vision. A Dakota shield was supposed to owe its efficacy more to the vision that had suggested the design on its cover than to the toughness of the hide. In a ceremony for bringing about the death of a tribal enemy, the Crow would blacken ceremonial articles since it was their custom to put black paint on one's face in token of a killing. Sometimes a warrior attempted to divine whether the party on which he was setting out would meet with success: if in peering into a mixture of badger and buffalo blood he fancied seeing an enemy's scalp, he felt encouraged to proceed; if he saw himself scalped, he abandoned the project.

The Arapaho even derived innovations in decorative design from inspiration by spirits. A generalizing Plains Indian is reputed to have said that while White men had new ideas, the Indians had dreams or visions; and one Blackfoot conceived the invention of the phonograph not as the achievement of a creative genius, but as the gift of a spirit that had revealed to the "inventor" just how the apparatus was to be constructed.

In short, for the Plains Indian supernaturalism was not the equivalent of churchgoing of a Sunday, but something that profoundly affected his daily life and offered an explanation of extraordinary occurrences.

VISIONS

Most North American Indians attached great importance to visions, and in the Plains these took precedence in the religious life. However, the spirits did not always appear to their prospective protégé, but might merely become audible to him, issuing instructions and promising definite benefits. In Siberia and parts of western North America supernatural visitants were not sought; in fact, often the spirit compelled a native to accept his guardianship much against the future protégé's wishes. In contrast, Woodland and Plains Indians deliberately went out to a lonely spot in order to obtain a revelation. Some Crow individuals received favors unsought when in a predicament. Occasionally it even happened that a spirit came under ordinary circumstances from a pure desire to befriend the mortal. However, the normal procedure was to go into solitude, fast and thirst for four days, and supplicate the spirits to take pity on the sufferer. A Crow usually cut off a finger joint of his left hand or in some other way mortified his flesh by way of arousing supernatural pity.

Certain tribal differences are noteworthy with respect to the vision quest. In the Woodlands, Ojibwa and Winnebago parents regularly instructed boys, possibly not over seven years of age, to fast in order to obtain the blessing of a spirit, and on the Plains the Hidatsa elders likewise prompted their chil-

dren to seek a revelation at an early age. But no
such admonition was customary among the Crow.
There a lad grew up, constantly hearing that all
success in life was derived from visions; hence, being eager for horses and for social recognition, an
adolescent would go out to fast, praying for rich
booty, for a chance to strike a coup, or for some
other benefit. A mature man or woman would seek
a vision whenever a special cause arose—if his children were sick, if he had lost his property, if he
longed to revenge the killing of a close relative, and
so on. Again, the Arapaho seem to have sought a
vision only as adults.

We naturally wonder what really happened on
such quests. There is no doubt that the vast majority of informants firmly believed in the reality of
the experiences they described. In order to explain
this phenomenon psychologically, several factors
have to be considered. First of all, the god seeker
was usually under a strong emotional impulse—either yearning to shine before his fellows or desiring
relief from want or disease or the grief over an un-
avenged kinsman. By seclusion in a lonely spot, by
his fast, by self-mutilation, he naturally intensified
his emotional state. What is more, the myths told
by his people and the accounts of the supernatural
experiences of contemporary tribesmen had left an
imprint on his mind and helped to shape the sense
impressions that came to him. His longings at the
time blended with the visionary pattern of his tribe
and with the sounds or sights actually experienced
under highly abnormal conditions so as to inspire
an interpretation of things seen and heard. Individual peculiarities likewise entered: an Indian of a
predominantly auditory type might imagine a

whole series of distinguishable sounds—the call of a bird, the rustling of leaves, the neighing of a horse, the speech of an alien tribe, and what not. If his was a decidedly visual type, he would see specific details, as when a would-be raider caught sight of a mount he was to steal—say, a bay horse with docked tail, heavy mane, and a zigzag line painted down its legs. A man who subsequently arranged his sensations for his own enlightenment or to give a clear statement to an audience was in the position of ourselves when trying to give a coherent account of a dream. Without trying to deceive or to invent, he would unconsciously bridge over obscure points, filling in the gaps, adapting his memories of the experience to one of the tribal vision patterns familiar to him from listening to earlier accounts.

A good example of such a pattern is the following. Several Crow informants independently tell how on their lonely vigil they saw a spirit or several spirits riding along, how the rocks and trees in the neighborhood turned into enemies who attacked the horsemen, but were unable to inflict any harm. The symbolical meaning of these apparitions is that the spirits are making the visionary invulnerable. This is, of course, a generally prized blessing, but several persons could not independently conceive the identical image of spiritual riders shot at by transformed bits of the landscape, especially when the very same motif appears also in traditional stories apart from the narration of the teller's personal experiences. Evidently the image, however it may have originated, became part of tribal folklore and was readily worked into the report of their revelations by persons who particularly craved invulnerability.

Again, it was certainly a part of the tribal pattern that most Crow Indians obtained their spiritual blessing on the fourth night of their seclusion, four being the mystic number within the area.

The supernatural beings who befriend man vary enormously in character. Animals were very frequent visitants of Plains Indians. Buffalo, elk, bears, eagles (sometimes conceived as birds producing thunder by flapping their wings), and sparrow hawks constantly figure in the narratives, but so also do quite lowly beasts such as dogs or rabbits. A Pawnee legend even describes the invocation of mosquitoes, and according to Cree tradition a mosquito gave one tribesman the gift of chieftaincy. Curious contradictions do not seem to have been recognized as such by the Indians. In a Crow story a rabbit pursued by a hawk promises to give supernatural power to an Indian if he will shield him from the bird of prey. Correspondingly, a Pawnee boy gets supernatural aid from mice who are unable to extricate themselves from a relatively simple difficulty. That is, though animals are possessed of supernatural powers, they may be dependent on mortals for specific services, for which they reward them. Celestial patrons are also frequent, stars figuring prominently among the Pawnee. Fanciful creatures of more or less human shape likewise appear in visions, e.g., a dwarf with a very powerful musculature. Sometimes the patron comes in human guise but in disappearing assumes his true shape or otherwise gives a clue to his identity.

The Crow interpreted the relationship between patron and protégé as that of a father and his child, and accounts of visions often explicitly quote the spirit as pronouncing the formula of adoption: "I will have you for my child." In any case the spirit normally taught the Crow a sacred song, instructed him just how he must dress in battle or if a man was to become a doctor what medicines or curing devices he must use, and frequently imposed certain taboos as to diet or behavior. Any infraction of the rules was liable to precipitate a loss of the guardian's protection or even a dire calamity. Often the visionary not only wore some token of his vision or painted it on, say, his shield cover, but also on the strength of successive visions assembled the ingredients to build up a "medicine bundle," a wrapper containing a set of sacred objects indicated by the spirit. A Pawnee bundle contained as a minimum one pipe, tobacco, paints, certain birds, and corn—all assembled in a container of buffalo hide that was hung from the wall of the lodge. The opening of a bundle and the treatment of its contents were accompanied by definite rites. As already stated, it is often difficult to tell whether the native consistently considered such objects sacred in their own right, in other words, made them fetishes wholly independent of any personal spirit, or whether they become sacred only as gifts of the spirit; very likely the attitude of a person varied at different times.

If because of visions, one individual worshiped above all a supernatural buffalo, another an eagle, and a third the morning star, the question arises how these several beings ranked in relation to one another. With the Comanche and the Crow this problem arose only when there was a clash of interests between tribesmen, each man falling back on the protection of his own guardian and the issue showing whose patron was the stronger. In the absence of a coherent system of the universe, the religious consciousness assigned priority to individual visitants. Thus, an Indian once told the author that a feather he cherished as a memento of his vision of a bird was the greatest thing in the world. At the opposite extreme stood the Pawnee (see page 182), who had brought their beliefs into a logical system, venerating a Supreme Being named Tirawa, a sky-dwelling creator who rules the universe, his commands being executed by lesser deities. Utterances by Dakota medicinemen suggest a similar fondness for metaphysical speculation and integration. A question that remains unanswered is whether the average Pawnee or Dakota individual in his daily life was actually guided by priestly generalizations or whether in practice, without overtly rejecting them, he followed the Crow pattern.

Though all persons coveted a revelation, not all were able to obtain one. Those who did not succeed naturally did not wish to be thereby doomed to failure throughout life. The Crow and some other tribes resolved the dilemma by permitting a successful visionary to sell part of his power to less fortunate tribesmen, adopting them as his supernatural patron had adopted *him*, making for each of his disciples a replica of his sacred paraphernalia, teaching him the sacred songs, and warning against breach of any taboo associated with his medicine.

SHAMANS

At the opposite pole from those unable to gain a personal vision were the Indians who, as demonstrated by their conspicuous success, had obtained exceptional power from the spirits. Such persons were said to be *maxpé* or *wakan* and in English may be called "medicinemen" or, to borrow a convenient Siberian term, "shamans."

According to the Wahpeton Dakota, their medicinemen lived a prenatal existence among the Thunders and enjoyed a knowledge, prior to birth, of all that would happen to them as mortals. Their social role began with maturity, when they received a sign from the Thunders to start performing shamanistic duties; any shaman disobeying the divine orders would suffer punishment or even be killed by the Thunders. The services rendered to tribesmen included curing the sick, discovering the whereabouts of the enemy, and helping to recover lost or stolen property. By way of proving his powers a shaman summoned people to large meetings, at which he performed tricks in order to establish himself as a wonder-worker.

The most elaborate organization for such miraculous performances appeared among the Pawnee. Their medicinemen in some measure partook of the nature of priests since they were trained, a great master of legerdemain being surrounded by a number of disciples. However, all medicinemen were supposed to obtain their powers from living creatures so that the subjective experience of the vision remained a vital element. In the late summer or early fall all the accepted masters at sleight-of-hand gathered in one of two earthlodges reserved in the village for that purpose and with the aid of pupils erected their several booths. A turtle effigy was modeled at the cleared fireplace, a new fireplace put on its back, and a ceremonially felled tree was planted by the Skidi Pawnee in the forked tail of an image representing a mythical water monster encircling the fireplace. The clay statue of a woman, life size, was set up on the south side, a large male figure of rawhide was placed upon a pole above the lodge, and many small human figures, also of rawhide, were attached about the assembly place. The fire symbolized the sun; the clay female, the moon; the large male effigy, the morning star; and the many little images, the stars.

After a dedication ceremony there was an impressive procession through the village, each shaman wearing a costume in mimicry of his animal protector. Then the participants reentered the lodge for a secret ritual, after which the door was opened for the spectacular show. Among other tricks there was the magical maturing of cornstalks before the onlookers' gaze; and the Bear shamans pretended to tear out a man's liver, to eat it, and then to make him rise unharmed.

Sleight-of-hand was a common technique for impressing the laity. The Iruska shamans of the Pawnee handled burning corn husks with their bare hands, took meat out of a kettle of boiling soup, and stood on red-hot rocks. These tricks were closely paralleled by the Dakota, who among other things shared a fire-walking feat with Arapaho, Gros Ventre, and Cheyenne performers. Another marvelous stunt, noted by Maximilian among the Mandan and Hidatsa, was to harbor some animal or plant inside one's body and have it emerge to the amazement of the spectators. The Prince actually saw a Hidatsa woman "dance a corncob out of herself," and another Indian professed to feel a buffalo calf kicking around inside his body. A Crow informant declared that when a certain song was sung a horse inside her would try to come out, protruding his tail from her mouth.

Sometimes Crow shamans offered a public competitive exhibition of their powers, one man or a group trying to overcome those pitted against them.

More important from the laity's point of view was the shaman's doctoring. The treatment of illness did not necessarily require supernatural power, for there were liniments, herbs, therapeutic potions, and other home remedies. However, in serious cases recourse was generally had to a practitioner who derived his techniques, even when rational, from a visionary experience. Because of the usually specific nature of the instruction given by the spirit, a doctor was likely to cure only particular ailments. Thus, he might treat only women in childbirth or men bitten by a snake.

Perhaps the commonest primitive theory of disease ascribes the cause to a foreign object in the patient's body; hence the physician tries to extract it, usually by suction, exhibiting to the patient and his kin the splinter, thorn, or what not that supposedly caused the disturbance. These notions occur also in the Plains. For example, in recent times a Crow named Bull-all-the-time cured several patients by sucking at the afflicted parts with a pipe-stem and pulling out, respectively, a bone, a black beetle, a morsel of meat, but he deprecated any competence in dealing with wounds or snake bites. The treatment by suction obviously implies sleight-of-hand.

Sickness would smite a shaman or his patient if rules laid down by his spiritual patron were disobeyed, whether willingly or not. Thus, it might be fatal for a sick man if a dog crossed his doctor's path. Anyone who ate food forbidden to him in a dream or vision was bound to suffer.

Though witchcraft was less pronounced than among the Pueblos, the Plains Indians did sometimes resort to effigy magic. In the 1890s, some Comanche suspected an interpreter of treason, made an image of him, and pelted it with mud; in consequence, they assert, he had a hemorrhage and died. The same people used to kill a sorcerer after he had repeatedly worked harm against his fellows. This act was in line with Basin custom, but at least the central Plains tribes probably did not proceed in this way, rather counteracting the malevolent shaman's magic by the aid of another shaman.

Other medical techniques included massage, smoking, bleeding, cupping, and applying burning sage. Arapaho doctors fumigated a sick infant with the smoke from heated roots or cedar twigs or made it inhale the fumes from herbs laid on hot coals. Though the sweatlodge (page 186) was prominent in ceremonialism, it was also used for medicinal purposes, at least by a number of tribes, such as the Arapaho and the Comanche.

PRIESTS

Whereas a shaman by definition acquires his status through a personal communication by supernatural beings, the priest need not have this face-to-face relationship with the spirit world but must have competence in conducting ritual. In other words, he has been trained for his activities. As stated, the medicinemen of the Pawnee were shamans by virtue of their animal mentors, but they were likewise priests in so far as they had to undergo special instruction. One might even speak of their ordination, for before being allowed to take a permanent place in the lodge each had to demonstrate his skill to the leaders, being ejected if he failed. However, the Pawnee had a number of other men who combined official standing with a knowledge of sacred songs in their sequence and of the meaning of ritual procedures. Accordingly, the tribe can properly be said to have had a priesthood. More particularly, the priests were associated with the sacred-bundle scheme that underlay Pawnee political organization. Each of the thirteen Skidi villages owned a bundle, which had to be opened at the first thunder in the spring, when the keeper made offerings and went through the traditional rites. Four of the bundles were preeminent, and a fifth, associated with the evening star, took absolute precedence; the priests of these bundles rather than the titular chiefs held supreme authority. Normally, the four priests in turn assumed responsibility for the welfare of the people for the period of a year and specifically for the success of the buffalo hunt. If this miscarried, the Evening Star priest was asked to supersede his officiating colleague. The priesthood was strictly hereditary, passing from its holder to the next of kin in the maternal line.

HEREAFTER

Some American aborigines, such as the Winnebago, were greatly concerned over the hereafter and the ability to travel thither in safety. This interest and anxiety seem to have been foreign to most Plains Indians. While sharing the universal aboriginal belief in a survival of the soul, the future was not a matter of great concern, there was no notion of rewards and punishments after death, no ancestor worship, no elaborate picture of posthumous exist-

24. A painted buffalo-skin robe collected by Lewis and Clark from the Mandan in 1805. The scene is supposed to represent a battle that took place in 1797. Courtesy Peabody Museum, Harvard University.

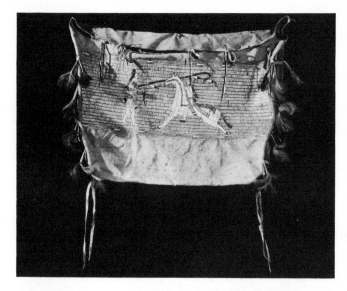

25. A quill-decorated sad-
dlebag from the Da-
kota.

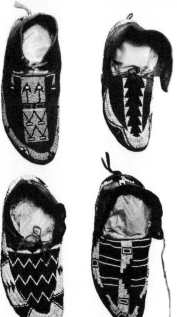

26. Dakota moccasins, il-
lustrating the variety
of design elements.

27. *Beaded and quilled pipe and tobacco bag from the Dakota.*

28. *A Dakota woman's bead-ornamented legging.*

29. *Crow sacred rock and offerings.*

30. *Face paint, headdress, and necklace of a Blackfoot medicine man.*

31. *Altar in the Adoption Lodge, Crow Tobacco Ceremony.*

32. *Entrance into the Adoption Lodge, Crow Tobacco Ceremony.*

33. *The leader of the procession in the Crow Tobacco Ceremony leaving the Preparatory Lodge with her pipe.*

34. The leader (center, with pipe) heading the procession to the Adoption Lodge, one of the stops on the way to the garden for planting, Crow Tobacco Ceremony.

35. *A model, showing one phase of the Arapaho Sun Dance.*

36. *The sacred doll of the Crow Sun Dance.*

ence. The usual conception was that the dead lived very much as they had while alive, hunting buffalo, playing games, and inhabiting the same sort of tipis as during their previous existence. Such beliefs as these rested largely on the reports of persons who had visited the spirit land, but returned to their fellows, *i.e.*, of people who were believed to have died but who recovered from their state of unconsciousness and sooner or later divulged their adventures while supposedly dead.

As might be expected, the Pawnee elaborated ideas on the subject, incorporating them into their general world view. Some souls traveled to the sky to turn into stars; cowards and men who died from disease joined the spirits in the south after traversing the Milky Way; chiefs and priests journeyed on a special road to a distinct destination; and shamans also had a spirit village of their own. According to one Pawnee view, the souls of people who died of illness, because seen by the Star of Disease, are taken to the South Star's home, whereas the Morning Star disposes of the fate of all others.

Concerning the soul concept itself, the Crow distinguished the ghost that haunts the grave and the soul that travels to the hereafter. They attributed souls to animals. According to the Mandan, a person had four souls, two of which, respectively, symbolized by white sage and the meadowlark, merged to form the spirit of the hereafter. The third was connected with its owner's lodge and loitered about it so long as traces of it remained, while the fourth sometimes left the village but periodically returned to frighten people.

Whether the Plains Indians as a whole recognized a supreme deity is a knotty problem. A positive answer seems established for the Pawnee. Their Tirawa existed in the beginning, wedded to Atira (Born from Corn or Vault of the Sky). He ordered the other gods where to stand and issued further commands to them through the Evening Star, the Mother of all Things. In accordance with his will the Morning Star mated with the Evening Star and the Sun with the Moon; the girl issuing from the former union as well as the boy begotten by the Sun were put on the earth, and the two married. Other deities also created human beings. The earth-dwellers acquired the rudiments of Indian culture and received from the gods the gift of ceremonial bundles, the associated rituals being revealed by the Evening Star. The Pawnee thus developed a rather complex mythology, strongly emphasizing the importance of celestial characters, all of them subordinate to Tirawa.

Certainly most of the other tribes had nothing like so coherent a scheme. The Crow, for example, by and large regarded the Sun as the outstanding supernatural being—he was invoked in prayer and on the vision quest, though he very rarely appeared to a would-be visionary; the sweatlodge was pre-eminently in his honor, and albino buffaloes were invariably offered to him. However, these Indians were not wholly consistent in regarding him as most powerful. In a crisis they relied primarily on their individual patrons, and they sometimes failed to distinguish him from the mythological figure called Old Man Coyote (page 139) whom they generally associated with the creation of the world, of man, and of human culture, but who is also in many episodes of his cycle an utterly unscrupulous rascal.

Ceremonialism

It is difficult to separate faith and observance, for the native who believes in supernatural beings will try to placate them by some act; and if he thinks that a certain procedure would bring rain or any other desired end, he will apply it. Accordingly, the foregoing account of *beliefs* could not be divorced from some statements about associated *practices*. In the following pages, however, attention is focused on relevant activities, the sum total of which is called "ceremonialism" or "ritualism," while its elements are conveniently labeled "rites."

Except for the western marginal peoples, such as the Comanche, who herein reveal their ultimate affinity with the Basin and Plateau Areas, the Plains Indians were markedly given to ritualism. Indeed, in this respect the Pawnee approach the Pueblos, who attained the highest development on the continent. The observances may be simple and brief, as when an Iowa, before smoking formally, offered tobacco to the sky spirit, puffing a mouthful of smoke toward him. At the other end of the scale were such four-day festivals as the Sun Dance and the Okipa of the Mandan, both of which required weeks of preparation. Such major ceremonies involved the entire tribe, at least as spectators and also in considerable measure as minor performers, even when portions of the ritual were enacted in secret. Other rituals, such as certain bundle ceremonies, were the private business of a limited group or even of a single individual; the performances might be of the utmost importance to those concerned, but obviously could not fulfill the requirements of a theatrical spectacle.

Rich as the Plains were in ceremonials, certain types prominent among other primitive tribes were absent or restricted. Thus, elaborate puberty rituals for girls, of outstanding importance in California, were either lacking (Crow, Arapaho, Blackfoot) or held only for a favored daughter (Dakota). Locally, observances at a girl's coming of age led to a four days' seclusion (Cree, Assiniboin), during which she was forbidden to scratch her head, except with a special stick, ate very sparingly, and practiced feminine activities, but such customs were dwarfed by coexisting rituals of a different order. In contrast to the Australians and the Tierra del Fuegians, there was no obligatory initiation of boys into a men's society that terrorized women. As a matter of fact, though menstrual taboos imposed some restrictions on the female sex, wives often aided their husbands in sacred rites, and in specific instances the highest ceremonial offices were open to women. Positively, ceremonialism was strongly affected by the central position of visions, which led to infinite diversification in details since individuals could add to or modify a traditional procedure on the basis of personal revelations, could found new subdivisions or offshoots of a religious fraternity, adopt novices, and so forth. A common supernatural patron might lead to a special organization (Dakota, Omaha): Omaha Indians blessed by supernatural grizzlies or buffalo, respectively, formed societies and danced in imitation of the animals. This fact, incidentally, shows that there was *some* impersonation in Plains ritualism, though considerably less than among many other Indians.

ELEMENTS OF CEREMONIALISM

Many rites were performed either separately or as parts of a larger whole. They include offerings and prayers, the solemn unfolding of the packs containing sacred objects, painting of the celebrant's face or body (Plate 30), sweating, the singing of sacred songs. A few of these merit some further account.

Prayers and offerings were commonly made and frequently the suppliant vowed that he would render gifts provided his wishes were fulfilled. Indeed, the Arapaho evolved a votive pattern for all major ceremonies, even those of military societies, a man pledging a performance if he escaped sickness or danger. The contractual relation assumed between the spirit and the worshiper is illustrated in the invocation of the Sun by a Kansa war captain:

"I wish to kill a Pawnee! I desire to bring horses when I return. I long to pull down an enemy! I promise you a calico shirt and a robe. I will give you a blanket also, O Wakanda, if you allow me to return in safety after killing a Pawnee!"

Shields, being sacred, were normally kept covered. Before exhibiting his own, a Crow chief would take some live coals, burn wild carrot root for incense, hold his shield above the fire, raise it a little, lower it, raise it a little higher, continuing in this way until the fourth time, when he lifted it aloft and began removing the two buckskin covers. This instance illustrates the effect of a sacred number on ritual procedure, significant acts being repeated accordingly. Often there were three feints; when walking out of a tipi toward the ceremonial lodge, the leader of the procession simulated an exit three times, each time withdrawing the foot put forward, and finally at the fourth time made the real start.

Tremendous importance was attached to songs taught in a vision; a Blackfoot doctor's power was supposed to lie primarily in his chants, which he was not allowed to sell as he might other sacred property. Plains Indians repeated songs in accordance with their mystic number. The most prominent number was doubtless four, but seven might coexist in the same tribe; the Blackfoot sang ritualistic songs by sevens, though four figured when they picked up ceremonial objects after three feints.

In part of the area the vapor bath was prized for its therapeutic value, and in recent times Crow and Blackfoot Indians have indulged in it as a sport. Yet its outstanding importance was ceremonial; some tribes considered sweating a necessary purification before taking part in any major ceremony. For sweating, the Indians erected a low dome-shaped structure of willow saplings, dug a fireplace in the center, put into it rocks that had been heated red-hot, and covered the little lodge with skins, making it quite dark inside. Water was poured on the rocks, making the participants sweat profusely. In order to permit them to cool off, an outsider removed the covering for a short time, then the operation was repeated. After the final (probably fourth) sweating, the bathers, dripping with perspiration, dashed into the nearest creek or in the wintertime wallowed in the snow. The sweat-lodge of the Crow was as a rule conceived as an offering to the Sun, but religious associations varied tribally, as did the details connected with the institution. The Blackfoot excluded women, whereas the Crow admitted them, though mostly as initiates into the Tobacco order. The number of willows for the frame varied according to the occasion: fourteen was usual among Crow and Blackfoot, but the Crow might use as many as a hundred, which number Blackfoot regarded as essential in the Sun Dance. As a rule, four persons joined in sweating themselves.

The sweatlodge is widely distributed in North America, being found from the Atlantic to the Pacific, though in California without vapor. The modern Finnish *sauna* and its Scandinavian equivalent in the sixteenth century involved procedures strikingly similar to the North American ones, thus raising the question whether the phenomenon could have been diffused from a single center.

A special space set aside in a ceremonial structure for arranging sacred objects or smoking them with incense is conveniently called an altar. The Blackfoot smudged their bundles in a plot behind the fire where the grass and surface soil had been removed. Their favorite incense was that from sweetgrass, but the plant varied with the bundle, as did the size and shape of the altar. The sacred plot was shaped into crescentic and other figures by means of colored earth. For one type of bundle it was proper to clear a 2-foot square of grass and cover it with white earth, then the crescent moon was worked out in black, bordered by yellow; two circles of the same colors symbolized the sun and the morning star, and two narrow oblongs in red represented sun dogs.

Altars of a different type were set up in the Sun Dance lodges of several Plains tribes, buffalo skulls being formally arranged in an excavated or cleared area. Near the center of the adoption lodge of the Tobacco order the Crow similarly cleared an oblong space at whose head the members afterward put down their medicine bags. Each of the longer sides was bounded by a row of willow arches resembling croquet wickets, and outside each row there was a parallel log of equal length. Within the altar were laid four rows of juniper sprigs (Plate 31). The altar represented the tobacco garden—the juniper, the tobacco itself in its green state—the logs were reckoned sacred, hence must not be burnt for firewood, but animal droppings placed on the altar might serve to light a pipe and to burn incense.

Compared with other primitive groups, the Plains Indians present some striking negative features in their ceremonial details. Masks were not wholly absent, for the Bull Dancers of the Mandan (Plate 19) wore buffalo heads and the Fool society of the Assiniboin, who acted like clowns in obedience to a spirit's revelation, wore grotesque masks. It remains true, however, that such disguise was markedly rare, in contrast to the Northwest Coast, Pueblo, and Iroquois Indians who had a profusion of masks. To some extent the absence of masks is explained by the slight development of carving in our area. In correlation with this deficiency, attempts at impersonation of deities were also rare, though by no means entirely absent. A conspicuous exception, besides that mentioned previously, occurred in the Okipa, where actors did assume the role of outstanding mythological characters.

MAJOR CEREMONIALS

Ceremonials of outstanding importance were not always the most spectacular. This applies to most of the rituals connected with bundles. The Arapaho recognized a "flat" pipe as the great tribal fetish. It was kept in a painted tipi (Plate 9), wrapped in a large pack of many pieces of cloth, and suspended so as never to touch the ground. An Arapaho might invoke the pipe to grant him long life and happiness, and he might present it with offerings. The keeper was the only one familiar with the orthodox version of the tribal myth and took four consecutive nights to tell the story. He directed the Sun Dance as well as other great ceremonies and was regarded with the utmost awe. But the observances connected with the holy of holies itself were unimpressive: the pipe had to be held and handled in the traditional way. Any dramatic features were coincidental, inasmuch as the pipe figured in the Sun Dance, and they were shared by tribes without this particular fetish.

Similar considerations apply to many forms of sacred pipe bundles in the area, some seventeen varieties of one type being found among the Blackfoot alone. The owners all enjoyed great esteem, but did not form an organization. The original pipe was revealed by the Thunder, a supplementary variety stemming from a bear who had thereby repaid a Blackfoot for the favors his daughter had granted the animal. The numerous appurtenances enclosed in the bundle include the fetus of a deer; squirrel, muskrat, mink, and bird skins; necklaces; and many other objects. It was obligatory for the owner to open the bundle at the first thunder in the spring,

also when someone in distress had vowed to the
Sun to dance with the pipestem or when the bundle
was transferred to a purchaser. Outsiders were supposed to derive benefits from a bundle, but above
all they redounded to the glory of the owner and
afforded him protection. He was, however, obliged
to submit to many fanciful and in part burdensome
rules: he was not allowed to point with any digit
but his thumb nor to pick up any object he found;
he had to hold his pipe in a particular way; he must
never sit on his bedding; and so forth. His wife had
to make smudge every morning and shift the position of the bundle in fixed sunwise sequence; and
under no condition was it to touch the ground. The
importance of these sacred pipes in Blackfoot society is manifest. Yet again the correlated ritual
is devoid of the spectacular element. When about
to open his pack, the owner invited an experienced
ritualist as aide and a few others to help with the
singing. The ceremony itself consisted merely in
opening the pack, in singing songs by sets of seven,
and in simple dancing—all this before a restricted
audience.

Intermediate in dramatic elaboration between
such performances and the Sun Dance are the
mystic rites that correspond to the Grand Medicine
Dance of the western Woodland tribes. Typical of
the Woodlands is supposed to be the Midewiwin,
the secret Medicine society of the Ojibwa, where
the candidate for admission was magically shot with
a shell, fell forward apparently lifeless, and was
restored by the older members. Actually this feature is equally characteristic of Southern Siouans,
such as the Iowa and Oto; indeed, the Omaha had
two organizations, the Shell and the Pebble society,

of which the supposed shooting and resuscitation was a cardinal characteristic. Apart from "killing" the novice, the members shot at one another to demonstrate their magical power. In short, this aspect of these societies was simply a startling shamanistic exhibition of power.

CROW TOBACCO SOCIETY

The Tobacco order of the Crow—which, as a result of new visions, split up into a number of chapters—planted a sacred tobacco, *Nicotiana multivalvis*, that was different from the species they smoked, *N. quadrivalvis* (page 28). Benefits accrued from the planting both to the members and to the tribe at large, and the prestige connected with affiliation induced people to pay heavy initiation fees to the sponsor who gave him the seeds and instructed him as well as usually also the tyro's wife, assuming a parental relationship toward them. During the winter the novice was usually taught four Tobacco songs and attended dances by his "father's" chapter. In the beginning of spring the highest officials of the several chapters met to discuss their dreams about the proper place for planting and settled on a site. These officials had received bags containing the members' seeds and prepared them for planting by mixing them with water, the droppings of game animals, roots, and other ingredients. For this labor the mixers were paid.

On the day after the preparation of the seeds the members, sometimes accompanied by the whole camp, set out for the garden after having been painted by the mixers. Outsiders were controlled by the military society serving as police at the time. The women carried large bags with seeds on their

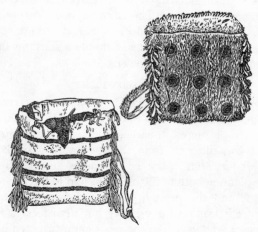

Fig. 44.   Tobacco bags used in the Crow Tobacco Ceremony.

backs (Fig. 44). Everyone assembled in a lodge, and the musicians intoned a song. One woman was far ahead of the line, and her chapter took precedence, for she carried a specially sacred otterskin. After four songs had been sung in the lodge, a woman walked round it and led the procession outside, being followed first by the other women, then by the men of her chapter, who took up a position to the right of the women. Then came the other chapters in turn until all of them formed a horizontal line. They proceeded toward the garden site, halting four times, and singing four songs at each stop. At the last station, possibly 100 yards from the goal, those carrying their tobacco bags turned them over to fast runners, who raced to the garden, where they laid down the bags; the winner of the race was sure to enjoy good luck that year and to have a good crop of tobacco. Various observances were followed at the stops, where the otterskin bearer offered the mixers a pipe to smoke, and they announced their dreams about the tobacco.

After the race the members came up to the site, cleared it, and prepared it by setting fire to the grass. The mixer of each chapter counted out a number of rows according to the size of the membership till the whole garden was divided up, a stick marking each group's plot. For each chapter a famous brave ran across the short side of the oblong that formed the garden and back again, reporting in a low voice, that he had been on a war party, struck a coup, and on his return found the tobacco prospering. The mixer, after proclaiming the message aloud and after three feints, punched a hole in the ground, thus ushering in the planting of the seeds.

When a chapter had completed this task, husband and wife cooperating, the men sang, both sexes danced in position and then feasted. After the planting, members would lie down at the edge of the garden, hoping to get a vision and a song about the tobacco.

A crudely fenced garden inspected in 1910 was about 60 by 6 yards, divided into six plots for the several chapters, each bounded by a row or rows of little willow wickets. Each couple within the chapter marked its section off by little stones and by setting up a distinctively shaped digging stick at either end. Two miniature sweatlodges were constructed at opposite sides of the garden to foster the growth of the sacred weed, and incense was burnt in them. A short distance from the site there was a large sweatlodge.

Formerly the adoption of novices took place immediately after the planting, but in later times it was postponed until the week of the Fourth of July festivities. Members of any chapter might attend the initiation, but only the initiating chapter received presents. The right to put up the adoption lodge with its altar was a greatly prized prerogative. There was a procession to it from a smaller preparatory tipi, in which the novice and the older members were decorated with face paint; the designs had all been revealed in visions, hence were the visionary's copyrighted property that could be transferred only by payments. Gray-bull had paid his own mother a horse, an ermine-skin shirt, quilts, and money for the right to use her pattern and sold it to Plenty-coups for four horses. When all members had been painted, dances were held in the preparatory tipi, the men drumming, a few shaking rattles, and the women gently swaying their bodies in position as they held unwrapped sacred articles. The wife of the man who owned the adoption lodge, holding a pipe, took up a position at the exit, while the men drummed and sang. After three feints she passed out of the tipi, followed by the women and then the men in a single file (Plates 33, 34). They halted four times, and at each stop four songs were sung. Then they entered the lodge, the musicians seating themselves on the west side of the altar, the women to the south and north. Immediately after the entrance a warrior went through roughly the same procedure as at the planting.

A man privileged to do so lit a pipe with trade

tobacco—never with the sacred species—and it was
solemnly smoked by the men. Thereafter the drum-
mers beat drums and sang, and members, mostly
women, would dance in accompaniment. Each held
a weasel skin or willow sprig or eagle feather fan
or the like in her hands. The dance simply consisted in moving the body in place while alternately
advancing and drawing back, or raising and lower-
ing, the clenched hands with a convulsive movement. Sets of dancers took turns. It was essential
that each novice should dance jointly, *i.e.*, in a horizontal line, with the four men who had taught him
songs during the winter. These procedures occupied most of the day except at noon during an
intermission for a feast and a distribution of gifts
from the novice's kin to the adopters. In the late
afternoon the terminal song was intoned, and at
its close the members all lifted willow sprigs or
drumsticks to symbolize and promote the growth
of the tobacco.

Either immediately after this ceremony or the
following morning, the novice or the married couple
who had been initiated joined their instructors in a
sweatlodge with tobacco bags on top of it. The
following morning the newly adopted was allowed
to pick out any "medicine" objects, including sacred
tobacco bags, paying for each article in turn and for
any coveted ceremonial privileges.

Between the planting and the harvest, members
of the order had to observe various rules, *e.g.*, they
must not play shinny after the sprouting of the
plant, lest it break down. During this period the
members often danced, in the simple way described, in order to hasten the growth of the to-

bacco. There were four formal inspections of the garden, either by the mixers or by inspectors reporting to them. When the wild cherries were ripe, the members—theoretically of all chapters on the same day—harvested the crop, returned to camp, and danced as they had during the adoption. If some plants were not yet mature, subsequent visits were made to the garden. After the final crop the members danced with the newly plucked tobacco in the adoption lodge. Finally the stems and leaves were plucked out, cut up fine, and thrown into a creek.

The Crow Tobacco society affords a good insight into Plains Indian ceremonialism. The ceremonies are highly composite. There is no central idea to which the various activities are logically subordinated. All the Crow identified the sacred tobacco with a star, but it is impossible to detect in the procedures a consistent astral cult. The origin tales do bring in one or more stars as founders of the order, but the chapters traced their beginning to all kinds of sources—weasels, a lizard, a crane, buffalo, or an eagle as the Sun's messenger. The performances themselves combine characteristic ritual ideas of the area—the altar, sweatlodges, incense smoking, facial paint, fourfold repetition. The notion that visionary blessings are transferable finds expression in the creation of innumerable special privileges, all finding payers of extravagant prices. Since the culture stresses military prowess, warriors get an opportunity to recount their deeds before a sizable audience, though their coups have nothing to do with either the stars or the avowed purpose of the ceremonies—the tribal welfare.

THE SUN DANCE

The Sun Dance ranks as the most conspicuous religious festival of about twenty Plains tribes. It was
not performed by the Pawnee, Wichita, Omaha,
and several other Southern Siouans, but elements
of it appeared among the Pawnee and Omaha. Because of the self-torturing associated with most of
its forms, the Department of the Interior prohibited
its performance in 1904, the ban being removed
in 1935, so that sundry tribes have held the Dance
since then, though modern conditions have introduced alterations. The festival was most highly
elaborated among the Arapaho, Cheyenne, and Dakota, most meager and recent among the western
marginal tribes. The Comanche, after being mere
spectators of the performance by their Kiowa neighbors, worked out a simplified copy of it in 1874;
the Ute adopted the dance about 1890 and subsequently made it their principal ceremony.

What holds true of the Crow Tobacco ceremonial
holds equally for the Sun Dance: it does not revolve
about the worship of a particular deity, the popular
English name for it being a misnomer, but is a
composite of largely unintegrated elements prominent in the area at large. The remarkable thing
about it is the wide distribution of many objective
features, while the interpretations and ostensible
motives for holding it vary widely. Quite general
was its tribal character: the Dance was performed
after the reassemblage following the winter dis-
persal, i.e., either in the late spring or early summer. Though in many tribes the performance was
annual, it hinged on some distressed tribesman's
vowing to have it held if he were relieved of his

worries. Among the Crow the only motive was an inconsolable mourner seeking revenge upon the tribe that had killed a close relative of his, so that years might elapse between successive ceremonies. A priest acquainted with the ritual conducted the Dance, first instructing the pledger in a preparatory tipi, while a large number of tribesmen not concerned with esoteric aspects brought in the requisites for the great ceremonial structure. Most groups stressed the solemnities associated with the central or the first pole to be set up for the lodge: they scouted for a suitable tree, had a specially qualified person—say, a chaste woman—chop it, and treated the fallen tree as an enemy on whom coup was to be counted. Before raising this pole, the builders put a bundle of brush, a buffalo hide, and offerings into the fork of the log. Commonly this bundle was explained as an eagle's or thunderbird's nest. The exceptional structure of the Crow was merely a huge tipi in shape; typical was a circular enclosure from whose crossbeams rafters extended to the fork of the central pole (Plate 35). Within the enclosure a cleared area with buffalo skulls figured as the altar. Before the main celebrants entered, warriors came in to dramatize military exploits (Crow, Kiowa, Arapaho, Cheyenne, Oglala, Hidatsa).

Generally the pledger and his associates, such as the members of his club among the Cheyenne, fasted and thirsted for several days, steadily gazing at the top of the central pole as they danced and prayed for power. The Crow pledger had to stare at a sacred doll (Plate 36) provided by his priestly mentor until it granted him a vision of a scalped enemy. Not absolutely general was the torture fea-

ture: certain participants had their breast or back
punctured so that skewers could be inserted, ropes
were attached at one end to the center pole, at the
other to the skewers, and the dancers strained
against the ropes until they had torn themselves
loose. The dance was extremely simple, the performers merely rising on their toes while blowing
whistles. As for the torture feature, it was completely lacking among the Kiowa, Ute, and Shoshone; only among the Dakota and Ponca did
the main celebrant practice such self-mortification,
while elsewhere it was voluntary, though usual, for
other dancers.

So many of the objective traits were alike
throughout most of the area that they must have
diffused from a single source. Yet the alleged aims
of the ceremony vary widely. We must infer that
the ceremonial *behavior* in the festival was older
and that the assumed objectives were subsequent
additions. It is also clear that the Dance was only
in part a religious ceremony and in large measure
served for the aesthetic pleasure and entertainment
of the spectators.

MODERN MOVEMENTS

Two modern religious movements require notice—
the Ghost Dance and the Peyote Cult.

The Ghost Dance derives its name from the belief that the Indians were to be reunited with their
dead. Its earlier form (1870) was developed by a
Paviotso Indian in Nevada who went into trances
and preached that the deceased were about to return to earth and that the ancient life was to be
restored along with the game animals then growing
scarce. In about 1888 the prophet's younger kins-

man Wovoka renewed the message. On the basis of a personal revelation granted to him, he taught his fellow tribesmen a dance that was to bring about the reunion with the dead. He combined this doctrine with ethical teachings, prohibiting fighting and enjoining peace with the Whites. Sometimes he blended Christian with pagan ideas, at one time even pretending to be Christ returning to renew the aging earth. This need for renovating the earth is an old and widespread American Indian conception.

Whereas Wovoka's predecessor had aroused no interest in the Plains Area, the younger messiah appeared at a time far more favorable to the reception of his cult. For one thing, means of communication had greatly improved, so that interested Indians living at a distance could easily visit the prophet. Secondly, by 1888 the disappearance of buffalo had wrought great hardships, which were aggravated by misunderstandings with the agents of the United States government. The Teton Dakota, Arapaho, Cheyenne, and Kiowa more especially seized upon what they supposed to be the new faith, though actually they completely changed its import. The peaceable Paviotso had never dreamt of rebellion against the government, whereas among the warlike Plains tribes this became a cardinal point of doctrine. Goaded into fury by their grievances, the disciples of Wovoka in the Plains substituted for his policy of amity a holy war in which the Whites were to be exterminated. As far as possible the dress and the ways of the hostile race were to be tabooed, while vestiges of the old life, such as the traditional games, were eagerly fostered. In revivalist mass meetings

men and women worked themselves into hypnotic
trances and, on coming to, announced what visions
they had seen—deceased kinsfolk, vast herds of
buffalo, and so forth. The Dakota more particularly
devised a kind of shirt, symbolically decorated, that
was supposed to make the wearer bulletproof.

Under the impetus of this cult, hostile demon-
strations broke out among the Teton under the
leadership of Sitting Bull, who was killed by Indian
police on December 15, 1890. A fortnight later
there was a battle at Wounded Knee, where 31
soldiers and 128 Dakota were killed. The armed
insurrection virtually ceased with this engagement,
but the excitement persisted for some time among
several of the tribes.

The most suggestive facts about the movement
are the radical change by the Plains Indians of the
imported Basin cult and the minor variations created within the Plains by the leaders of the several
tribes affected. Particular developments are likewise of interest, such as the religious flavor im-
parted by the votaries to old games. The Pawnee,
for instance, carried shinny balls or hoops in their
dances and tried to induce visions with their aid;
they also came to treat the hand game as a ceremony, its proper procedure being revealed in visions.

Weston La Barre in his study of the Peyote Cult
describes peyote (*Lophophora williamsii* Lemaire)
as "a small, spineless carrot-shaped cactus growing
in the Rio Grande Valley and southward." Its round
top, the only part visible above the ground, is cut
off and dried to form the "button." The plant is not
to be confused with the north Mexican mescal
(*Agave americana*). Containing nine narcotic alka-

loids, peyote produces visual hallucinations and other physiological derangements, including dilated pupils. The first effect is exhilaration, followed by depression, nausea, and wakefulness, and ultimately the partaker has brilliant color visions lasting for several hours.

The cult centering about this narcotic is recent in the Plains, not reaching the Kiowa before *ca.* 1870 and hardly becoming conspicuous there until about fifteen years later; but Mexican natives used the plant as early as the sixteenth century, and the Cora practiced a peyote ritual in 1754. Since the species is not indigenous north of Texas, most of the Plains peyotists are obliged to make expeditions to its home or to purchase it. As in the case of the Ghost Dance, the Plains Indians greatly modified the religious notions developed in the original center of diffusion. In Mexico the main objective of the seasonal ritual was curing, success in war and in corn growing or the deer hunt; there was considerable dancing, but no society of peyote eaters, no exclusiveness, even women taking part in the performances. In the Plains, doctoring, though as a rule important, was not essential; warfare was stressed in the earlier period; dancing was generally lacking; the ceremony can be performed at any time; and the peyote worshipers form an organization, which at first excluded women. The Mexicans assemble outdoors, the Plains Indians in a tipi; the Plains tribes stress smoking, which plays no great role in Mexico, but do not combine their Peyote Cult with ritual races and ball games, which loom large in Mexico. Notwithstanding such noteworthy differences, there are likewise many parallels in the two areas. To mention only a few, in both regions peyote is collected on a ceremonial trip, the sessions are held at night, followed by a ritual breakfast, in which parched corn, sweetened water, and boneless meat are prominent.

The earliest form of Plains peyotism, as practiced by the Kiowa, exhibits a number of features characteristic of ancient Plains supernaturalism. Meetings are held in accordance with a vow, on the pattern of a Sun Dance; the desire for a vision through the peyote takes precedence of the doctoring motive; there is a preparatory sweatbath; and four appears as the sacred number. As to organization, the sponsor of the meeting is responsible for the expense involved and supplies the peyote; he selects the leader of the ceremony, who is assisted by a drummer and a fire tender. The leader's regalia include a staff, a gourd rattle, an eagle-bone whistle, a drum partly filled with water, and cedar incense. Essential for a performance is the peyote altar, usually built of clayey earth in a crescent shape.

Given the Plains pattern of visionary experiences as the basis for modifications in ritual, the Kiowa prototype came to be considerably altered in accordance with leaders' individual revelations. In some tribes even Christian elements entered, including Bible reading; the three Osage officials are said to represent the Trinity; a bird image of ashes made by the Oto is interpreted as the Spirit descending at Jesus' baptism. As a matter of fact, peyotism is shot through with symbolism, both pagan and Christian. The leader's staff is the "staff of life" for a Wichita, the Saviour's staff for an Iowa.

Because of the supposedly evil effects of peyote—a mooted issue—many attempts have been launched to prohibit its use. As a countermeasure an inter-tribal Native American Church was founded. It is worth noting that the cult spread to various Woodland and Basin groups as well as to originally Southeastern tribes settled in Oklahoma.

The earliest finds of archaeological material in the Plains date back possibly over 10,000 years—so far back that its makers cannot be regarded as the ancestors of the Indians under consideration in this book, though they were doubtless of the same race. It is, however, interesting to note that the area was inhabited thousands of years ago by hunters who manufactured tools of the ancient types known as "Folsom" points, *i.e.*, thin stone points skillfully worked by pressure, large longitudinal flakes being removed from one or both faces.

Of direct relevance to our subject have been the archaeological researches of the past twenty years by William D. Strong, Waldo Wedel, William Mulloy, and others. Working back from sites known to have been occupied by particular tribes in historic times, they have been able to unfold the story of culture in earlier periods, though so far only in limited portions of the total area. Nevertheless some definite results stand out. Before the coming of the horse, Nebraska and the Dakotas appear to have been for some time inhabited by semisedentary peoples. That is, contrary to the picture of later times the Pawnee and the Mandan rather than pure hunters set the tone in this region. Pawnee sites of *ca.* A.D. 1800 indicate large villages of earthlodges with plenty of horse remains and articles of Caucasian origin as well as distinctive aboriginal pottery. Sites of the same district on the Platte and Loup rivers, Nebraska, probably dating back to A.D. 1600, reveal no signs of contact with Whites, and the large earthlodge villages of this period harbored far superior pottery and a greater abundance of stonework. The conclusion is that during the two centuries aboriginal Pawnee culture declined.

To a still earlier period belong many small villages with mostly, though not exclusively, square earthlodges. Pottery is abundant, and ornaments of shells indigenous to the Gulf coast prove connection with the Southeast. Roughly contemporary are settlements of small, scattered, unfortified earthlodges, half underground, rectangular or square dwellings being definitely in the majority. Clay rather than stone pipes of elaborate and realistic shape are characteristic; abundant vegetable remains, such as charred maize, and many bone hoes demonstrate considerable farming. Just south of the Platte-Missouri confluence a unique site has plenty of remains of squashes and gourds but no trace of maize, and deer bones outnumber those of buffalo. Typical of the same settlement are small houses with reed-thatched roofs and a dearth of stone implements, compensated for by much fine work in bone and antler, including awls and beads.

At Signal Butte, in westernmost Nebraska, Strong found clearly separable layers, the top one containing earthenware like that on the Upper Republican, while the two older strata have no pottery at all. In stone projectile points, the highest and the lowest horizon differ sharply. The upper stratum has tiny chipped points resembling those of the Upper Republican and of the earliest historic Pawnee. In the lowest stratum leaf-shaped points recall those found in Nebraska and elsewhere in association with extinct species of mammals.

The sequence in the subarea best explored to date, then, is as follows: At first there was, as elsewhere, a purely hunting stage. Later, agriculture, mainly based on maize, was developed to a considerable degree, though hunting remained important. The economy was thus intermediate between that of the virtually altogether agricultural Pueblos and of the purely hunting equestrians of the historic Plains.

A star example of the changes undergone by some tribes is furnished by the Cheyenne. In the eighteenth century they occupied a settlement on the Sheyenne River in east-central North Dakota; this was destroyed by the Ojibwa in *ca.* 1770. Excavation demonstrated a village of possibly seventy circular earthlodges very much like the type found on the Upper Missouri in historic times. Cache pits contained vegetal remains, broken pottery, buffalo bones, and various indications of White contact. By way of contrast, a Cheyenne camp site of the early nineteenth century showed no trace of agriculture or of earthlodges but contained numerous trade objects. It would seem that within the space of fifty years the formerly semisedentary Cheyenne had completely given up farming and permanent dwellings in favor of buffalo hunting and tipis.

If several centuries ago Nebraska and the Dakotas were inhabited by natives of a relatively complex way of life, Montana seems to have had outposts of that culture. About five miles southeast of

Glendive, in the easternmost part of the state, William Mulloy discovered a site with one small earth-lodge and twenty cache pits. Abundant remains in the neighborhood suggest that perhaps most of the occupants of the settlement lived in temporary dwellings. Several circumstances render this site especially noteworthy. The district lies within the territory of the historic Crow, whose language is so close to Hidatsa that they cannot have separated more than a few centuries ago. A westward migration is supported by both Crow and Hidatsa tradition, and this movement was accompanied by a loss of farming, so that Crow history broadly parallels that of the Cheyenne. Given these basic facts, a transitional stage is a reasonable assumption, and the site near Glendive meets the conditions. Buffalo shoulder blades indicate the sort of hoeing practiced until recently by Hidatsa women and the pottery—not made by the historic Crow—seems most closely related to that of the Mandan-Hidatsa (Plate 15), both in its uncoiled technique and its simple decoration. The stone tools point in the same direction, duplicating types previously known from the Mandan. Many small scrapers chipped only on the back and worked into a flat convex edge at one end closely resemble an authentically Mandan blade in the United States National Museum.

Though the correspondence is not complete and should not be expected to be so, it is thus likely that the occupants of the Glendive site were Crow Indians still retaining a good deal of their Hidatsa cultural heritage "before they had sloughed off entirely their old semisedentary mode of village life and pottery-making and when they had not yet acquired the horse" (Wedel).

Another significant series of archaeological discoveries proves that pottery without agriculture was once very widely distributed in Montana, even in the extreme North and Northwest. The relations of this ware are as yet obscure; some details point toward the western Great Lakes or the upper Mississippi Valley. We cannot contend that the ceramic art ever *flourished* in Montana or is very ancient there. In Pictograph Cave, near Billings, the single stratified site so far examined, pottery exists only in the upper layer and with Caucasian remains, indicating manufacture by the direct ancestors of historic inhabitants of the region. Nevertheless, the finds enlarge the range of the ceramic art in North America and support traditions of northern Plains tribes hitherto treated with reserve (page 61).

The archaeological exploration of Texas has also brought to light interesting connections. In the Panhandle, many-roomed stone and adobe buildings prove Pueblo influence, while the pottery points overwhelmingly to the utilitarian cord-marked ware of the central Plains. The few Pueblo-like sherds that have been found help, however, to fix the approximate date of the culture as between A.D. 1300 and 1450. In the contemporary eastern Pueblo of Pecos, New Mexico, various implements connected with the hunt and skin dressing prove that the borrowing extended in both directions. The people of the Panhandle practiced at that period partly an agricultural, partly a hunting economy. Possibly, because of serious droughts, they migrated, so that Coronado found the Canadian River Valley to be the home of nomadic buffalo hunters.

In the Texas section of the Llano Estacado the remains are quite different, the pottery discovered indicating a marginal Pueblo culture. The same influences appear to the south.

In north-central Texas, on the Upper Brazos and Upper Red Rivers, a few sherds of trade Puebloan pottery accompany a mixed economy of semisedentary Plains type and Pueblo hand mills. It has been suggested that the bearers of this culture were Wichita, but prior to 1700 evidence is lacking that this tribe lived south of Oklahoma; it can be traced archaeologically only as far south as central Kansas. Thus north-central Texas in, say, A.D. 1450 was inhabited by an as yet unidentified semisedentary people. Still farther east the sites fall within the Caddoan section of the Southeastern Area. The Caddoans visited there by the Spaniards in 1542 had cotton blankets and turquoise, both of which they must have obtained from the Pueblos. A connection between the Southeast and the Southwest, say, in 1400, is further suggested by ceramic resemblances due to mutual borrowing and greater than can be ascribed to mere trade. However, there is very little similarity between Southeastern sites in the wooded sections of eastern Oklahoma, western Arkansas, northwestern Louisiana, and northeastern Texas on the one hand and central or southern sites of clear-cut Plains type. At present the Pawnee cannot be archaeologically connected with fellow Caddoans to the south and southeast, though linguistic affiliation points in that direction.

As the Cheyenne and Crow cases illustrate, a combination of archaeological with historical and linguistic findings greatly aids us in the reconstruction of the past. For some tribes the written records suffice to give us a fairly clear picture of cultural developments.

The Plains Cree are one of the best-known instances. When first mentioned by the chroniclers of the *Jesuit Relations* in 1640, the Cree had nothing to do with our area, being an eastern Woodland people living toward Hudson Bay. In 1666–1667 they were roving hunters, canoers, and gatherers of wild rice who shared with other forest dwellers the region between Hudson Bay and Lake Superior. Hostile to the Dakota, they were friendly to the Assiniboin. With the coming of the Hudson's Bay Company, the Cree turned trappers to supply the traders with furs. The demand for beaver made them penetrate farther west, displacing the older inhabitants with the aid of the Europeans' guns. By about 1730 a detachment of Cree was reported south of the Saskatchewan, and they had certainly reached Lake Winnipeg. Though not yet adapted to the new habitat, they had already largely changed their old economy for, as a result of their specialization as trappers, they were now depending on the traders for weapons, clothing, utensils, and even food. They still paddled about in canoes, thus enjoying great mobility. The advantage due to firearms, however, decreased as other tribes likewise got guns.

The change, which affected only part of the Cree, was rapid, but came by stages. In 1772 the western advance guard was impounding buffalo, but still clung to the canoe. In fact, a few survivals of the old culture, such as snowshoes, remained for good. But to all intents and purposes the Plains Cree, after somewhat tardily taking up equestrian life, became thoroughly assimilated Plains people, sharply separated in outlook and customs, though not in speech, from the Eastern Cree.

Other Woodland tribes, who lived farther south, sharing the widespread maize culture of the East, completely abandoned farming in favor of the buffalo chase. The Cheyenne have already been cited in this connection. When first mentioned in 1673 they lived in westernmost Wisconsin and the section of Minnesota between the Mississippi, Minnesota, and Upper Red River. Pressed by the Dakota, who were themselves pushed out by the Ojibwa, they migrated westward. In 1804 Lewis and Clark found them in the Black Hills country of present South Dakota. The Cheyenne, too, turned into pure buffalo hunters, but also played the part of middlemen in procuring English goods from the Hidatsa and passing them on to the Arapaho and other tribes. It is probable that the basic mutation did not affect all the Cheyenne at once, but at first only their westernmost outposts while the laggards were still to some extent raising corn.

The story of the Dakota runs parallel with that of the Cheyenne. When first seen by Whites in the seventeenth century, they were a forest people occupying the territory from the Upper Mississippi to the headwaters of the Minnesota. They embraced many politically distinct subdivisions, but a sense of unity persisted, and their three dialects did not differ materially. "They fought other people, but ordinarily not each other" (Mekeel). The Teton, migrating as far as the Black Hills, Wyoming, and southeastern Montana, became the embodiment of Plains nomadism, while the Santee and other eastern sub-groups retained the old semi-agricultural economy. The differentiation cannot be wholly due to European contact, for as early as 1700 Le Sueur notes the Teton's lack of canoes and wild rice. At all events, the Dakota as a unit must have been an originally Woodland people, a large branch of which became buffalo hunters to the exclusion of farming.

The Assiniboin speak a language closely akin to the N dialects of Dakota. In 1640 they were already distinct from the parent tribe and inhabited the vicinity of the Lake of the Woods and Lake Nipigon in southern Ontario. They became intimately connected with the Cree, sharing in the transformation undergone by that tribe. In Lewis and Clark's day they were also in close contact with the villagers of the Upper Missouri. As might be expected, their culture is largely a blend of Dakota and Cree traits.

The Southern Siouans may be summarily dealt with. None of them occupied *high* Plains country, and some of their traditions indicate the lower Ohio River as an earlier home. What is more, the language of the Iowa-Oto is closely related to Winnebago, the speech of an unquestionably Woodland people. Skinner finds a series of stages between the Winnebago at one extreme and the Ponca at the other, the Iowa, Oto, Omaha, and Ponca marking the steps toward a full-fledged Plains culture. None of them turned into pure hunters, but even the historic Iowa surrounded buffalo, dressed skins with elk-horn scrapers, crossed rivers in bull-boats, traveled with travois, and had rival military clubs. The Omaha also had some military societies, though overshadowed by other organizations. They lacked the Sun Dance, but did practice the ceremonial chopping down of a tree that is so conspicuous and widespread a feature of that festival. Among the Ponca there were several military organizations; in part they obtained them from the Teton and passed them on to the Omaha. The Ponca also celebrated a full-fledged Sun Dance. All in all, the Southern Siouan culture was a mixture of Plains and Woodland features.

While all the tribes just considered came from the eastern Woodlands, the Caddoans of the Plains —Pawnee-Arikara and Wichita—can be connected specifically with the Southeast. This holds true especially if, in accordance with many scholars, the Iroquois of New York are regarded as originally native to that area. In this connection it is worth emphasizing that eminent linguists consider Iroquoian and Caddoan closely related stocks and that the unquestionably Iroquoian Cherokee were met by De Soto (1540) in the southern Alleghenies. To the great resemblance between Pawnee and Iroquois pottery may be added the exceptionally large number of small triangular, unnotched arrowheads found in Iroquoian and Caddoan sites. The Southeast as a whole is marked by the deposition of human remains in bone-houses; and though such ossuaries are not known from the historic Pawnee, early sites indicative of the Pawnee do reveal such structures. Again, prehistoric square earthlodges on the Republican River strongly recall a type discovered in Arkansas. Unknown in the period of Caucasian contact, they may well represent the antecedent of the historic circular earthlodge. Grass houses, typical of the modern Wichita and observed by Coronado in 1541 along the Arkansas River, are a variant of this type. A striking parallel between the Skidi Pawnee and the Natchez of the Lower Mississippi is the torture of a captive stretched out in a frame. The cutting open of the victim's breast is reminiscent of an Aztec ceremony (southern Mexico), but the immediate historical connection seems to be with the Natchez. Considering that the Caddo proper and other members of their family are indigenous to the Southeast, it is justifiable to trace the Plains Caddoans to the vicinity of the Gulf of Mexico, say to southern Texas, even though clear-cut archaeological proof is lacking. We may picture the Pawnee as originally skillful Southeastern farmers, who also did considerable hunting. As they pushed farther west and north, they probably—like the historic Caddo—took more and more to the buffalo chase. This explains the abundance of buffalo bones on archaeological sites within their territory. However, in getting more and more horses the Pawnee tended to emphasize this aspect of their economy, and though they kept on farming, the art of pottery declined. Considering that in the later periods they often raided the Southwest, they remained remarkably free from Pueblo influences. Thus, the stone hand mill, so characteristic of the Pueblo Area, was conspicuously rare, wooden mortars of the Eastern type prevailing.

The Arikara must be considered a fairly recent offshoot of the Pawnee since their speech differs only dialectically. They moved north, became neighbors of the Mandan and Hidatsa, and are probably responsible for some elaborations in the culture of the Upper Missouri.

In all the foregoing cases the Plains were invaded from the east. There were likewise incursions from

the opposite direction. From the subarctic Athabaskan region came the Sarsi, linguistically an offshoot
of the Beaver Indians first discovered toward the
end of the eighteenth century around the upper
Saskatchewan and Athabaska Rivers. Numerically
weak, they attached themselves to the Blackfoot
and assimilated the ways of their more powerful
neighbors, even achieving sketchy replicas of the
military associations and the Sun Dance.

Of much greater importance in Plains history
were the Uto-Aztecans. The three groups significant
in this context—the Wind River Shoshone, Comanche, and Ute—all belong to the Shoshonean branch
of the family. Some other Shoshoneans also partook
of Plains culture, but only sporadically and to a
minor degree. Since by far the majority of Shoshonean tribes lived in the Basin Area and southern
California, our three groups doubtless ultimately
came into the Plains as relative newcomers from
the west; *i.e.*, they formerly inhabited an area of
marked simplicity. Accordingly, on the whole they
passively took on Plains features, absorbing essentially material rather than social and religious traits.
One vital exception, however, must be made. The
Shoshone provided horses for the Crow and the
Blackfoot (page 42). In the southern Plains, the
Comanche, being near the Spanish settlements,
played a corresponding role; the Ponca regarded
them as their masters in horsemanship and in packing horses. Apart from such services, it is possible
that the distinctive parfleche style of the Crow was
influenced by the Shoshone.

How soon the Shoshoneans turned into Plains
Indians remains uncertain. The "Teyas" of the Spanish chroniclers have been regarded as Comanche,

but this is merely a possible interpretation. The earliest unquestionable reference to this people goes back to 1701 and places them near the headwaters of the Arkansas (Colorado); in 1705 they were found in New Mexico. Since Comanche and Shoshone differ only dialectically, their separation cannot date back many centuries. That they or the parent tribe had adopted buffalo hunting as their main subsistence basis by *ca*. A.D. 1700 may be accepted as certain.

The Blackfoot and the Arapaho-Gros Ventre languages, though Algonkian, differ so sharply from other Algonkian tongues as to indicate for their speakers a long period of separation from eastern and central members of the stock. It is therefore plausible to assume that they are "ancient occupants of the northern true plains, or rather of the foothills of the Rockies and the plains tributary thereto" (Kroeber). In the south, the Kiowa cannot be traced outside the Plains Area on the basis of historic documents. Linguistically, some scholars link them with the Tanoan family of the Rio Grande region, in other words, with the easternmost Pueblos. The Athabaskan Kiowa-Apache, too, are apparently old inhabitants of our area, centering in southwestern Oklahoma. As a small group they attached themselves to the Kiowa for the celebration of the Sun Dance as though a band of the larger tribe, but otherwise preserved their identity; the two peoples communicated with each other mainly by gestures. The case of the Plains Apache (page 9) is problematic. The "Querechos" or "Vaqueros" described by sixteenth-century Spanish chroniclers as nomadic hunters have been generally identified as "Apache"; but the Jicarilla Apache who seem to have come closest to the Plains pattern turn out to have practiced considerable farming before the American occupation, and the oldest survivors in 1934 insisted on the ancillary and comparatively recent use of the tipi. In consequence, doubt is cast on the traditional equation "Querechos = Apache." Finally, the archaeological evidence cited indicates prehistoric Pawnee residence in the Plains, as does the Spanish reference to grass houses of presumably Wichita and almost certainly Caddoan construction.

Thus, though many other groups may well have been in the area in aboriginal days, the strongest claim for early Plains residence may be made for the eastern Shoshoneans, the Blackfoot, Arapaho-Gros Ventre, Kiowa, Kiowa-Apache, Pawnee, and some other Caddoans.

8 ACCULTURATION

Acculturation has been defined as the changes produced in the cultures of peoples in continuous contact with each other. When the two groups differ in complexity, the simpler culture is likely to be more receptive than the other. Such was the relative status of Indians and Caucasians, the latter more frequently playing the donor's role. Thus occurred the assimilation of the White man's clothing, utensils, tools, firearms, and horses. Yet the process was not wholly one-sided, for maize was the Indian's gift to European civilization, and the specific variety planted on the Upper Missouri proved a boon to White settlers in the area.

Automatically the recipients of laborsaving devices dropped their ancient handiwork and processes of manufacture except where emotional attachment led them to retain what was old, as in ceremonials. In this sense there were cultural losses as well as gains. By no means all possible material traits were accepted, even where the advantages were obvious. The Plains tribes accepted cattle as the closest approach to the moribund buffalo herds, but did not take at all kindly to milking, churning, or cheese making. Further, some elements of the Caucasian culture were, for some reason, introduced much later than necessary; the Crow, for instance, did not get wagons until 1874.

It is necessary to distinguish acculturation that happened through the sheer contact of Indians with Whites and the acculturation due to deliberate planning on the part of the United States government. Far-reaching results were caused by the mere coming of traders and later by the construction of railroads. The rapid interchange of ideas by different tribes at the time of the Ghost Dance would not have been possible in the era of more primitive transportation.

The general policy of the government was to civilize the natives in the sense of making them literate, English-speaking, Christian farmers like their White neighbors. This aim created formidable problems. In the first place, many tribes, having either always or at least for decades been nomadic hunters, did not wish to take up fixed residences. But even the semisedentary Plains Indians were not ready to emulate the example of Caucasian agriculturists. For one thing, their farming tools were hoes and dibbles, involving techniques quite different from ploughing with domestic livestock. No less serious was the sociological transformation involved, for in the old days women planted, whereas under the new order the men were expected to do the work. At first, then, any men who took up ploughing were likely to lose face and to be jeered at. Apart from everything else, much of the land allotted to the natives was unsuitable for husbandry or required irrigation. The task of the agency officials appointed to teach the Indians farming was therefore an arduous one. Some Indians managed to lease their land to Whites, some simply killed off and ate whatever cattle were issued to them. Again, in matrilineal tribes, confusion arose when officials insisted on having land inherited from father to son.

One outstanding change in adaptation to an industrial civilization was in the direction of individualism. The Plains Indians were indeed intensely individualistic in matters of prestige, but economically they were often the reverse, sharing food freely with anyone and other chattels at least with kinsfolk. A potentially successful farmer would thus be held back in his economic progress by a host of needy spongers if he clung to tribal ethics. On this point individuals widely varied, some for a long time being willing to forego material prosperity rather than to flout ancient custom.

With regard to education, the government provided schooling on and off the reservations. For a long time the boarding schools like that at Carlisle, Pennsylvania, were far more effective since the children, removed from parental and tribal influences, had to learn English and to make adjustments to American life. In other respects the results were less advantageous: alienated from his people, the returning young man or woman was at least for some time a stranger in his own country. These "educated Indians" could, however, play an important part as interpreters and as spokesmen of their people in dealings with United States officials.

An important personality problem, for the males, was finding a suitable substitute for the ancient goals. With the buffalo gone and warfare a thing of the past, they found it very hard to discover any objectives that made life worth living. Some strongly expressed the sentiment that they preferred the old existence with all its hazards, but with the chance for glory, to the pedestrian career of a farmer or mechanic.

Education was to a considerable extent offered by missionaries of various denominations. The effectiveness of their religious instruction is difficult to judge. It depended on the length of time the Indians were exposed to such efforts and on the individual character of both the natives and the missionaries. With the older people, aboriginal paganism lingered for a very long time. Moreover, aboriginal religion was definitely neither propagandist nor dogmatic, so that an Indian could very well combine Christian doctrines with ancient belief in the reality of spirits who appeared in visions. In those recent cults which favored proselytizing, such as the Peyote Cult, Christian teachings easily blended with native ideas.

Conditions have been so different for the several groups on the Plains that no generalizing sketch of their acculturation can do justice to all the facts. The issue has depended on such factors as when the particular tribe was put on a reservation, whether they remained in their historic territory, whether or not they had had markedly hostile clashes with government agencies, whether missions or schools had been established. Within the last half century, assimilation to White ways has certainly progressed. To take the Omaha, in 1910, of those under forty years of age 90 per cent had some knowledge of English, many of them spoke it well. All lived in houses, using tents only in the summer. Except for about twenty men in a population of 1,270, all males dressed in citizens' clothes, while the older women had taken to a compromise between native and White dress and some of the younger ones

wore White clothing. Ninety-five per cent of the
people used carriages and buggies. Ninety per cent
of the children spent a reasonable portion of the
year in school. Two Omaha were lawyers, two
merchants, three or four engaged in real estate or
stock business, several in government service, a
large number were making good homes for themselves as farmers.

Although the Omaha, then, largely attained the
goal originally set by the Bureau of Indian Affairs,
there were currents and crosscurrents in the recent
history of the Plains Indians. From 1933 until 1945
Commissioner John Collier headed the Bureau and
applied the policy of fostering native custom so far
as it did not conflict with the necessities of modern
civilization. Thus became possible the revival of the
Sun Dance in modified form.

Apart from developments directed from above,
there have been "pagan" survivals, such as exist
even in remote rural communities of western Europe and of America. In 1931 an old Crow would
not eat a cake till he was assured that it had not
been made with eggs, which had been tabooed to
him in a vision. A middle-aged man at that time
carefully kept his medicine bundle where it could
not be polluted by the presence of menstruating
women. The Arapaho were rigidly maintaining the
mother-in-law taboo only twenty years ago and
probably still are. Rather generally there has been
the omnipresent struggle between progressives and
conservatives, the former favoring rapid adaptation
to modern conditions, the latter trying to salvage
what they could of ancient usage.

9 CONCLUSION

A few general facts emerge from a consideration of the data. The tribes dealt with are properly regarded as representing a distinctive mode of life during the period of Caucasian contacts. Dependence on the buffalo, residence in skin-covered tipis, use of the horse for the hunt and for transport, the peculiar style of decorative and of pictographic art, the sign language, the ideology of warfare, the Sun Dance and less conspicuous features of supernaturalism are outstanding features widely prevalent in our area and not similarly combined elsewhere.

However, culture areas are merely convenient ways of classifying peoples, and we must recognize that a different alignment is possible and equally legitimate. The semisedentary tribes clearly form a subgroup within our area; and they could properly be united with the western Woodland tribes of Wisconsin and Illinois to form a Wisconsin-Southern Plains Area. This consideration applies with special force to the Southern Siouans. The Omaha, Oto, and Iowa share with the Winnebago, Menomini, Sauk, and Fox many traits not typical of the high Plains. To take one feature, the game of lacrosse is highly characteristic of the eastern half of the United States and suggestively lacking in our area—except among the Iowa, Oto, Eastern Dakota, and their offshoot, the Assiniboin. To take another feature from a different sphere of culture, the Southern Siouans have the same form of patrilineal clan organization as the Central Algonkians and the Winnebago, and with it went the same mode of classifying relatives (page 103). In vital aspects of social life, the Omaha resemble the Algonkian Menomini of the Woodlands more than they do their fellow Siouans. It is a matter of choice whether we stress the set of traits connected with the buffalo hunt and, in later times, with the horse or stress the complex which the Southern Siouans brought from the Woodlands in migrating westward.

From a broader point of view, we must first of all recognize Plains traits that go back to a hoary antiquity and were pan-American, e.g., the technique of stone chipping, the dog as a domesticated animal, the firedrill. Then there are elements not so widely found, yet general north of the Rio Grande; the vision quest, lacking only in the Pueblo Area, would be an example. Another set of traits would include those penetrating from the west and southwest. Under this head fall the sinew-backed bow, hard-soled moccasins, and probably some decorative designs. This influence, however, is overshadowed by the features shared with the Eastern tribes of the continent and, like the Cree snowshoes, demonstrably carried west in the contact period. Altogether the Plains culture thus appears as a specialization of the Woodland cultures, modified by subsequent borrowings from elsewhere and by regional adaptations to a new environment.

The horse stimulated mobility and with it brought far-reaching contacts among hitherto remote tribes so that over an immense territory cultural leveling occurred. This was most noticeable as regards external features, but was by no means confined to them. The Comanche, peripheral to the typical representatives of the Plains, retained vestiges of their affinity with the Basin Area. Yet it is remarkable how many specific items they came to share, though some of them very late, with the most typical peoples of the Plains. Their mystic number was four, not five, as of some Basin Shoshoneans. Their practice of the vision quest and their attitude toward guardian spirits strongly recall Crow phenomena. Though in slightly developed form, military societies existed and so did a whole series of sentiments and practices associated with warfare on the Plains. There was the glorification of valor, the axiom that a man ought to die young as a warrior, the recital of coups, the scouts' swearing on a pile of buffalo droppings, the theoretical appropriation of all loot by the leader of a raid, the occasional assumption of a "contrary" role (page 113) by men courting death.

Leveling of another kind occurred when some tribes lost earlier features and at the same time adopted the horse and a fuller adaptation to the buffalo chase. Thus, those Cree who entered the Plains lost the canoe and became equestrian nomads; the previously corn-growing Cheyenne lost agriculture and fixed habitations as they specialized in buffalo hunting; the Pawnee did not go so far, but grew less intensive cultivators and more ardent hunters.

Important as Caucasian contacts were in precipitating westward migrations and in introducing the horse, the *creative* power of the innovations should not be exaggerated. The consequences seem merely "a logical development of the type of life described by Coronado" (Eggan). It is a curious fact that what figures as the fully developed Plains culture did *not* evolve among the tribes that first acquired horses; neither the Apache nor the Shoshone-Comanche nor the Nez Percé were Plains tribes in the fullest sense. The simple explanation is that many essential aspects of Plains culture were preexistent in the "Eastern Maize Area," not dependent on horse breeding, and came to be imported into the Plains by migration either of peoples or of ideas from the Woodlands. This appears clearly from the earlier sources.

In the first place, the buffalo was far from unknown in the East and probably a much more important game animal in prehistoric times than it became later. Robes of buffalo skin were worn in the Southeast, shields were of buffalo hide, the horns furnished ornaments on headdresses as well as material for spoons and dishes. As among the Hidatsa, hoes were made of buffalo shoulder blades. The hair was woven into cords, belts, and garters, which recalls the bags of buffalo wool seen among the Oto, Kansa, and Osage (Skinner). Though the animals grew scarce in the Southeast in colonial days, they occurred in large numbers in what is now Kentucky, northeastern Arkansas, Tennessee, especially in the western section of the Gulf region. The Creek even had a Buffalo clan in ancient times.

Farther north there were likewise local differences in the distribution of the species. The Menomini wove buffalo wool and wore a cap of buffalo skin in one of their dances, but in Catlin's day (1832) they had to go far to hunt the animal. The Winnebago went to the prairie after buffalo, and one of their clans was named for the species; the Ojibwa drove herds into enclosures. For the Miami, buffalo were the principal game and furnished the material for robes; these Indians set fire to the dead grass and surrounded the herd, driving it toward the hunters' ambush. Attention has been called to the effectiveness of such methods in early contact times.

What is more, though the relative importance of fishing, hunting, and cultivating varied from one Eastern tribe to another, the economic pattern of the Illinois and Miami was precisely that of the semisedentary Plains peoples. The Illinois of *ca.* A.D. 1700 would leave their villages in communal quest of large game in the winter, returning toward May to plant maize, beans, and pumpkins; as among the Mandan, Hidatsa, and Omaha, women farmed and men hunted.

Nothing was more characteristic of the Plains than the functioning of a police force during the collective hunt or in travel. It so happens that our earliest report of the institution (1680) is for the Santee Dakota, properly a Woodland group. Louis Hennepin, who wrote *A New Discovery of a Vast Country in America* (London, 1698), had met a company of men from that tribe and been offered of their meat when suddenly came retribution:

> Fifteen or sixteen Savages came into the middle of the Place where they were, with their great Clubs in their Hands. The first thing they did was to over-set the Cabin of those that had invited us. Then they took away all their Victuals and what Bears-Oil they could find in their Bladders, or elsewhere, with which they

rubbed themselves all over from Head to
Foot. . . .

We knew not what these Savages were at
first; but it appear'd they were some of those
that we had left above the Fall of St. Anthony.
One of them, who call'd himself my Uncle, told
me, that those who had given us Victuals, had
done basely to go and forestal the others in the
Chase; and that according to the Laws and
Customs of their Country, 'twas lawful for them
to plunder them, since they had been the cause
that the Bulls were all run away, before the
Nation could get together, which was a great
Injury to the Publick; For when they are all
met, they make a great Slaughter amongst the
Bulls; for they surround them so on every side,
that 'tis impossible for them to escape.

All the characteristic elements of this phenomenon, the so-called soldier killing, appeared in other
western Woodlands groups either during journeys
or when engaged in a major economic enterprise.
At the rice harvest the Menomini and the Winnebago police forbade anyone to trespass on the fields
before the day fixed. The war chiefs of the Sauk and
Fox restrained tribesmen from singly returning to
the village from a hunt and destroyed a transgres-
sor's canoe and property. In about A.D. 1700 an
Illinois

would not dare separate from the mass to go
and hunt when they are on land, for immediately a band of young men who are guards
would run after him to make him return, break
his arms and tear off all that he had on him.
These savages have established this kind of law

among themselves because those who go in advance would cause the animals to flee while killing only a very few of them, which would oblige them to go much farther to find some.

In other words, this typical "Plains" institution was observed east of the Plains by the earliest travelers and as quite independent of any direct or indirect stimulus due to White contact.

Turning to supernaturalism, the Delaware and other Indians of the Atlantic Coast—not to mention tribes farther west—sent boys to fast for a vision at or before puberty, as did the Hidatsa and the Omaha. The sweatbath of the Huron and the subsequent plunge into a river figure in Lafitau's work on Indian customs (1724). The Huron shamans practiced the Pawnee trick of putting their arms into boiling water and handling live coals as early as 1620, and similar miracles are reported from New York Indians fifty years later.

The roach found in certain ceremonial organizations of the Plains was the characteristic daily men's hairdress among the Pawnee, Osage, and Iowa. It was equally typical of the Sauk and Fox and in 1665 attracted the attention of David Pieterz de Vries on Manhattan Island: "Their hair is shorn at the top like a cock's comb."

Finally, Plains militarism, which sharply contrasts with Pueblo, Basin, and Plateau attitudes, corresponds closely to the spirit of the tribes east of the Mississippi before and after the coming of the horse. The suggestion sometimes offered that the craving for horses or other economic values was required to evoke warlike undertaking is preposterous in the light of the evidence. The Powhatan of Virginia, early colonial observers expressly state, seldom warred "for lands or goods, but for women and children, and principally for revenge." In later times, the theft of horses naturally became a main objective in the Southeast, but prior to their introduction retaliation and social advancement were the motives for war expeditions, the main difference from the Plains being the inordinate importance attached to scalps. Just as in the Plains, a leader lost standing if he lost any followers, religious sanctions loomed large, and the raiders carried with them the equivalent of a war medicine bundle.

The same attitude prevailed farther north. In 1632 an observer declared that the Huron went to war "without other pledge or hope of recompense than of honor and praise, which they value more than all the gold in the world." Something very much like the coup existed among several Eastern tribes: a Huron or Illinois took an enemy prisoner by merely touching him. An Illinois captain had to pacify the family of a follower killed on a raid. The Miami leader reaped all the glory of success, but also the disgrace of failure. The system of sending out scouts and having them make a formal report offers another parallel. Naturally, the resemblances multiply as one approaches the Plains. Thus, the war-bundle concept, rudimentary among the Delaware of 1774, flourished full-blown among the Menomini, Sauk, Fox, and Winnebago. Recital of one's deeds in public was characteristic of Menomini and Winnebago. The latter valued touching a foeman higher than killing him, they taught their young the universal Plains maxim that it was well not to die of old age but as a young fighting warrior, and,

like Cheyenne or Crow, they swore oaths to affirm
the correctness of their claim to a war honor.

In short, vital ingredients of the Plains culture existed before European influences, though not necessarily all *in* the Plains. Further, in the Plains themselves Coronado in 1541 already distinguished the
two main subcultures of the area—the villagers' and
the nomads'. The people of Quivira planted corn
and built houses of "straw," and there were "other
thickly settled provinces around it [one settlement]
containing large numbers of men." By way of contrast, the Querechos and Teyas "do not have any
crockery . . . do not make gourds, nor sow corn,
nor eat bread. . . ." They depended for sustenance
on the flesh of buffalo, for fuel on buffalo dung. "A
Teya was seen to shoot a bull right through both
shoulders with an arrow, which would be a good
shot for a musket." These people lived "in tents
made of the tanned skins of the cows," and the tents
were transported by pack dogs. Pemmican, travois,
the sign language are specifically attested by the
Spanish chroniclers. However much the Woodland
Indians and Caucasians brought into the Plains
later, the ecological pattern of the culture area had
been created before the discovery.

Imperfect as the picture of the natives by their
earliest White visitors is, we do not get the impression that the nomads of the Plains were laboring
under the wretched standards of living of the aborigines of the Basin. Coronado's men came upon a
settlement of 200 tipis, which suggests a band of,
say, 1,000 people. Later, but still before the horse
had reached them, possibly in 1740, the Piegan
could muster against the Shoshone 350 warriors,
representing a probable population of 1,500. Fi-

nally, at least the southern nomads were in a position to enrich their life by trading with the Pueblos, exchanging robes for corn and what not; this intercourse could easily involve additional cultural loans.

It remains true that the Plains Indians at any period we can clearly grasp are not so sharply set off from the Woodland peoples as these are from the Basin or the Southwestern tribes. Nevertheless, the effective ecological exploitation of the buffalo created something distinctive, and the cultural complex resting on this basis obviously antedated the horse, the fur trade, or any other White influence. On this fact rests the justification for speaking of an aboriginal culture area.

HINTS FOR FURTHER READING

There are a number of not over-technical books giving more or less complete descriptions of particular Plains tribes. The following may be recommended:

BOWERS, ALFRED W., *Mandan Social and Ceremonial Organization*, University of Chicago Press, Chicago, 1950.

CURTIS, EDWARD S., *The North American Indian*, Vol. 4 [Crow], The University Press, Cambridge, Mass., 1909.

FLETCHER, ALICE C., and FRANCIS LA FLESCHE, "The Omaha Tribe," 27th Annual Report, Bureau of American Ethnology, Washington, D.C., 1911.

GRINNELL, GEORGE BIRD, *The Cheyenne Indians*, Yale University Press, New Haven, 1923.

LOWIE, ROBERT H., *The Crow Indians*, Farrar & Rinehart, Inc., New York, 1935.

MC CLINTOCK, WALTER, *The Old North Trail* [Blackfoot], Macmillan & Co., London, 1910.

WALLACE, ERNEST, and E. ADAMSON HOEBEL, *The Comanches; Lords of the Southern Plains*, University of Oklahoma Press, Norman, Oklahoma, 1952.

There is no general book on the archaeology of the area, but the following essays give a fair picture of modern methods and results:

CHAPMAN, CARL H., Culture Sequence in the Lower Missouri Valley, in *Archeology of Eastern United States*, pp. 139–151, James B. Griffin, ed., The University of Chicago Press, Chicago, 1952.

EGGAN, FRED R., The Ethnological Cultures and Their Archeological Backgrounds, in *Archeology of Eastern United States*, pp. 35–45, James B. Griffin, ed., The University of Chicago Press, Chicago, 1952.

MULLOY, WILLIAM, The Northern Plains, in *Archeology of Eastern United States*, pp. 124–138, James B. Griffin, ed., The University of Chicago Press, Chicago, 1952.

STRONG, WILLIAM DUNCAN, From History to Prehistory in the Northern Great Plains, in *Essays in Historical Anthropology of North America*, Smithsonian Miscellaneous Publications, Vol. 100, pp. 291–352, Washington, D.C., 1940.

WEDEL, WALDO R., Culture Sequences in the Central Great Plains, in *Essays in Historical Anthropology of North America*, Smithsonian Miscellaneous Publications, Vol. 100, pp. 291–352, Washington, D.C., 1940.

Among the numerous more popular books on the area a few may be cited as interesting and instructive:

GRINNELL, GEORGE BIRD, *Blackfoot Lodge Tales*, Bison Books, University of Nebraska Press, Lincoln, Nebraska, 1962.

LINDERMANN, FRANK B., *American: The Life Story of a Great Indian* [Crow], The John Day Company, New York, 1930.

LINDERMANN, FRANK B., *Red Mother* [Crow], The John Day Company, New York, 1932.

MARIOTT, ALICE, *The Ten Grandmothers; a Contribution to the Ethnology of the Kiowa Indians*, University of Oklahoma Press, Norman, Oklahoma, 1945.

SCHULTZ, J. W., *My Life as an Indian* [Blackfoot], Doubleday, Page & Co., New York, 1907.

SCHULTZ, J. W., and JESSIE L. DONALDSON, *The Sun God's Children* [Blackfoot], Houghton Mifflin Company, Boston, 1930.

The best of the early observers often give a marvelously clear picture of Plains Indian life before it was thoroughly modified by White influence. Some remarks on several of the authors listed below are indicated.

Catlin (1796–1872) was an American painter who visited many tribes in the United States and is especially good on the Mandan, whom he observed in 1832. Prince Maximilian of Wied Neuwied (1782–1867), a trained German naturalist, had already distinguished himself by his travels in Brazil when in 1832 he set out for a two years' journey to the Indians of the Upper Missouri. He studied the Mandan shortly after Catlin and gave an excellent description of their culture a few years before they were reduced by the smallpox, besides offering briefer observations on various other tribes. Carl Bodmer, a Swiss artist who accompanied the Prince, made numerous drawings of high documentary value. Henry and Thompson were intelligent British fur traders in the Blackfoot country about the turn of the nineteenth century. Denig became a bookkeeper for the American Fur Company at Fort Union near the mouth of the Yellowstone in about 1843 and played a prominent part in that region. Married to an Assiniboin chief's daughter, he enjoyed exceptional opportunities for observing his wife's tribe and also neighboring Plains peoples. The work cited was probably written about 1854. Lewis and Clark's famous expedition (1804–1806) was stimulated by President Thomas Jefferson. Starting from St. Louis, they ascended the Missouri and the Jefferson Rivers, crossed the Rockies, descended the Columbia, and reached the Pacific. They recorded many priceless observations on the Indians met. In addition to their Original Journals there are several works summarizing their scientific results.

BRADBURY, JOHN, *Travels in the Interior of America, in the Years 1809, 1810 and 1811*, Smith & Galway, Liverpool, 1817.

CATLIN, GEORGE, *Illustrations of the Manners, Customs and Conditions of the North American Indians*, Henry G. Bohn, London, 1848.

DENIG, EDWIN THOMPSON, "Indian Tribes of the Upper Missouri," 46th Annual Report, Bureau of American Ethnology, Washington, D.C., 1930, pp. 375–628.

HENRY, ALEXANDER, and DAVID THOMPSON, *New Light on the Early History of the Great Northwest*, edited by Elliott Coues, Francis P. Harper, New York, 1897.

KURZ, RUDOLPH FRIEDRICH, Journal; an Account of His Experiences among Fur Traders and American Indians on the Mississippi and the Upper Missouri Rivers during the Years 1846 to 1852, Bureau of American Ethnology, Bulletin 115, Washington, D.C., 1937.

LEWIS, M., and W. CLARK, *Original Journals of the Lewis and Clark Expedition* (Thwaites edition), Dodd Mead & Co., New York, 1904.

MAXIMILIAN, PRINCE OF WIED, *Travels in the Interior of North America*, translated by H. Evans Lloyd, London, 1843.

WINSHIP, GEORGE PARKER, ed., *The Journey of Coronado, 1540–1542, from the City of Mexico to the Grand Canyon of the Colorado and the Buffalo Plains of Texas, Kansas, and Nebraska, as told by himself and his followers*, A. S. Barnes & Co., New York, 1904.

Technical monographs on Plains cultures or particular phases of them will be found in Bulletin XVIII and in the Anthropological Papers of The American Museum of Natural

History; the Annual Reports and Bulletins of the Bureau of American Ethnology; and the Anthropological Series of the Field Museum of Natural History, Chicago.

Most monographs on the Plains Indians give bibliographies in which additional references may be found. In addition, a very useful compendium, the *Ethnographic Bibliography of North America,* by G. P. Murdock (third edition), Human Relations Area File, New Haven, Connecticut (1960), lists a great many books, short papers, etc. on the areal cultures.

INDEX